Schooner Days
IN DOOR COUNTY

Walter M. and Mary K. Hirthe

Endorsed and Registered by
the Association for Great Lakes Maritime History
as Publication B1

Thanks for your interest in schooner!
I hope you find a "North Bay" that
inspires you.

R. A. Hirth
July 23, 2019

Reprinted 2012 by
The Wisconsin Marine Historical Society

Published by Graphic Arts Studio, Inc.
28W111 Commercial Ave.
Barrington, IL 60010
www.gasink.net

ISBN 0-89658-061-X

Printed in the United States of America.

5 4 3 2 1

CONTENTS

25th Anniversary Foreword by Henry N. Barkhausen

Preface   vii

Acknowledgments   ix

Introduction   x

I   Where is the *Two Friends?* – A Story of North Bay   3

II   Shipbuilding at Little Sturgeon Bay, 1866 to 1874   15

III   Three of a Kind – A Story of Pilot Island   33

IV   The Long Journey of the *Windsor* to Cana Island   43

V   The *William Aldrich* – She Outlived Her Time   49

VI   The Reign of the *Ebenezers* – A Tale of Three Schooners   63

VII   From Lumber to Leisure – The *Lily E.*, ex-*Louisa McDonald*   71

VIII   The Discovery of the *America*   81

IX   Official No. 135665 – The *Emma L. Nielsen*   85

X   The *Farrand H. Williams* – A Scow Schooner   91

XI   The *Lummy* – The *Lomie A. Burton*   99

XII   The Perils of *Pauline*, – and *John*, – and *Edward*   105

Chapter Notes   119

Appendix A – Data for Vessels Built or Rebuilt at Little Sturgeon Bay   133

Appendix B – Enrollments and Registers for Vessels Built or Rebuilt at Little Sturgeon Bay   134

Bibliography   137

Index of Vessels   138

Index of Proper Names   141

FOREWORD

Illustrations can often be the primary appeal and emblem of authenticity of a publication on local history. *Schooner Days in Door County* is an absolute treasure- trove of rare photographs dating from the glory days of sail on Lake Michigan to the final chapter written by the aging schooners that eked out a marginal existence in the first quarter of the last century.

But the authors also give us unprecedented insights into the maritime commerce of the day, illuminating the entrepreneurial energy of ship owners and captains and their willingness to risk the gales that were commonly encountered on early and late season trips in order to earn extra income, usually at higher freight rates. Their accounts highlight the havoc caused by fall gales like that of October 1880, which trapped some forty vessels in North Bay and Bailey's Harbor, and left the Lake Michigan shore literally strewn with wrecked and stranded vessels. The records cited also emphasize the tenacity and resourcefulness of captains and salvage operators who were able to release many of these ships under the most difficult conditions. Most of them had to be rescued multiple times over the years.

Schooner Days offers diverse views of Door County. Today, Little Sturgeon Bay is a quiet harbor, generally by-passed and overlooked by tourists and summer residents. The authors have made a major contribution researching and bringing to life the surprising lumbering, shipping and ship-building activity that took place here from 1856 to 1877 when Little Sturgeon was a significantly more important commercial community than Sturgeon Bay, the county seat. The surprising number of first class sailing vessels that were built or re-built here are carefully documented, many with photographs.

Another eye-opener, detailed a number of times, were the extraordinary efforts made by Door County life -saving station crews, not only in saving lives, but saving the vessels as well. They often worked around the clock relieving exhausted crews at the pumps, physically unloading cargo to lighten the vessel, and carrying out anchors and manning windlasses in an effort to kedge the ship off reefs and beaches.

In fact, constant pumping of the bilges of these old schooners was a way of life in their fading years after World War I. There was simply not enough revenue from the diminishing number of cargoes of cedar posts, slabs, potatoes, cordwood, hay or fruit to make the necessary repairs and replace the rotting canvas.

All this and much more is meticulously recorded in this handsome volume. In compiling it twenty five years ago, the Hirthes were actually engaged in a pioneering effort. They were the first to utilize such a wide range of resources in researching and writing on Great Lakes maritime subjects, combining material culled from contemporary newspapers, vessel enrollments from various customhouses, insurance records, admiralty and civil court reports and Life –Saving station logs together with extensive collections of photographs.

Walter and Mary Hirthe have been mentors and an inspiration to scores of divers, researchers and writers and we will all continue to benefit from their contributions to our understanding and appreciation of local maritime history.

Henry N. Barkhausen
April, 2012

To all those who lived the schooner days in Door
. . . and to those who wish they had

Walter M. Hirthe 1927-1991

PREFACE

Although much has been written about the era of sail on the Great Lakes, the desire for complete and documented material has not been satisfied. This book provides factual accounts of the "great white-winged fleet" that served as the primary means of transportation during much of the last century.

Before the Civil War, most of the sailing vessels on the Great Lakes were brigs or barques, which were square-rigged, that is, they had square sails on their masts. These sails were supported and spread by long spars tapered toward the ends called yards. A brig had two masts—a foremast and a mainmast—each having at least two yards for carrying square sails; and a barque, or bark, had three masts—a foremast, a mainmast, and a mizzenmast—with at least two masts carrying square sails. These vessels dominated the trade routes of the world, and it was only natural that they would be the first to appear on the lakes, since many of their builders, owners, and masters had migrated from salt water.

In contrast to the square riggers, the schooner was a fore-and-aft rigged vessel having two or more masts with sails supported and spread by spars called gaffs. Another spar called a boom was attached to the bottom, or foot, of the sail. With the booms pulled in toward the center line of the vessel by means of lines called sheets, the sails were fore-and-aft. By rotating the booms around the masts, the vessel could be made to respond to the direction of the wind. Early Great Lakes schooners typically had two masts, with the smaller sail on the shorter foremast and the taller mainmast nearly amidships in the middle of the vessel from front (bow) to stern (back).

After the Civil War, changes in rig were commonplace as the brigs and barques began to disappear to be replaced by the schooners. The reason for this change was twofold: (1) the schooners were faster when sailing into the wind, that is, "beating up wind" and (2) the schooners had a simpler rig and were therefore easier and more economical of equipment and crew. The main course for vessels on the Great Lakes was from east to west (Buffalo to Chicago) or vice versa. Since the prevailing winds are west to east, the vessels were either sailing with the wind, called running before the wind, or into the wind, called beating. Although the square-rigged vessels had an advantage when sailing with the wind, they could not sail into the wind nearly as well. For this reason and because their outfit (sails and rigging) was more expensive and difficult to handle, the schooners replaced the square-rigged sailing vessels.

The design of the schooner was refined for use on the Great Lakes during the 1840s and 1850s. One of the builders who contributed most to this process was William W. Bates of Manitowoc, Wisconsin. In 1852, he launched the first distinctive Great Lakes schooner, named the *Challenge*. Although her features were not new, she combined a number of them into a new model that was well suited for the lakes. The hull of the *Challenge* was shoal (not deep in the water), flatbottomed, sharp ended (narrow in the bow and stern), and had a center board. She had a clipper-type bow with a long spar called a jibboom to carry sails called jibs well out in front of the bow. The *Challenge* revolutionized the design of sailing vessels on the lakes because of her dependability and speed, which was reported to be in excess of 13 knots (about 15 miles per hour).

The *Challenge* was followed by the schooner *Clipper City* in 1854 and the schooners *Stephen Bates* and *Belle* in 1856. Over the next 10 years, builders turned to the schooner as the sailing vessel on the lakes, and the notation "rig change" from brig or barque to schooner became the cause for issuing new enrollments for many vessels. Even the earlier schooners, which were usually two masted, experienced a rig change to three masts, and in some cases an increase in length, as the owners, masters, and shippers pursued speed, just as their counterparts were doing on the oceans of the world.

Although sailing craft date back to ancient times, the demise of sailing did not occur on the Great Lakes until the development of larger, efficient, steam-propelled vessels. The settlement of Door County coincided with the peak of the schooner era on Lake Michigan. In reviewing this era, we have the opportunity to relive shipbuilding at Little Sturgeon Bay, 1866 to 1874, followed by the long decline of the commercial schooner into oblivion. By the turn of the century, the number of schooners had been greatly reduced, and they no longer ran to Buffalo or other eastern ports but only served in the trade along the shores of Green

Bay or Lake Michigan, or to and from islands such as Washington, Rock, and Chambers.

Door County was on the main track of all the important trade on the Great Lakes. Great Lakes trade began with the arrival of sailing vessels and steamboats at Green Bay from the east and continued with the establishment of the principal ports of Milwaukee and Chicago. The first cargo consisted of immigrants and the merchandise necessary to their survival in the "west." The piers of Door County were the first settlements in the area and provided the natural resources—lumber, limestone, lime, ties, telegraph poles, cordwood, and the like—for the construction of the new cities and transportation systems—railroads and steamboats—that ultimately replaced the schooner.

Therefore, the schooners of Door County provide an excellent vehicle with which to observe this era of the sailing ship on the Great Lakes and to appreciate its importance in the development of our nation. As we prepared this book, we questioned whether we could create interesting accounts of the schooners based only on fact. We believe that we have succeeded and hope you will enjoy these stories of the schooners and the people and places they served in Door County.

ACKNOWLEDGMENTS

Without the contribution of many individuals and institutions, this manuscript could not have become a reality. We wish to express our sincere appreciation to all who assisted and encouraged us in this work. We owe a very special thanks to the following for their efforts in our behalf:

Mr. Robert Angwall
Mrs. Marion Augustine
Mr. Henry N. Barkhausen
Mr. G. Kent Bellrichard
Mr. Floyd G. Boyce
Mr. James Brotz
Mr. Michael J. Burda
Fr. Edward J. Dowling, S.J.
Mr. Fred Erskine
Dr. Charles E. Feltner
Mrs. Jeri Baron Feltner
Rev. Wolfgram Fliegel
Ms. Lynn Frederick
Mr. Greg Gregory
Mr. Kenneth R. Hall
Mr. Chan Harris
Mr. James J. Jetzer
Mr. Aldrich C. Krones
Mr. C. Patrick Labadie

Mr. James A. Larsen
Mrs. Meta Lawrie
Mr. George A. Leonard
Mr. Orval O. Liljequist
Mrs. Suzette J. Lopez
The Milwaukee Public Library
Mr. Carl A. Norberg
Mr. David L. Pamperin
Mr. Steve Radovan
Mrs. Ruth Revels
Mr. Herman Runge
Mr. Charles A. Scheffner
Mr. John R. Steele
Mr. David Trotter
Mr. Arni Wegner
Mrs. Edwin Wilson
The Wisconsin Marine Historical Society
Dr. Paul Woehrmann
Mr. Rich Zaleski

INTRODUCTION

The material in this book was selected from articles we had written on the marine history of the Great Lakes. The first story represents our introduction to the subject in the fall of 1969 at our summer place on North Bay, about five miles north of Baileys Harbor on the Lake Michigan side of Door County.

On a cold and windy day, two skin divers came to our cottage to ask the question "Where is the *Two Friends*?" Their research had led them to believe that the Canadian barque *Two Friends* had been lost in North Bay during the great storm of October 1880 known as the Alpena Gale because of the tragic loss of the Goodrich Transportation Co. side-wheel steamer *Alpena*.

Our reply to the divers was "Over there," as we pointed northeast across North Bay to a reef at the entrance to Lake Michigan, "just off Marshall's Point." Although the weather was severe, these determined divers disappeared after receiving directions to this relatively inaccessible area on Lake Michigan in northern Door County.

Their question piqued our interest in the *Two Friends*, and we decided to learn the details of her loss. From articles in newspapers for a period of almost a year after the storm and from certificates of enrollment issued at the Port of Milwaukee in 1881, we found that the *Two Friends* had been released from North Bay, rebuilt as a schooner, and renamed *Pewaukee*. In subsequent years, she was converted to a steam barge, reduced to a tow barge in the stone trade, and finally sunk to serve as a dock in Sturgeon Bay in 1913, 33 years after her "total loss" in North Bay.

As a result of this discovery and other accounts of disasters on the Great Lakes, we soon realized that published information on the era of sail in Door County, and on all of the lakes, was limited and, in some cases, lacking in detail and accuracy. Therefore, we began to research this subject, with special emphasis on the schooners that were built in or served Door County and the western shore of Lake Michigan, including Green Bay. The sailors, masters, owners, and pier settlements associated with these vessels are a vital part of their stories.

The principal shipbuilding center in Door County during the era of sail was Little Sturgeon Bay, and a detailed account of this early settlement with its shipyard and dock

and the people who played a role in its rise was essential to our work.

Shipwrecks have marked the history of sailing vessels, and the violent storms that rendered repeated blows on Pilot Island in Death's Door, where the schooners found it difficult to maneuver in the best of weather, and on Cana Island, which lies out in Lake Michigan exposed to the north, south, and east, were the cause of many disasters. We have included two chapters that describe the loss of sailing vessels on these rock-bound islands in the waters of Door County.

Although wooden ships were known for their durability, some schooners survived the wind and waves for extraordinary lengths of time. The records of the *William Aldrich*, 1856 to 1916, and the first *Ebenezer*, 1846 to 1904, allow us to review this era in a continuous manner. The old-timers experienced many changes: the migration from the eastern ports where they were built to ports on the western lakes where they were lost or abandoned; the changes in rig from brig or barque to topsail schooner, from two masts to three and then in some cases back to two with the advent of the so-called Grand Haven or jackass rig; the decline in insurance classification or rating from A or A 1 to 00, not insurable; the change in cargo from passengers and merchandise to coarse or bulk freight; and finally, the change in routes from Buffalo to Chicago to a shorter run in the coasting trade.

Even today, much evidence of this era remains, and with the discovery of the schooner *America* in 1977 and the schooner *Emma L. Nielsen* in 1980, we have the opportunity to study these time capsules from the past. Since few construction drawings of schooners built before 1880 are in existence, much of their detail can only be obtained from careful underwater archeological surveys of their remains.

In the chapter about the *Farrand H. Williams*, we feature the scow schooner, a shallow draft schooner ideal for service in the many small harbors that dotted the Great Lakes. Although scows were usually small and only carried two masts, they were workhorses on the lakes because they served as lighters to transport cargo into and out of shallow harbors and rivers and as carriers from port to port.

In researching the final chapter, we were surprised to meet Capt. James Larsen a second time. In the story of North Bay, Chapter 1, we met him in 1880 as the young fisherman who rescued the crew of the *Two Friends,* and in the last chapter, he is an old captain on board his son's schooner, the *Edward E. Skeele,* when she is wrecked in the North Channel some 41 years later.

Vessel data were taken from the certificates of enrollment issued at the custom houses of the ports. Currently, these certificates of enrollment reside in the National Archives, Washington, D.C. These documents give the owner(s), master, and physical dimensions, including the tonnage. The relationship between vessel tonnage and length was first prescribed in the United States in an act of August 4, 1790, and was replaced by a different system of tonnage measurement in 1864.

In the old system of measurement (OM), a ton was equal to 95 cubic feet of cargo-carrying capacity. In an act of May 6, 1864, cargo capacity was expressed in tons of 100 cubic feet, using a formula that took into account the shape of the hull and the enclosures above the deck. The tons calculated by this method are also referred to as the "total tonnage" or "gross" tons. An act of August 5, 1882, allows deductions for crew space, storerooms, machinery, and the like, which resulted in "net" tonnage. Therefore, for the period before 1864, tonnage is given as tons OM, from 1865 through 1882 as total tons, and after 1882 as gross and net tons.

Other primary references included the annual reports of the U.S. Life-Saving Service, wreck reports filed with various agencies, and insurance registers that originated in Buffalo before the start of the Civil War. The Inland Lloyds, for example, was a group of insurance companies that prepared a book each season known as the Inland Lloyds Vessel Register, designed for the "private use only" of the participating companies in the prosecution of lake insurance and not to be promulgated to the public. A letter from the office of Inland Lloyds, dated Buffalo, March 20, 1882, best describes the purpose and use of these books:

Dear Sir:

This classification of hulls has been prepared for the exclusive convenience and guidance of the Insurance Companies (and their agents) composing "THE INLAND LLOYDS."

It is not claimed that the valuations are exact, but approximate. For these reasons allow no one besides yourself and employees to inspect this book. Should you, in reply to inquiry, name the registered value of any vessel, invariably inform such person that the value of the vessel is approximate only.

On Demand of the undersigned, this book is to be returned to the head office of the Inland Lloyds, at Buffalo.

Yours truly,
Edw. B. Smith
Chairman Executive Committee

Vessels were divided into three classes: A, B, and 00 (cyphers), with the following grades to each class: A 1*, A 1, A 1½, A 2, A 2½, B 1, B 1½, B 2, 00. Vessels classed 00 were not insurable. Monthly supplements to the register were issued, embracing such corrections, changes, and additions as were required. This system of classification started before the Civil War and evolved during the era of sail.

Newspaper accounts of the time provided some of the descriptive materials, which have been supplemented with our knowledge of the area. In this manner, we hope that we have maintained reasonable accuracy in our accounts so that they can be used in future work.

Schooner Days
IN DOOR COUNTY

CHAPTER ONE

Where is the *Two Friends*?
A Story of North Bay

"Where is the *Two Friends*?" This question was asked by two skin divers on a cold and windy day in the fall of 1969. "Over there," we said, pointing to the northeast across North Bay to a reef at the entrance to Lake Michigan, "just off Marshall's Point." Although the weather was severe, these determined divers disappeared after receiving our directions to this relatively inaccessible area on the Lake Michigan side of northern Door County, Wisconsin.

The location we had given for the final resting place of the *Two Friends*, a nineteenth century sailing vessel, was consistent with books [1] and charts [2] concerning the marine history of the Great Lakes. Since that time, we have reviewed much of this history and will now relate the true life story of the *Two Friends*.

She was built in 1873 at Port Burwell, Ontario, by Lemuel McDermond for George Suffel, et al. of Port Burwell. The *Two Friends* is listed as a schooner in the 1875 classification of the National Board of Lake Underwriters [3] and the 1879 Lake Hull Register of the Association of Lake Underwriters, [4] but is referred to as a barque in other references of the time. For insurance purposes, these registers give her tonnage as 319, value $19,000, and class A 1 in 1875; and tonnage 396, value $12,000, and class A 1 in 1879.

The *Two Friends* was one of many vessels on Lake Michigan October 16, 1880, during a storm that has been described by many as the worst in memory. It is referred to as the Alpena Gale because of the loss of the Goodrich Transportation Co. side-wheel steamer *Alpena*. Mansfield [5] provides the following description of the storm:

> One of the storms that have great cause to be remembered in lake shipping circles swept over Lake Michigan October 16, 1880. The weather on October 15 was warm and pleasant, the thermometer ranging from 60° to 70°. Light northerly winds prevailed over Lake Superior and southerly over Lake Michigan. The storm began about midnight on the 16th with easterly shifting to southwesterly winds at the Straits of Mackinac, and southwesterly from Grand Haven southward. Violent southwesterly gales on Lake Michigan raged all day of the 16th and part of the 17th. The temperature dropped from 65° to the freezing point, and snow fell as far south as Chicago. The loss of life was very great, nearly 100 souls going down on the Goodrich liner *Alpena*, Grand Haven to Chicago. This vessel was last seen about 30 miles from Chicago. In all about 90 vessels were wrecked or badly damaged, and 118 lives were lost as a result of this storm.

A contemporary account of the nature and intensity of this storm is given in the *Door County Advocate:* [6] "The blow which set in from the south early Saturday morning is said by all who had an opportunity to see its effects on the bay and lake to have been one of the severest ever encountered in this latitude. As a consequence a large num-

The Goodrich Transportation Co. steamer *Alpena* was lost in the great storm of 1880, which has come to be known as the Alpena Gale. Courtesy of the Wisconsin Marine Historical Society.

ber of vessels have been wrecked and driven ashore at the foot of Lake Michigan, many of them being damaged so that they will have to be abandoned. Upward of twenty craft have found the beach between Kewaunee and Death's Door, a distance of fifty miles."

In North Bay, a fleet of nearly thirty vessels had sought refuge from the storm. The sailing vessels were mostly of the larger class and were either bound for Buffalo loaded with grain or on their way to Chicago with lumber, iron ore, or coal. They included the *Floretta, Louisa McDonald, Lem Ellsworth, Col. Ellsworth, George Murray, Montauk, Naiad, Jennibel, Lucy Graham, T. Y. Avery, G. Pfister,* and the *Two Friends,* the latter deeply laden with salt.

The *Two Friends* was the last to arrive, and as the bay was crowded to capacity, she was compelled to anchor in an exposed berth directly at the mouth, where it was very rough because the sea had an unbroken sweep from the lake. She came to with both anchors out at 3:00 P.M. on the sixteenth, and two hours later dragged ashore on the

northerly side of the bay. She immediately swung broadside to the sea and fell over on her starboard side, or offshore. Thus exposed, her deck was swept of everything movable in a short time, the cabin smashed in, the boat washed from the davits and stove in pieces on the rocky shore, and the crew driven to the rigging. Accounts of their rescue by a local fisherman, James Larsen of Sister Bay, are given in the Annual Report of the U.S. Life-Saving Service,[7] in Frederickson,[8] and in the *Door County Advocate.*[9] From the Life-Saving Service report:

Although several other vessels were aground up the bay none of their people were yet ashore, and the only persons on the beach at that time were James Larsen, a fisherman of the locality, and his hired assistant, Ole M. Rasmussen. They were before long, however, joined by the crew of one of the other stranded vessels who had landed their own yawl. Larsen begged their aid with their boat, but this was refused, the captain offering in excuse that his boat could not live in such a sea as was running where the bark lay. They, however, aided him in an effort to throw a small line to the vessel by means of a shot-gun, but the dis-

The schooner *Lem Ellsworth* was a canaller built for trading through the Welland Canal locks before they were lengthened in 1882. The *Ellsworth* foundered in Lake Michigan about May 18, 1894, with a cargo of stone from Jacobsville, Michigan, to Chicago. Wreckage was found near Kenosha a week later, but nothing was ever heard of her crew of seven. Courtesy of the Wisconsin Marine Historical Society.

The gold medal awarded to James Larsen by the U.S. Life-Saving Service for his daring and sacrifice in the rescue of the crew of the *Two Friends* in North Bay. Courtesy of Mrs. Frederick Timmerman.

tance, one hundred yards, was too great, and the attempt failed. This idea was doubtless due to his previous training as a surfman at one of the life-saving stations on that coast. With the approach of night a driving snow-storm set in and as the vessel showed signs of breaking up, the situation of the people in the rigging became very alarming. The party on shore were now dropping off one by one to seek shelter, believing that nothing further could be done until daylight next morning. This left Larsen and his comrade alone. The two remained some hours longer watching the vessel and listening to the piteous cries of the people for help, which could plainly be heard above the howling of the gale, until the brave Larsen could stand it no longer, and he resolved to get a boat at all hazards and attempt the rescue alone, although Rasmussen, who himself was a boatman, tried to dissuade him from it. It should be stated that Larsen's own boat had been driven on the rocks by the gale and damaged so badly that it was unfit for use. But for this he would have ventured out soon after the bark struck. He at last succeeded at about 10 P.M. in borrowing a light, fourteen-foot clinker-built boat from William Marshall, the superintendent on the North Bay property, in spite of the remonstrances of several persons, among whom were captains of vessels in the bay, who derided his earnestness and characterized the project as foolhardy; some going so far as to say that no one but a lunatic would think of going out to the wreck in such a sea, and that he would surely lose his own life. In fact, so strong was the opposition and the belief that Larsen would be dashed back against the rock-bound shore, that it was only when he offered to deposit with the owner the money value of the boat that he obtained consent for its use. Un-

deterred by the many objections, he sent for the boat, which had to be carried some distance through the woods, and then fastening a small line about his waist, he took his seat, and when a favorable moment presented shoved off, and in seven trips brought the bark's crew, one at a time, safely ashore, the entire operation taking him just one hour and a half. The last man was landed precisely at midnight. He had several narrow escapes, the boat being swamped no less than five times, and the utmost difficulty was encountered in getting the numbed and almost exhausted men off the wreck. This was done by their lowering themselves from the jib-boom, it being too dangerous for him to go alongside or even lay in his oars.

James Larsen was awarded a gold medal for his daring and sacrifice, the highest award within the province of the Life-Saving Service to bestow. Born in Denmark in 1855, Larsen immigrated to the United States in 1871, settling in Racine, where he married and continued to reside for nine years until he moved to Door County. Later Larsen moved to Marinette, Wisconsin, where he became a shipbuilder and master, and represented Marinette County in the state legislature. James Larsen died at Kenosha, Wisconsin, in May 1923 and was buried at Fish Creek, Wisconsin, not far from the site of his heroic deeds.

By the end of the gale, the *Two Friends* was referred to as a total loss. From the *Door Country Advocate* of October 28, 1880: "The Gardner [10] reports the bottom out of the schooner Two Friends, ashore at North Bay, and the vessel is a total loss. She had been stripped." Later in the same column: "The tug Champion left Detroit two or three days ago to assist the schooner Two Friends, ashore at North Bay. The Two Friends is, however, a total loss, and the Champion's long journey will be in vain." From Frederickson: [11] "A century old anchor from the bark Two Friends is now used as a lawn decoration at Gordon's Lodge at North Bay, near Bailey's Harbor, Wisconsin. Recently, the remains of the Two Friends have been found by skin divers on Marshall's Reef in North Bay. She lies in about twenty feet of water." However, despite the above, the *Two Friends* did not meet her end in North Bay. In fact, she was quite "young" at the time of her experiences in one of the greatest storms of all.

Within a week after the storm subsided, only the two schooners that were seriously damaged remained in North Bay—the *G. Pfister* [12] and the *Two Friends*. On October 29, the *Pfister* was pulled from the rock shore by the tugs *Champion* [13] and *Oswego* [14] and was towed to Manitowoc by the *Champion* for repairs, leaving only the *Two Friends*.

Evidence of her afterlife began to appear in the *Door County Advocate* of December 30, 1880: "Wm. Marshall,

S. B. GRUMMOND,
---OWNER---
First-Class Tugs for Wrecking, Raft-Towing, Etc.
SIXTEEN STEAM PUMPS, ROTARY AND WORTHINGTON,
Improved Horizontal, Straight Base Hydraulic Jacks.

Tugs:

LEVIATHAN,

WINSLOW,

M. SWAIN,

CHAMPION.

Tugs:

JOHN OWEN,

WM. A. MOORE,

AND

OSWEGO.

SUBMARINE DIVERS, HAWSERS, LIGHTERS, ETC.
OFFICES OPEN DAY AND NIGHT. SATISFACTION GUARANTEED.

Wrecking Tugs LEVIATHAN and CHAMPION, stationed at Cheboygan, with plenty of Wrecking Material on Board and in Warehouse.

Office and Warehouse on Dock, Foot of First St.,   DETROIT, MICH.

An advertisement for S. B. Grummond of Detroit, featuring the wrecking tug *Winslow*. Note that the large wreckers *Leviathan* and *Champion* were stationed at Cheboygan, Michigan, to recover wrecks in the Straits of Mackinac, Lake Michigan, or Lake Huron. Courtesy of Fr. Edward J. Dowling, S.J.

of North Bay, reports that the Canadian schooner Two Friends, which was driven ashore at that place during the October storm, still remains in about the condition she was after the blow. Her hold full of salt has been entirely washed out, not a particle remaining. Mr. Marshall has a claim of $150 against the owners of the vessel for boarding and caring for the ship-wrecked crew, which the underwriters have promised to liquidate."

William Marshall, who lived on the north point of North Bay, known as Craignair, was a native of Scotland, born in the village of The Bridge-of-Dee in 1839. He left Scotland in the spring of 1868 and sailed right for North Bay to be in the employ of George A. Thompson, who was the owner of considerable land in Liberty Grove Township, part of the property being located on the north side of North Bay. Thompson's holdings were sold at a United States marshall's sale at Milwaukee in the late 1870s to Richard Irvin and Co., bankers and brokers in New York. After this sale, William Marshall became the superintendent of the property.

The *Door County Advocate* gives an interesting and

picturesque description of the area under the heading[15] "Among the Pines:"

North Bay is an indentation of this peninsula, on the Lake Michigan side, about ten miles from the Door, and nine miles from Bailey's Harbor. It is not far from four miles long by two miles in width, and supplies safe anchorage for vessels during gales from almost any direction. On the southern and western shores it is marshy, but the land lies high and dry on the northern side, and the clearings already made indicate that in good time some of the best farms in the county will be found here. William Marshall, who resides on the northern shore, a mile or so up the bay, has sixty acres under plow, and is raising some excellent crops. As a gardner he has probably no superior in the county, the vegetables and other products raised by him having won numerous premiums at the fairs of the agricultural society. He is the agent of an eastern company which owns large tracts of land in the vicinity, and devotes as much of his time as is necessary to the interests of his employers, the remainder being given to working his farm, which he cultivates with the energy and ability characteristic of his native Scotland. Mr. Marshall has a wife and seven children, and resides in a handsome frame house not far from the shore, the grounds around it being beautified by the evergreens which grow so freely that it was only necessary to remove those that were not necessary to the adornment of the landscape.

And from a later paragraph: "During last winter about two millions of feet of pine logs were banked on the shore of North Bay by Bailey & Marshall and Thomas Farrell for the use of Sturgeon Bay Lumbering Co. For several months the employes of that company have been engaged in bringing these logs to the mill on the scows built for that purpose. The shallowness of the water near the banking ground prevents the loading of the logs at the shore, making it necessary to tow them out half a mile, where they are then picked up by the derrick on the scow *Home*[16] and piled upon the scows prepared to receive them."

In December 1880, while Marshall was at Sturgeon Bay, some party or parties visited the *Two Friends*, cut away one of the spars, and carried off a portion of the wire rigging of the vessel. The wreck had been purchased from the insurance companies by Wolf & Davidson of Milwaukee, and William H. Wolf went to North Bay with his family to look after the vessel. Wolf & Davidson was the largest shipyard in Milwaukee, occupying 11 acres at the confluence of the Milwaukee and Kinnickinnic rivers. The Kirtland, Wolf & Davidson Wrecking Co. was affiliated with the yard and owned the wrecking tug *Leviathan*.[17] She was one of the most successful wreckers on the lakes, under the command and management of Capt.

Charles E. Kirtland, with Capt. John V. Tuttle as port captain.

The opening of the 1881 season saw tugs scurrying over Lake Michigan to recover the wrecks resulting from the storms of 1880. Owners and underwriters were anxious to return their vessels to service because of the shortage of shipping created by the large losses in vessel property and by increases in grain and ore traffic in general. Many contracts had been let, and tug owners and wreckers had a great deal more work than they could handle in a single spring.

The schooner *Nabob*[18] had run on a reef near Cana Island, a few miles south of North Bay, on the evening of September 24, 1880, just a few weeks before the Alpena Gale. The site of the stranding was on a smooth, sloping shelf rock on the point separating Little and Mud (Moonlight) bays. She was abandoned to the underwriters, who contracted with Kirtland, Wolf & Davidson to release their vessel. Captain Kirtland had gone to the *Nabob* with the *Leviathan* early in October and brought the canvas and rigging of the wrecked schooner to Milwaukee. Workmen had prepared the vessel for launching by lifting her about two feet to ensure a successful release. With everything nearly ready, the great gale had struck, driving the *Nabob* out high and dry and postponing her rescue until spring.

Kirtland, Wolf & Davidson had also purchased the schooner *E.C.L.*[19] for $800 in the fall of 1880 as she lay

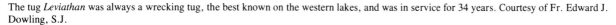

The tug *Leviathan* was always a wrecking tug, the best known on the western lakes, and was in service for 34 years. Courtesy of Fr. Edward J. Dowling, S.J.

badly listing on the beach near Henderson's Pier on the north side of Sister Bay. She had failed to ride out a gale at anchor in Sister Bay on November 21 and went on the beach. The *E. C. L.* was owned and sailed by Capt. Claude H. Oellerich of Milwaukee and was not insured. The last enrollment of the schooner was surrendered at Milwaukee on November 20, 1880; cause of surrender: total loss. However, it was the business of the wrecking company to recover badly damaged vessels to be rebuilt in the yard of Wolf & Davidson and sold at a profit for all.

The owners of the *Leviathan* also had an offer of $1,000 from an insurance company in the fall of 1880 to recover the schooner *George H. Warmington,* [20] which had been scuttled on the rocks to prevent pounding between Big and Little Summer islands. Since she was frozen in, the wreckers could not get to her, and this job was also delayed until spring. The underwriters let the same contract to the *Leviathan* in the spring of 1881, but for $1,500. Thus, Kirtland, Wolf & Davidson had commitments to rescue the *Warmington* on the Summer islands, the *Nabob* near Cana Island, the *E. C. L.* in Sister Bay, and the *Two Friends* in North Bay—all in a single spring.

Stranded vessels were recovered according to two basic procedures: (1) they were simply pulled off the shore by brute force using the individual or combined power of a tug or tugs or (2) if they were well out of the water, they were raised by jackscrews, placed on ways, and then pulled into deep water. If the bottom was soft, tugs could dredge a channel with the action of their propellers to assist in the release of a vessel.

The use of jackscrews required that wreckers work in the water for extended periods of time, and this could not be done until the water began to warm up later in the spring. In all wrecking operations, some of the factors to be considered were the position of the wreck, the length of time required for the operation, the temperature of the water, and, in early spring or winter, the movement of the pack ice that drifted in and out with the direction of the prevailing wind. As a general rule, vessels in exposed positions were to be rescued first to prevent further damage from wind and ice, but if the release required working in the water, their recovery was delayed until later in the spring.

On April 16, 1881, Captains Kirtland and Tuttle received a letter from Escanaba stating that no trouble would now be experienced in getting to the *Warmington* because the ice had gone out between St. Martin's, Poverty, and Summer islands. The lake was also clear between St. Martin's and Rock islands, but a heavy easterly wind

would again place an embargo on the wreck. A letter received in Milwaukee on the eighteenth from the shipkeeper of the *Nabob* said that the vessel was clear of ice. As the *Leviathan* departed for the *Warmington* on the afternoon of the twenty-second to take advantage of this "window in the weather," the time had come to reap the great harvest of 1881.

The information with regard to the *Warmington* proved to be correct, as she was easily pulled off at 7:00 A.M. Tuesday April 26, towed past Sturgeon Bay on the twenty-seventh, and docked in Milwaukee on the twenty-eighth. A survey of the schooner was made on May 2 by John B. Merrill and John H. Blend at Wolf & Davidson's dry dock. At first glance, she appeared only slightly damaged, but on close examination it was seen that nearly two-thirds of her bottom and keel had been badly chafed and would have to be replaced. The *Warmington* also had to be thoroughly refastened, have her ends raised up, and be recaulked. Wolf & Davidson estimated that the total cost of repairing would be $10,000. The schooner was taken out of dry dock on May 24 and left for Escanaba after the needed repairs were made to her upper works. According to insurance registers, this rebuild lowered her classification from A 2 to A 2½ but increased her value from $18,000 to $20,000.

The *Leviathan* left Milwaukee on May 3 for the *Nabob* near Cana Island and the *Two Friends* in North Bay. The work of releasing the *Nabob* was deferred until warmer weather after Captain Kirtland had verified the necessity of raising the schooner with jackscrews, which would have required his crew to work waist deep in the icy water of early May.

The *Leviathan* steamed on to Cheboygan, Michigan, to obtain a steam pump and other appliances for raising the *Two Friends.* The expedition arrived at North Bay during the weekend of May 7, and the crew engaged in filling the hold of the *Two Friends* with cedar posts to increase her buoyancy. The release of the wreck was not accomplished until about the seventeenth, after the hull had been patched by a diver, Peter J. Crowley. Because of other commitments, Captain Kirtland left the *Two Friends* in North Bay to be towed to Milwaukee at a more opportune time.

He turned his attention to the Canadian schooner *W. R. Taylor,* [21] sunk at Northport, Michigan, with 25,000 bushels of corn. The *Taylor* ran ashore on the Manitous in the fall of 1880 but was towed into Northport, where she was allowed to sink because it was so late in the season. However, Captain Kirtland received a telegram from Captain Tuttle to abandon the job, as her owners did not want her raised at the time. This change was due to a mis-understanding between the owners and underwriters as to where the *Taylor* was to be repaired. The tug *Winslow*[22] of Detroit raised the schooner and towed her to St. Catharines, where she received the necessary repairs.

The *Leviathan* went to the rescue of the *Nabob* on May 20, but Captain Kirtland intended to tow the *Two Friends* to Milwaukee if the water around the former was still too cold. He succeeded in getting steam pumps on the *Nabob* but was prepared for a long and tedious job because she had to be screwed up and placed on ways. While his crew was laboring on the stranded schooner, marine insurance men in Chicago, the home port of the *Nabob,* alleged that the schooner could have been released long ago if the wreckers at work on her had been earnest in their efforts. These men engaged an attorney to take evidence of seamen and others for the purpose of proving their position. The *Chicago Inter-Ocean* of May 26, 1881, said of the affair: "Capt. Kirtland is the wrecker, and it will be hard to prove by the evidence of any men that he does not try to get every craft he goes after. There is no better and no more faithful and honest wrecker anywhere on the lakes than Capt. Kirtland. The case will probably not stop the movement of the world. And meanwhile, if the water becomes warm for work in it about her, Captain Kirtland will have the *Nabob* in port."

On the same day, a dispatch was received from Captain Kirtland reporting that he had the *Nabob* on ways, and the wreckers did not experience any difficulty working about the schooner because the water was quite warm. A telegram on June 9 reported that he would succeed in releasing the schooner with two more days of fine weather. The *Nabob* was moved over 100 feet on Saturday June 11, but the hawser parted, and the *Leviathan* went into Baileys Harbor in the evening to obtain another. After three weeks of hard work, the tug released the *Nabob* on June 14 and towed her to North Bay. The *Leviathan* steamed to Escanaba for coal and another steam pump before towing the *Nabob* to Milwaukee, where they arrived the evening of the eighteenth.

On June 21, the *Leviathan* departed for Sister Bay with the steam pump used on the *Nabob* and the diver Crowley to work on the *E.C.L.* and bring the *Two Friends* to Milwaukee at an opportune time. Captain Kirtland said that no difficulty would be experienced in releasing the *E.C.L.* if Crowley could patch up some of the holes in her bottom. She could then be pumped out and the cargo of wood removed from her hold. However, the bottom of the schooner was so bad that she could not be pumped out, and the

expedition ceased work on the *E.C.L.* during the first week of July. At last it was the *Two Friends'* turn. The *Leviathan* returned to the wreck in North Bay, where she had been waiting to be towed to Milwaukee for almost two months. This action supported the integrity of Captain Kirtland, since the *Two Friends,* the only wreck owned by Wolf & Davidson that could be recovered, was the last to be brought into port.

Capt. W. T. Spencer of the bulk freighter *Minnesota*[23] arrived in Milwaukee from Escanaba on July 11 and reported that the *Leviathan* had towed the *Two Friends* a considerable distance but was compelled to beach her as she was taking water too fast. It was thought that she could be successfully towed to Milwaukee by putting 300 more posts into the hold and patching up the starboard bow. The *Leviathan*, with the wreck in tow, finally arrived in Milwaukee on July 14, almost nine months to the day after the disaster in North Bay.

Captain Kirtland returned with the *Leviathan,* but diver Crowley did not. It seems that Crowley's work was unsatisfactory, and Captain Kirtland discharged him at Escanaba. This so enraged Crowley that he attacked the captain with brass knuckles, knocking out several teeth and badly cutting and bruising his face. Captain Kirtland went to his home to recover but returned to his place of business in about 10 days. However, his injuries had not sufficiently healed, forcing him to remain in bed for a longer convalescence.

The *Leviathan* quickly turned around for Sister Bay, where she arrived on July 18 to continue work on the *E.C.L.* Because it was impossible to free her of water, she was stripped of everything of value in order to save enough to pay back the money spent in her purchase, and then abandoned.

After two weeks of delays, Wolf & Davidson placed the wreck of the *Two Friends* in dry dock. A thorough search of the remains revealed that she would need an entire new bottom; new keel, except for a small place forward; new deadwood aft; new decks and deck frames; and a full set of new spars. Her stern and bottom were by far the most injured parts of the craft. It was thought that when the schooner *Warmington* was released, she was one of the worst wrecked vessels ever taken from the beach, but inspection of the *Two Friends* revealed the fact that she was much worse. Most of the craft's outfit was saved after the disaster and could be utilized, but considerable rigging and sails were stolen at North Bay. In addition to the repairs already mentioned, the *Two Friends* would need a new stern post, a rudder and rudder post, a new steering

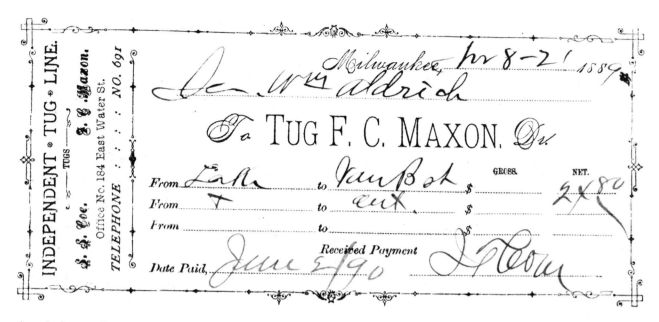

A receipt for a tow from Lake Michigan to VanBuren Street, Milwaukee, and back. Although the tow occurred on August 21, 1889, the bill was not paid until June 2, 1890, which was the usual procedure. Courtesy of Arni Wegner.

apparatus, a number of timber heads and tow posts, a new windlass, bulwarks and a portion of new rail, slight repairs to her top sides, and a new cabin. The cost of putting the vessel in condition for sea was variously estimated from $9,000 to $11,000, outside of whatever gear was saved.

While examining the vessel, Capt. Thomas Davidson called attention to the work done by Peter Crowley, the driver, to patch up all serious holes in the vessel's bottom. On the port side forward, a few feet below the watermark, several boards were nailed over an area that was wholly uninjured. Captain Davidson claimed that there was no need of boards there and that they had been nailed on in order to deceive the owners of the vessel about the amount of work done by Crowley. The latter had libeled the *Two Friends* to recover some $200 in wages he claimed were due him for the work done.

The *Two Friends* was thoroughly rebuilt in a short time, came out of dry dock on August 16, 1881, and was rechristened the *Pewaukee*. Since the *Two Friends* was a Canadian bottom, it was necessary for Wolf & Davidson to prove that they had significantly increased her value in order to be able to register the vessel. Collector Hall of the Milwaukee Custom House received a letter from Assistant Secretary of Commerce J. A. Upton instructing him to document the schooner *Pewaukee*, formerly the Canadian schooner *Two Friends*, as an American bottom, satisfactory evidence having been given that Wolf & Davidson expended three times the amount originally paid for the

craft, when on the beach, in rebuilding her and fitting out. The first enrollment of the schooner *Pewaukee* was issued at the port of Milwaukee on October 7, 1881, with the official no. 150233 assigned to the vessel. Her measurements were 310.26 gross, 294.75 net tons, and 135.4 x 25.7 x 11.0 feet, with three masts. She was placed in the iron ore trade between Escanaba and Chicago or Cleveland with a reported value of $15,000. For insurance purposes, the schooner rated A 2 with a value of $10,000 in the 1882 Inland Lloyds Vessel Register.

Although the wreck of the *Nabob* was delivered in Milwaukee by the *Leviathan* on June 18, she still lay with her nose on the bank of the river near Wolf & Davidson's yard at the end of summer. She was awaiting the action of some of the underwriters who had been so critical of Kirtland, Wolf & Davidson for not delivering her earlier in the spring. The *Nabob* was libeled by the United States marshall at Milwaukee in September for a claim of $7,800 held by the wrecking company for the cost of recovery.

Wolf & Davidson purchased the wreck at the marshall's sale for $1,015. They rebuilt the schooner in the winter of 1881–82 and renamed her the *Waukesha* on April 4 in honor of the hometown of William H. Wolf's wife. The first enrollment of the *Waukesha* was issued at the port of Milwaukee on April 20, 1882. Her dimensions were essentially unchanged in the rebuild, but the rig was changed from two to three masts. The value and classification of the schooner increased from $5,000 to $9,500 and from B 1- to A 2½ respectively. Capt. Julius Hagen of

Milwaukee was the first master of the *Waukesha* and served in that capacity through the season of 1886, when she was sold to F. H. Head of Chicago, the last principal owner. The schooner foundered with a cargo of salt at her anchorage off Muskegon, Michigan, in a heavy gale on November 7, 1896, to become a total loss. Six of the crew of seven were lost in the disaster.

The schooner *Pewaukee* went from the iron ore trade into the lumber trade in the fall of 1886 when Michael Hilty of Milwaukee became the principal owner, with John Nelson as master. For the season of 1887, the schooner rated A 2½ with a value of $6,000, down from $10,000 after the rebuild by Wolf & Davidson in 1881. On October 25, 1887, the schooner was bound for Garden Bay on the Garden Peninsula of Upper Michigan. At 6:00 A.M. she went on Detroit Island Reef near Detroit Island in the dreaded Death's Door and was soon carried up on to the shoal by the heavy sea that was rolling in at the time. The *Pewaukee* was on the reef pretty hard, raised about 6 inches all around, but was leaking very little, there being

not more than 4 inches of water in her. Detroit Island Reef, the site of numerous shipwrecks, is exposed to wind and sea from the north, east, and south, and unless the schooner was released, she would soon become a total wreck.

A telegram asking for assistance was received in Sturgeon Bay in the afternoon, and the wrecking tug *Jesse Spaulding*, [24] with full outfit, was chartered to the *Pewaukee* by Capt. John V. Tuttle of Milwaukee, who now represented the St. Paul Fire & Marine Insurance Company, which had insurance on the vessel. This was the same Captain Tuttle who had served as port captain for the *Leviathan* when she recovered the wreck of the *Two Friends* in North Bay. The expedition left Sturgeon Bay for the scene of the disaster that same evening.

The *Pewaukee's* crew, with the help of the lifesaving men from the Plum Island Station, stripped the schooner, which was said to be fast going to pieces. The tug *Spaulding* returned to Sturgeon Bay on the thirty-first, having failed to release the vessel, which her owners had aban-

A drawing of the schooner *Waukesha*, ex-*Nabob*, after she was rebuilt by Wolf and Davidson. Courtesy of the Wisconsin Marine Historical Society.

doned to the insurance companies. The last enrollment of the *Pewaukee* was surrendered at Milwaukee on November 4, 1887; cause of surrender: total loss. This declaration usually served as the death notice of a vessel, but sometimes it merely notified the underwriters that the owners wished to collect their insurance. In the case of the *Pewaukee*, ex-*Two Friends*, it proved to be the second time that the announcement of her passing was premature.

On the same day, November 4, the schooner *Pewaukee* was towed into Sturgeon Bay, having been released on the third by the tugs *George Nelson*[25] and *Spaulding*. She was leaking badly because her bottom had been pretty well scraped on the rocks. Leathem and Smith's 12-inch centrifugal pump was still on board to keep her afloat as she was towed to Manitowoc, where a survey was held on November 10. The *Pewaukee* was found to be in much better condition than expected, having lost none of her shape. She required a new forefoot, about 25 feet of new keel, and one piece of plank; and her bottom and center board box would have to be recaulked. The cost of repairs amounted to about $700, but this, with the general expense of $4,500, would bring the total cost to the underwriters to $5,200, equivalent to a total loss. The *Pewaukee* was insured for only $4,000, making a total outlay for the insurance companies of $9,200, while they owned the vessel worth about $5,000. On January 23, 1888, a new enrollment for the schooner *Pewaukee* was issued at the port of Milwaukee because she was reclaimed, with C. H. Bigelow as the principal owner and John V. Tuttle as master.

The next transition in the career of the *Pewaukee*, ex-*Two Friends*, occured in 1888. She was sold to John Leathem and Thomas H. Smith of Sturgeon Bay, and according to enrollment no. 6 issued at the port of Milwaukee on July 23, she received an engine and boiler to become the steam barge *Pewaukee*. As a steamer she would be much more profitable to her new owners than as a schooner. The propeller *Pewaukee* measured 310.26 gross, 228.07 net tons, but there were no changes in the dimensions of the hull: 135.5 x 26.4 x 10.8 feet, with one deck and three masts.

Leathem and Smith placed the *Pewaukee* in the lumber trade between Menominee and Chicago for the season of 1889 at a rate of $1.50 per 1,000 feet, which was maintained throughout the season. The propeller was laid up on November 28, having made a total of 36 trips during the season. Her average cargo was 325,000 feet of lumber, for a total of 11,700,000 feet transported to market, with the return to Leathem & Smith of $17,550.

Vessels with wooden hulls were harshly treated by wind and ice whether they were powered by steam or by sail. Seventeen years after her conversion to steam by Leathem & Smith, the *Pewaukee* was encountering the same difficulties experienced by the old schooners. On September 1, 1905, the *Pewaukee*, bound from Sturgeon Bay to Petoskey, Michigan, entered Baileys Harbor in tow of a tug during a heavy southeast gale. Her crew, consisting of Captain Morrison and only one other sailor, attempted to anchor but could not lower the anchors. The lifesavers at Baileys Harbor Station answered the signal of her whistle and boarded her. Finding no gear for lowering the anchors, they hoisted one over the side with handspikes. On September 2, the *Pewaukee* began to drag, and the station crew went aboard and worked the other anchor overboard. They found 4 feet of water in her hold and summoned a tug to pump her out. On the fifth, the lifesavers again went aboard the *Pewaukee* to raise the anchors by the force of much labor. The propeller then departed for the east shore to deliver her cargo of stone. The U.S. Life-Saving Service estimated the value of the vessel as $2,000 and the cargo as $700.

After almost 20 years of service as a steam barge, the *Pewaukee* was reduced to the lowest type of commercial vessel—the tow barge—in 1907. She was cut down to a barge at 353 total tons with one mast and no machinery to serve in the stone trade for the Leathem & Smith Towing & Wrecking Co. of Sturgeon Bay. The stone barge *Pewaukee* was relegated to the boneyard on October 7, 1912, with a tug shoving her up in the mud south of the shipyard. In October 1913, the barge was raised from the bed of mud north of Liberty Street in Sturgeon Bay with the use of two pumps and taken to the crushed stone quarry at the mouth of Green Bay for the final act. The old wooden hull was filled with stone, sunk, and used as a breakwater to protect the shore at the quarry. On November 10, 1913, she was reported exempt, that is, no longer in service as a commercial vessel, having been converted into a dock in Sturgeon Bay.

Thus ended the long life of the *Two Friends*, 40 years—some 33 years after her "total loss" in North Bay and 26 years after she supposedly passed out of existence in Death's Door. The account of the *Two Friends* is not unique. Rather than being the story of a particular sailing vessel, it represents the experiences of most vessels that survived the changes that occurred from the days of sail to the mastery of the lakes by steam. She was born as a barque, changed to a schooner, converted to a steam barge, reduced to a tow barge, and degraded to a dock between

1873 and 1913. The account also serves to point out the principal bulk trades in which vessels were prominent during this period: the grain trade, the iron ore trade, the lumber trade, and the stone trade. As the years progressed, most of these trades were dominated by larger steam vessels, leaving the schooners only the coastwise trade or exceptional freights where smaller quantities of bulk goods were transported.

We hope that the two divers who asked us "Where is the *Two Friends*?" finally have a proper answer.

CHAPTER TWO

Shipbuilding at Little Sturgeon Bay, 1866 to 1874

The largest city in Door County, Wisconsin, today is Sturgeon Bay. But before Sturgeon Bay, there was Little Sturgeon, situated on the shore of Little Sturgeon Bay just a few miles to the west. Little Sturgeon Bay juts southward into southern Door County from Green Bay, with Green Island and the twin cities of Marinette and Menominee to the northwest. To the northeast lie the headlands that anchor the shore of Green Bay and provide the harbors for northern Door County on the bay side.

Hjalmar R. Holand[1] has given an excellent account of the rise and fall of Little Sturgeon. This small village had the largest shipyard in Door County prior to the turn of the century. The vessels built and repaired at Little Sturgeon Bay saw lengthy service on all of the Great Lakes.

The driving force for the development of Little Sturgeon was Freeland B. Gardner of Chicago. Gardner's first establishment in the area was begun in 1850 at Pensaukee, Wisconsin, 23 miles north of Green Bay on the west bay shore. By 1857, it consisted of a large steam mill and a water mill for sawing lumber, a large boardinghouse, and a few houses. It was located at Pensaukee because of the good hardwood timber for shipbuilding in the vicinity and the abundant farmlands in the surrounding region. A dock was also built so that small steamers could load without difficulty. Lumber vessels, however, were loaded outside by scows.

In the early 1850s, Gardner moved to Little Sturgeon Bay, and on October 18, 1854, he bought the old homestead of Increase Claflin, the first pioneer in Door County. A large steam mill capable of sawing long timbers for bridges and vessels was completed in the fall of 1856. On Monday morning July 6, 1857, while all hands were busy in and around the mill, it caught fire from the smokestack, and the fire spread so rapidly that nothing of value was saved. The loss of the mill, provisions, and about 250,000 feet of lumber amounted to $65,000, with no insurance. The brig *Fanny Gardner*,[2] which was lying at the mill dock, was barely saved from burning. The mill was rebuilt, and the establishment expanded over a period of time to include a shingle mill, warehouses, limekilns, a shipyard, and docks. This chapter will document the construction and records of those vessels associated with the

golden age of Little Sturgeon Bay and relate some of the history of this early lumber settlement.

When Joseph Harris started the *Door County Advocate* in 1862, he debated whether to move the newspaper to Little Sturgeon since the only road to Green Bay passed through Little Sturgeon. It was said that Sturgeon Bay was the county seat but Little Sturgeon had the business. The first issue of the *Advocate* addressed the attention of farmers to an advertisement of the F. B. Gardner Saw and Flouring Mill.

In the August 16, 1862, issue of the *Advocate*, an article entitled "Shipbuilding" stressed the advantages of the Green Bay area for this industry. In part, it said,

> We call attention of shipbuilders to our Green Bay districts, as also to vessel proprietors, as a cheap and commodious locality. From the city of Green Bay northward to its connection with Lake Michigan, on both sides of the Bay, oak and other fine timber abounds, and can be obtained and furnished for ship building for one-third the cost than at more distant easterly localities, and of a far superior quality. We affirm 'that we do know' when we so assert as witness the *Parmelia Flood*,[3] built in Green Bay, the *F. B.*[4] and *Fannie Gardner*,[5] built at Pensaukee, and last, the *Two Fannies*, built the past winter, at Peshtigo. We fully believe that the Green Bay district is to be first of all ship building points on the Great Lakes.[6] No other locality has as fair timber or as easily and cheaply obtained. We invite attention to the fact of those whose business it is to build ships or to have them built.

However, because of the Civil War, shipbuilding did not begin at Little Sturgeon until 1866.

The brig *F. B. Gardner* was laid up in winter quarters at Little Sturgeon Bay in December 1865. This vessel had been built in 1855 at Sheboygan, Wisconsin, by Alfred Gilson for F. B. Gardner. During the winter of 1865–66, the *Gardner* was lengthened 60 feet[7] and converted into a barque. The white oak logs used in the lengthening were gotten out of the woods by Gardner's men and rafted to Little Sturgeon Bay. The rebuilding of the *Gardner* was under the supervision of Messrs. Spear and Newall.

Thomas Spear came to Wisconsin in 1857 from the state of Maine, where he had built many saltwater vessels. He located in Fort Howard (Green Bay), Brown County,

The *F. B. Gardner* in later years in the St. Mary's River at Sault Ste. Marie. The remains of the *Gardner* were located by divers in 1982. Courtesy of Fr. Edward J. Dowling, S.J.

with his wife, Amanda (Preble) Spear, and two sons, George O., age 17, and Albert Marshall, age 15. Thomas Spear continued his trade with much success and built the *Parmelia Flood* at Green Bay. The vessel, a full-rigged barque, was sent to the Atlantic laden with oak staves but was abandoned at sea while on a voyage from New Orleans to Liverpool in 1863. In 1860, Spear went to St. Louis, Missouri, but returned to Wisconsin in 1861 and resided at Peshtigo, Marinette County, for two years. Thomas Spear designed and built the barque *Two Fannies* at Peshtigo for the Peshtigo Company with his son George O. and a crew of 35 shipbuilders, mostly from Maine. Construction of the vessel began in December 1861, and the barque was launched in May of 1862. The *Two Fannies* was one of the largest vessels on the lakes, measuring 563³¹/₉₅ tons OM, with a carrying capacity of 30,000 bushels of grain or 400,000 feet of lumber.

Thomas Spear proceeded to Red River on the Green Bay shore in 1863 and erected a sawmill, which was destroyed by fire on Tuesday morning April 27, 1865. A large quantity of sawed shingles adjoining the mill also burned, and as result of the heavy loss, Thomas Spear moved to Gardner's establishment at Little Sturgeon Bay. At Little Sturgeon, he was assisted by his sons, George

O., an expert caulker, and Albert Marshall, who became an expert carpenter.

The reconstructed *F. B. Gardner* was launched on July 3, 1866, as part of the Fourth of July celebration at Little Sturgeon. Her rig was changed from a barque to a schooner in the spring of 1872. The *Gardner* served almost 40 years after being rebuilt at Little Sturgeon. In later years, the schooner was cut down to a barge with only two masts, and on September 15, 1904, while in tow of the steam barge *D. Leuty*,[8] the *F. B. Gardner* caught fire on Lake Huron between Port Sanilac and Forester, Michigan. She burned to the water's edge to become a total loss.

At the same time the *F. B. Gardner* was being rebuilt, the tug *Union*, owned by Gardner, was lengthened and converted into a freight and passenger boat. The *Union* had been built at Pensaukee in 1862 as a side-wheel steam tug, S. C. Fowles master carpenter, for towing purposes at Gardner's two sawmills at Little Sturgeon Bay and Pensaukee. The rebuilt *Union* was launched on April 13, 1866, and received her outfit in Green Bay. The steamer was placed in service on the west shore between Green Bay and Menominee, which was also the route of the side-wheeler *Queen City*.[9]

Gardner sold a one-half interest in the *Union* to A. C.

Brown of Green Bay, according to an enrollment issued on June 6, 1866, at Milwaukee, and the rival steamboat lines were consolidated. The *Queen City* and the *Union* ran on alternate days between Green Bay and Menominee. Early in 1867, these bay steamers were put into a stock company consisting of F. B. Gardner, A. C. Brown of Green Bay, Jesse Spaulding of Chicago, Isaac Stephenson of Marinette, and Samuel M. Stephenson of Menominee. The Green Bay & Menominee Navigation Co., William J. Fisk secretary, purchased the *Union*, with September 4, 1867, the date of the new enrollment. The West Shore Line of Green Bay, Lewis J. Day secretary, owned the *Union* in 1869, with Thomas Hawley of Green Bay as master.

Captain Hawley became a one-quarter owner in 1874 and sole owner in 1876. The *Union* was renovated by a Green Bay artist before the season of 1877, and were it not for various familiar landmarks about the hull, a casual observer would hardly have recognized the steamboat. A spread eagle adorned each paddle box, and the rather ancient whistle had given place to deep-toned chimes. The *Union* ran between Green Bay and west and east shore ports until the fall of 1879, when one of her wheels was badly smashed in the vicinity of Escanaba, Michigan. It took several days to make the return passage to Green Bay with one wheel. Captain Hawley had already commissioned John Gregory to build the side-wheel steamer *M. C. Hawley*[10] at Fort Howard to replace the *Union*. The *Hawley* received the machinery of the *Union* and a new boiler costing over $2,000. The dismantled *Union*, lying at Fort Howard in April 1880, broke away from her moorings during a heavy storm and went to pieces. Thus ended the eventful career of the old craft.

The summer of 1866 also saw the construction of the steamboat *John Spry* at Little Sturgeon by Thomas Spear for F. B. Gardner & Co., but she was not fitted out at Fort Howard until the spring of 1867. Her machinery was installed by Tim S. Hudson of Fort Howard, and she went into towing service at Pensaukee. The *Spry* served as a steamer and a tug on both sides of Green Bay in the interest of F. B. Gardner for 10 years. William H. Baptist of Green Bay, formerly a superintendent at Little Sturgeon, purchased the *Spry*, as recorded on an enrollment issued at Milwaukee on May 3, 1877. A devastating tornado destroyed Pensaukee on Saturday evening July 7, 1877. The *Spry*, lying at the dock, was leveled to the main deck, nothing but the engine and a small portion of one wheelhouse remaining on board. The steamer was rebuilt and sold to the estate of F. B. Gardner in the fall of 1882, with F. J. Page of Oconto as ship's husband.

The last owner of the *Spry* was A. J. Cointe of Little Suamico, Wisconsin, who purchased the vessel from the estate in 1884 for $500. She was valued at $6,000 and insured for $3,500, so this will give some idea of the depression in vessel property at the time. The *Spry* was fitted out as a freight and passenger boat and placed on the Fox River between Green Bay and Fond du Lac. While lying at a wharf about 3 miles north of Wrightstown, 10 miles south of Green Bay, on November 4, 1885, a fire started somewhere around the boiler and was under such headway when discovered that some of the men asleep on board had to jump overboard to escape. The steamer *John Spry* burned to the water's edge, and the last enrollment was surrendered at Milwaukee on November 23, 1885; cause of surrender: vessel burned, total loss.

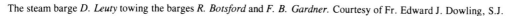

The steam barge *D. Leuty* towing the barges *R. Botsford* and *F. B. Gardner*. Courtesy of Fr. Edward J. Dowling, S.J.

In July 1866, Gardner purchased the powerful Mississippi River steamer *Ozaukee* for use as a tug at his establishments at Little Sturgeon and Pensaukee. She came from the Mississippi by the Fox and Wisconsin rivers, arriving at Green Bay on July 9. The *Ozaukee* was built in 1857 at Port Washington, Wisconsin, with Alva Trowbridge as the managing owner. She was rebuilt and refitted for regular passenger service at Little Sturgeon before the season of 1867. Her cabin was enlarged and upholstered, and everything furnished to contribute to the comforts of her passengers. The *Ozaukee* was scheduled for two trips a week between Sturgeon Bay and Green Bay and a weekly trip to Egg Harbor and Fish Creek. The steamer *Ozaukee* caught fire and was burned to the water's edge while lying at the dock at Little Sturgeon on December 2, 1870. The fire originated while the crew was ashore at dinner and was discovered bursting out of the pilothouse. The hull was comparatively uninjured, but the upper works were entirely destroyed and the machinery badly damaged. She was not insured and was valued at about $8,000. The hull was hauled out and the *Ozaukee* immediately rebuilt at Little Sturgeon, with the machinery installed at Pensaukee.

F. B. Gardner & Co. sold the vessel to Albert M. Spear in December 1875 for $2,000, and in May 1877 the *Ozaukee* was purchased by F. J. Page of Oconto for towing purposes along the Green Bay shore. She was sold to parties at Ashland in 1878 and engaged in towing on Lake Superior. On May 27, 1884, the paddle steamer *Ozaukee* foundered in Lake Superior at Bad River, Wisconsin, and was a total loss. The disaster was caused by heavy seas, which broke over her while she was out in the lake. The crew succeeded in making their escape to the shore in a small boat.

The first large vessel built at Little Sturgeon was the *Pensaukee*. Preparation for construction of this 177-foot barque began in December 1866. Fourteen ship carpenters were brought in from Canada. Altogether, 60 carpenters were at work on this, the fiftieth vessel built by Thomas Spear. Unusual care was taken in the construction of the new vessel, using nothing but the best quality timber. On the day of her launch, the ways broke down, letting the stern drop on the ground. No damage resulted from the mishap, and the *Pensaukee* was launched on May 11, 1867. As a barque, she had three masts and a carrying capacity for 35,000 bushels of wheat or 400,000 feet of lumber. The cost to Gardner for the vessel was $60,000, which proved to be an excellent investment.

In five consecutive weeks during the fall of 1870, the *Pensaukee*, carrying over 700 tons, made five round trips between Pensaukee and Chicago and at no time carried less than 475,000 feet of lumber, which had to be loaded and unloaded. Gardner sold the barque to James S. Dunham of Chicago during the season of 1872, and a good run was sailed from Chicago to Buffalo in five days of November 1872. The *Pensaukee* was rerigged as a schooner in 1874 and continued to record fast sailings out of Chicago for Dunham. In August of 1876, she made the round trip between Chicago and Bay City, Michigan, in 11½ days, including 4 days in loading, and during the season of 1877 a round trip to Buffalo from Chicago in 14 days.

Many of the sailing ships that were on the lakes in the great gale of October 15 and 16, 1880, suffered some damage, and the *Pensaukee* was no exception. The schooner was en route to Chicago from Cheboygan, Michigan, with her hold and deck loaded with lumber when the storm struck. She made the anchorage at Plum Island in Death's Door but pounded out the backing of her rudder on the rocks, broke her steering gear, and began leaking badly, besides suffering damage to canvas. After the damage had been sustained, the deck load was jettisoned at a loss of $1,235.

The new tug *A. W. Lawrence*[11] of Sturgeon Bay was dispatched to tow the *Pensaukee* to her home port of Chicago for repairs. The tug stopped at Sturgeon Bay and picked up the crew of the schooner *Ann Maria*[12] of Ludington, another victim of the gale. The *Ann Maria* waterlogged and was abandoned off Portage, Michigan, where her crew was picked up by the schooner *Reindeer* and landed at the Lake Michigan entrance to the canal on October 19. The *Pensaukee,* in tow of the *Lawrence,* arrived in Chicago on the twenty-fourth to be placed in dry dock on the twenty-fifth. The rudder and steering gear were readily repaired, and the schooner came out of dry dock only five days later at a cost of $1,200.

The *Pensaukee,* Capt. O. E. Lawson in command, was driven ashore light in the September blow of 1883 and suffered severe damage. She cleared Chicago on August 29 with 38,523 bushels of corn and 200 barrels of pork to arrive at Collingwood, Ontario, on September 3. On the return trip, the schooner struggled in heavy weather at night off Lighthouse Point about a mile below Cheboygan, Michigan. It was raining, blowing hard, and very thick, with all hands on deck to keep a strict lookout. They could see the light on the point but thought that they had enough water to clear. Suddenly, breakers appeared ahead, the signal for dangerous shoal water, but it was too late to avoid striking the bottom. The *Pensaukee* went on with full force, well out of the water at 4:00 A.M. Friday, September 7.

The sea kept working the schooner in until she came to rest, with 2 feet of water under the bow and 7 feet aft, on a rock shelf covered with 3 feet of sand. The *Pensaukee* began to leak and filled with water to the level of the lake. Captain Lawson and the crew came ashore on Saturday noon to negotiate for assistance to dredge her out. The wrecking tug *Champion*[13] of Detroit, which was stationed at Cheboygan, and a small tug were sent to the wreck, and the tug *Sweepstakes*[14] put a steam pump on board the *Pensaukee*. The water was so shallow that the *Champion* could not get close enough to be of service, but the small tug dredged the sand away from the hull. Progress was slow because northerly winds kept filling up the channel with sand. The tugs were able to slue the stranded vessel only a short distance each day, for example, 140 feet on the twelfth. Finally, the schooner was pulled off by the *Champion* on September 17 to be towed inside the harbor at Cheboygan. After coaling, the tug towed the *Pensaukee* to Manitowoc for repairs in Rand & Burger's dry dock as per instructions from her owner, James S. Dunham.

The schooner was valued at $20,000 and insured for $14,400, placed as follows: State of Pennsylvania, $4,400; Boston Marine, $4,000; Western Assurance, $2,000; Thames and Mersey, $4,000. The cost of rescuing the vessel was $3,000, with the cost of repairs about $4,000, but Dunham took the opportunity to have the *Pensaukee* thoroughly rebuilt because she had been classed down to B1 for insurance purposes by Inland Lloyds for the past three years.

The *Pensaukee* was renamed *James G. Blaine* by Dunham on enrollment no. 41 issued at the Port of Chicago on December 11, 1890. He sold her to the Waide Transportation Co. of Chicago according to an enrollment issued on April 5, 1900. The *Blaine* was reduced to an "x" schooner with two masts and a capacity for 672,000 feet of lumber to serve as a tow barge, or consort, a vessel dragged about the lakes by a steam-powered craft. Two years later, Charles H. Ripsom of Oswego bought the barge and sold her to Walter K. Fullum of Buffalo in 1904. The last owner of the *Blaine* was the George Hall Coal Co., which registered the vessel at Ogdensburg on May 28, 1907.

The *James G. Blaine,* born in a bay on a western lake and christened *Pensaukee,* was lost on an eastern lake just after her forty-first birthday. The *Blaine* was in command of Capt. Samuel LeFlam; on board with him were Mr. and Mrs. W. Meyers, first mate and cook, and four deckhands, all residents of Ogdensburg. The barge left Charlotte, New York, at 11:15 A.M. Tuesday, July 7, 1908, with the barge *Walter A. Sherman,*[15] Capt. Matt Hourigan of Oswego, both being in tow of the tug *William L.*

Proctor,[16] Capt. A. McDonald. The *Blaine* was loaded with 1,014 tons of slack coal consigned to the George Hall Coal Co. at Prescott, Ontario. At 9:00 P.M., the tow ran into Oswego to pick up the barge *Argosy.*[17]

They left Oswego and had been running about half an hour when a gale struck, compelling them to return to Oswego for shelter. The *Proctor* landed the barges at the new pier just before 2:00 A.M. Everything went well until early in the morning, when it was discovered that the *Blaine* had sprung a number of bad leaks from pounding against the pier. It was feared that she might sink, and it was decided to shift her into the shoal water of the old harbor.

About 6:30 A.M., the *Proctor* took her in tow, and hardly had the tug commenced to round her consort into the river before the towline broke. Another one was quickly passed, but that likewise gave way. Then a third, a new 8-inch line, was thrown from the *Proctor,* but it faired the same fate as the other two, snapped as though it were a piece of twine as soon as the tug started to pull.

By that time the wind and strong current working out of the new harbor had carried the *Blaine* abreast of the lifesaving station, close to the east pier. The *Proctor* was also in shoal water, and it was feared for a time that she might be dashed on the rocks. However, Captain McDonald abandoned his efforts to keep the *Blaine* from beaching to save his own boat. A minute after the third tow line parted, the barge began to strike bottom. She struck fast 500 to 600 feet northeast of the station and 100 yards from shore under the Fort Bank, a place dreaded by sailors endeavoring to make port in a northwester.

Meanwhile, Capt. Frederick Anderson of the lifesaving crew had launched the surfboat, and the work of rescuing the crew was underway five minutes after the *Blaine* hit the rocks. It was apparent to the lifesavers that the barge would go to pieces in a short time. Mrs. Meyers was taken off first, with some difficulty, and before the last of the seven were safely in the surfboat, the foremast fell. Fortunately, the crew had huddled aft awaiting rescue, thereby escaping death or serious injury under the maze of the splintered mast and rigging.

The crew had hardly been safely landed in the lifesaving station before the starboard side of the *Blaine* caved in. She began to disintegrate so quickly that most of the belongings of the crew were lost. Half an hour after she first struck, the barge was a total loss; by 8:00 P.M., the soft coal had been washed away and the remains consisted of a spar and a few timbers washed up on the beach by the big combers. The estimated value of the vessel was $4,000 and the cargo $1,750.

The schooner *Lake Forest*, built in 1869 at Little Sturgeon Bay, taken on the Detroit River. Her 3,400 yards of canvas made her one of the fastest schooners on the lakes. Courtesy of Fr. Edward J. Dowling, S.J.

The amount of lumber cut at Little Sturgeon Bay during 1867 was 4,500,000 feet. A lath and shingle mill were added during the winter of 1867–68, and the gristmill was improved. Gardner sold the mill property, including the steamer *Ozaukee,* to Erastus Bailey and Tristam Vincent in February 1868. Preparations for the building of another large vessel began at Little Sturgeon in the summer of 1868. The new schooner was being built for Messrs. Bailey and Vincent by Thomas Spear and son to be finished in time for the opening of navigation the next spring. She was built sharp forward with a clean run aft to be a staunch, fast vessel. The schooner was launched on April 17, 1869, and named *Lake Forest* in honor of the city in which the owners lived. She looked well in the water, and it was felt that her 3,400 yards of canvas, together with her clean run, would make her one of the fastest schooners on the lakes. The *Lake Forest* left for Chicago

early in May with a cargo of lumber under the command of Capt. R. J. Stubbs. Gardner officially acquired the schooner on March 19, 1870, but sold her two days later to Henry S. Halsted of Chicago.

Predictions about her speed proved correct. On Wednesday evening September 22, 1875, the *Lake Forest* left Chicago, loaded 353,000 feet of lumber at Whitehall, Michigan, and departed for Buffalo on Sunday morning. She arrived at her destination Wednesday night, making the whole trip in a little over seven days. In October 1876, the *Lake Forest* was reported to have made the run from Sheboygan to Chicago in nine hours, but as is the case for all modes of transportation, the price of speed is often disaster.

A year later, the schooner, Captain Nelson, was bound from Buffalo to Chicago with coal in an easterly gale with fog and a heavy sea. She struck on Thunder Bay Island

Reef one mile due south of North Point, Lake Huron, at 11:30 A.M. on October 10, 1877. The wreck was discovered by Keeper J. S. Matthews of Life-Saving Station No. 4 (Thunder Bay Island), who started to her assistance with the lifeboat and a crew of eight men. By the time they reached her, the schooner had jumped the reef and anchored, leaking badly. Her rudder had been carried away, sails split, and bulwarks stove in. One of the ten men on board, Peter B. Olson, had been killed by the falling of the foreboom when she struck, and the other nine were completely exhausted from pumping. Since the vessel was already sinking, the lifeboat crew relieved the men at the pumps to keep the *Lake Forest* from going down.

Shortly afterward, Captain Nelson boarded the lifeboat and started for Alpena, about 5 miles distant, to procure the services of a tug and fresh men to save his schooner. On the way, the schooner *J. B. Kitchen*[18] was observed 4 miles away flying signals of distress. She was bound for Cleveland from Fayette, a furnace town on the Garden Peninsula of Upper Michigan, with pig iron and a crew of eight. The *Kitchen* was leaking, her booms and gaffs were broken, her canvas was blown away, and her exhausted crew had water in the hold gaining on them. The lifeboat headed for the *Kitchen,* took off Captain Herington, and bore away for Alpena, where the two captains engaged three tugs to assist their schooners.

They steamed out under cover of land for North Point, with the lifeboat in tow and fresh men to relieve the crews at the pumps. The sea was running so high between the point and the stranded vessels that the tugs were unable to reach them, but the lifeboat succeeded in getting alongside each schooner and transferring the men. Both craft were safely brought into the harbor by the tugs the next morning, the sea having subsided somewhat. The estimated amount of the loss to the *Lake Forest* and her cargo was $3,000; for the *Kitchen* the amount was $1,000. The *Lake Forest* had to receive nearly an entire new keel at Chicago before she could be returned to service.

During September 1880, the *Lake Forest,* Capt. H. H. Kramer, accomplished one of the fastest, if not the fastest, trips on record during the previous 25 years. She left Ford River, Michigan, about 7 miles south of Escanaba, on a Tuesday evening with 500 tons of ice and reached Buffalo at 9:00 P.M. Friday, making the trip in exactly three days. To our knowledge, the only run to which it can be compared was made by the barque *Canada* in 1854, when she sailed from Chicago to Buffalo in three days and eight hours.

If the colloquialism "leaker" did not originate with sailing ships, it should have. After years of exposure to the

Another view of the *Lake Forest* on the Detroit River. In October 1876, she was reported to have made the run from Sheboygan to Chicago in nine hours. Courtesy of Fr. Edward J. Dowling, S.J.

forces of wind, water, and ice, which worked their wooden hulls and tore out the caulking, they leaked continuously and had to be pumped out constantly, usually by hand-operated bilge pumps. The U.S. Life-Saving Service came to the rescue of the leaker *Lake Forest* at least twice in her later years. On April 26, 1902, about three weeks after the schooner had been sold to James E. Erickson of Milwaukee by James T. Johnson of Chicago, she was sighted by the lookout of the Frankfort Station 4 miles to the north flying a distress signal. The station crew pulled to the schooner at once and followed her into port. The *Lake Forest* had sprung a leak en route to Milwaukee from East Tawas, Michigan, and the crew had become exhausted at the pumps trying to keep her afloat. She was loaded with cedar logs and had 4 feet of water in the hold. The lifesavers pumped the schooner out and returned to the station after making arrangements to provide further assistance if the master, Captain Ketteas, should signal. While lying at a wharf near the Old Chicago Station on October 21, 1904, leaking badly, with her crew exhausted from incessant pumping, Capt. James E. Erickson requested assistance. A crew of surfmen pumped her out and assisted her to the dock, where she was to discharge a cargo of lumber from Manistique, Michigan. At the time, the *Lake Forest* was valued at $4,000 and the cargo at $4,200.

These encounters with Lake Michigan were but the beginning of the end for the *Lake Forest.* Her last owners were Christ. Nerdrum, James E. Erickson, and Theodore J. Kjeldass, all of Milwaukee, each owning one-third. The last enrollment for the schooner *Lake Forest* was surrendered at Chicago on March 7, 1910; cause of surrender: dismantled and converted into a barge. She was not enrolled as a barge, so her official record ends here.

In the fall of 1869, Messrs. Bailey and Vincent sold the Little Sturgeon Bay mill property back to Gardner. The shipments from Little Sturgeon for the 1869 season were 5,000,000 feet of lumber, 8,000,000 cut shingles, and 150 cords of wood. For the next two years, there was a pause in shipbuilding, but Gardner continued to develop the Little Sturgeon plant. He built an addition to the mill and a large shed, 420 feet long and 40 feet wide, to store shingles in. During the season of 1870, 11,000,000 shingles were cut with one machine; the largest number cut in one day was 95,000. A patent limekiln was erected near the point of the bluff for the purpose of supplying Green Bay and the west shore with lime. In March 1871, Gardner purchased a steam dredge in Chicago and brought it to Little Sturgeon to deepen the channel to the dock.

The mill at Little Sturgeon cut 106,000 shingles with a Valentine machine and 6,100 feet of lumber with one circular saw in one and one-quarter hours on July 20, 1871. The total of six day's sawing by the one machine, from July 19 through 25, was 602,500 shingles. The mill had no stop exceeding five minutes for three months' running time.

Great fire storms ravaged 1,280,000 acres of Wisconsin and Upper Michigan in the fall of 1871. The so-called Peshtigo Fire included large areas of southern Door County and Kewaunee County, particularly on the Green Bay side. On Sunday night October 8, 1871, Peshtigo, Wisconsin, a booming town of 1,700 people was wiped out of existence in the greatest forest fire in American history. Loss of life and property in the great fire that occurred on the *same night* in Chicago did not match the toll of death and destruction visited on northeastern Wisconsin during those same dreadful hours. The town of Peshtigo was built around a woodenware factory, the largest in the county. Every building in the community was lost, and the tornado of fire claimed at least 800 lives in the Peshtigo area alone.

One of the hardest hit settlements in Door County was Williamsonville, just a few miles south of Little Sturgeon Bay, near Brussels. The Williamson brothers came to Door in the late 1860s, to what was said to be the most desolate part of the peninsula—Gardner Township. Not

being foreign immigrants, they had arrived in the wilderness with more resources than the European settlers. The brothers took possession of 480 acres of timberland and became shingle makers. Instead of making shingles one at a time by hand, as was the practice, they erected a shingle mill. They built a home, a barn, a boarding house, a store, a blacksmith shop, and a number of shanties for the millhands. Since Little Sturgeon Bay was a safe harbor, they could haul wagonloads of shingles to the dock for shipment on lake vessels. From April 22 to July 19, 1871, 21 vessels and propellers loaded lumber and shingles at Little Sturgeon for Gardner, and 6 vessels loaded shingles for Williamson Bros.

There were 76 persons living in Williamsonville, including 15 women and 16 children. The fire tornado that had already consumed New Franken to the south struck Williamson's mill on October 8, 1871. It destroyed the settlement and claimed the lives of 59 persons, including 11 women and 14 children. The site of this tragedy is now a county park, Tornado Memorial Park, 10 miles southwest of Sturgeon Bay on Highway 57.

From Williamsonville, the fire swept north to Little Sturgeon. The establishment was hard pressed by the fire and was saved only by the extraordinary vigilance of Wil-

A map of the Peshtigo Fire area in Wisconsin and Upper Michigan. Broken lines indicate the approximate area devastated—some 1,280,000 acres. The insert map outlines Wisconsin and Upper Michigan and shows the estimated burned-over portions of the two states. Courtesy of Robert W. Wells.

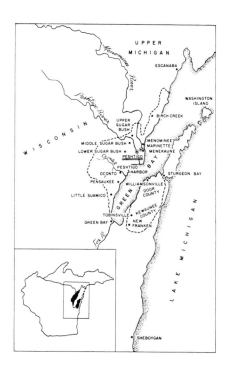

liam H. Baptist, Gardner's superintendent. He rallied the hired hands, and with the bay at their backs to supply water, they managed to save the settlement. Baptist served as a relief agent after the fire and furnished sufficient lumber to put up a dozen shanties in his town. He also cleared out roads and forwarded stoves and stores with his own teams.

The steamer *Union* played a prominent role in the rescue of refugees from the fire and carried the first news of the disaster to the outside world. The *Union,* Captain Hawley, made trips three times a week between Green Bay and Marinette, touching at Pensaukee, Oconto, and Menominee as well as Peshtigo. The steamer *George L. Dunlap* [19] was built to carry passengers and freight for the Chicago & Northwestern Rail Road between Green Bay and Escanaba until the railroad was built to connect these cities in 1872. The steamer *St. Joseph* [20] was owned by the Goodrich Transportation Co. and left Chicago for Green Bay every Friday evening, with a stop on Sunday at Fish Creek, Menominee, Peshtigo, and Oconto. All three steamers were in Menominee the night of the great fire.

After the fire had destroyed Peshtigo, it roared north to the twin lumber towns of Marinette and Menominee along the Wisconsin-Michigan border. Captain Hawley estimated that 300 refugees crowded aboard the *Union* that fateful night. He allowed the steamer to drift down the channel toward the bay, only using her power to keep the wind from shoving the vessel against the Michigan bank of the river. The captain explained later that the channel was so narrow and the smoke so thick that he did not dare steam down the river for fear the *Union* would run aground. Fires were burning on both sides before the steamer reached the river mouth, but Hawley took his vessel through unscathed to the safety of Green Bay, Lake Michigan. The *Union* remained on the bay overnight before returning to Marinette.

Once the residents of Marinette were convinced that their own losses were minor by comparison, they reacted promptly. Isaac "Ike" Stephenson, the leading timber king of Marinette, dashed off messages asking for help. He entrusted the messages to Captain Hawley, who agreed to send them as soon as he could get to the city of Green Bay. By the time the *Union* unloaded its passengers at Marinette, survivors from Peshtigo were beginning to straggle in. Captain Hawley took some of them aboard, including a number of injured, and steamed for Green Bay. It was not until the evening of October 9, when the *Union* arrived at Green Bay, that the first news of the great disaster at Peshtigo was dispatched to the rest of the nation.

The only significant activity in Gardner's shipyard during this period was the rebuilding of the barque *Norman.* The *Norman* had been built with three masts in 1848 at Sacketts Harbor, New York, by Ellenwood for D. C. Littlejohn, Henry Fitzhugh, and James Peck. Gardner bought the barque from Howard C. Gardiner of Chicago before the season of 1865, sold it to Joseph McGee (4/6), Capt. Patrick Meyers (1/6), and Capt. Thomas Meyers (1/6), all of Chicago, before the season of 1867, and acquired it a second time on April 21, 1870, according to enrollments issued at Chicago on these dates. The *Norman* was laid up at Little Sturgeon in December 1870 to be rebuilt from the water's edge at a cost of about $5,500. The vessel was not hauled out but left in the ice, where new planks were placed in the hull starting one plank below the waterline. On her first trip to Chicago, in May 1871, the *Norman* sprung a leak near Little Sister Bay and was compelled to put back to Little Sturgeon. The trouble was in the old planking below the waterline, which was quickly repaired before she departed a second time for Chicago. James S. Dunham of Chicago purchased the barque before the season of 1873 and changed the rig from a barque to that of a schooner, like the *Pensaukee.*

After 50 years of service, 28 years after the rebuild at Little Sturgeon, the schooner *Norman* was showing her age. While underway from Manistique to Chicago with a cargo of lumber, she sprung a leak and put into Frankfort for shelter on November 9, 1898. The master and sole owner, Capt. Henry Hust, asked assistance of the station crew to pump her out because his crew was exhausted. Surfmen worked all night but were unable to gain on the water. Captain Hust decided to let the schooner fill with water and sent for a steam pump. He sold the cargo of wood, discharged it, had the schooner pumped out, and made temporary repairs before returning to Chicago. The last enrollment of the *Norman* was surrendered at Chicago on June 22, 1901; cause of surrender: dismantled and abandoned as unfit for service.

The Chicago fire spurred the demand for building materials of all kinds, and F. B. Gardner's mill at Little Sturgeon responded to the need. In the winter of 1871-72, the logging camps of F. B. Gardner & Co. got out about 8,000,000 feet, and the sawmill was extensively remodeled. One of the old boilers was torn out and replaced with two new ones, making four 24-foot boilers in position. The old engine was replaced by a new, more powerful one. The old Valentine shingle machine was replaced by a new machine of greater cutting capacity. A new circular saw was put in that doubled the lumber-cutting power of the mill, and a new gang edger was installed. A stave ma-

The *Halsted*, built in 1873 at Little Sturgeon Bay, taken in the St. Mary's River at Sault Ste. Marie. She was designed for a capacity of 38,000 bushels of grain or 500,000 feet of lumber. Courtesy of Fr. Edward J. Dowling, S.J.

chine that had been in the Pensaukee mill was also installed at Little Sturgeon. These additions and improvements nearly doubled the capacity of the mill.

In the fall of 1872, two new patent limekilns were completed on the point near the old one. The lime manufactured from the three kilns, a capacity of 200 barrels per day, and large quantities of limestone for building purposes were shipped to Chicago. To facilitate these shipments, a solid dock was constructed, with 150 feet of frontage and a wing that extended back from one end. The water was 17 feet deep at one end on the front and 24 feet at the other end. The dock was built of squared timber and logs, securely bolted with iron bolts, stayed with piles, filled with stone, and protected by boiler iron from the action of the ice.

The next large schooner built at Little Sturgeon was the best known of all because of her longevity. Construction of this vessel by Thomas Spear, master carpenter, began late in 1872. The schooner was intended for Gardner, but because of business reverses, it was completed for Henry S. Halsted of Chicago and named the *Halsted*. Her construction was superintended by Capt. John G. Keith, who was the first master. Her three spars, sails, and rigging were the work of John Wood, later Captain Wood, who

accompanied Captain Keith as mate for nearly all the time he was in command. The schooner *Halsted* was launched on May 1, 1873. She had a carrying capacity of 500,000 feet of lumber and measured 496.53 total tons. Like her predecessor the *Lake Forest*, the *Halsted* proved to be a fast and able vessel. In November 1873, the *Halsted* made the round trip between Milwaukee and Buffalo in 11½ days. Another fast sailing was made in November 1874 from Chicago to Escanaba and back to Milwaukee with a cargo of iron ore in 4½ days.

An excellent description of the record of the *Halsted* was given in the *Door County Advocate* of December 13, 1883, after she had arrived in Sturgeon Bay for the winter layup and repairs: "The *Halsted* has had her share of adventure, and had she not been a strongly-built vessel would probably now be under water. About three years after she came out she collided with the bark *City of Painesville*,[21] on Lake Erie, and while the *Halsted* was not much injured, the bark went to the bottom in five minutes. A year later she encountered the schooner *Jane M. Scott*, of Oswego, in the straits of Mackinac, losing her jibs and receiving other damage, but continuing to Sheboygan, where she was to load."

Actually, the *Halsted* had encountered the coal-laden

24

A painting of the barkentine *City of Painesville*, which was built in 1867 at Fairport, Ohio, by D. E. and J. E. Bailey. Courtesy of Fr. Edward J. Dowling, S.J.

schooner *J. Maria Scott* [22] in the Straits of Mackinac while bound from Milwaukee to Cheboygan, Michigan, for lumber on the night of November 9, 1875. The *Halsted* had her port bow stove in, staysail boom broken, and two jibs torn. The *Scott* lost her bowsprit and jibboom, and was leaking badly after the collision. She was taken through to Chicago for repairs by the tug *Crusader.* [23] The *Halsted* continued to Cheboygan, loaded a cargo of lumber, and returned to Milwaukee, where the damages sustained, including several broken frames, were estimated at about $2,000. Owner Halsted libeled the *Scott* for $2,500, and the *Halsted* was repaired in the Union Dry-Dock Yards at Buffalo in the spring of 1876. However, the owners of the *Scott* did not settle the $2,500 judgment rendered against her until early in January 1880. With interest and costs, the total amount paid was $3,384.46.

Continuing from the *Advocate,*

In the spring of 1881 she was beached on Celia Shoal, in the straits of Mackinac, and had her forefoot knocked off. She was loaded with grain for Buffalo, and after being hauled off went on to her destination. When she arrived at Buffalo Capt. Keith was paid off and Mr. Wood was promoted to the command of the vessel.

With the exception of her decks the *Halsted* is almost as sound as when she was launched. When she was built she was thoroughly salted, between two and three hundred barrels being used, and the application has been renewed every winter since that time. Capt. Wood now has forty barrels on board for present use, and as much or more has been put into the vessel every year, making not far from six hundred barrels used since her construction. The *Halsted* cost $45,000 and has a capacity of about 38,000 bushels. She has just had a thorough washing-out, and during the winter will receive a new deck and be otherwise put in good repair. Her seams are so tight that

when she was pumped out, a few days ago, she had less than six inches of water, although she had not been pumped before for three weeks.

The crew of the Evanston Life-Saving Station, Lake Michigan, rescued 10 men from the stranded *Halsted* on Thanksgiving Day, November 24, 1887. The schooner had left Buffalo for Chicago on November 12 with 950 tons of coal and had experienced thick and heavy easterly weather on the voyage. During a dense fog, Capt. George Pollock lost his bearings and struck on the rocks near the village of Glencoe, Illinois, about 8 miles north of the station, at 10:00 P.M. on the twenty-third. There was a high sea running, and the captain wisely scuttled the *Halsted* to prevent her from pounding to pieces. The breakers swept the decks, forcing the crew to the cabin roof, where they spent a terrible night soaked to the skin and almost frozen.

In the morning, they found that they were within a few hundred yards of a line of high bluffs but that the surf was rushing in with such fury it would be little better than suicide to attempt to reach the shore in their yawl. It was not until 9:30 A.M. that the schooner was accidently discovered by a resident of Glencoe who happend to walk down to the beach. He promptly telegraphed Evanston, and the station keeper, Captain Lawson, mustered his crew of college boys, procured several horses, and set out for the wreck with the surfboat and beach apparatus.

The roads were good only part of the way, and after a hard tramp over hills and along the beach, the lifesavers arrived at 11:30 A.M. The bank was steep and some 80 feet high, but fortunately a pathway of fair width led to the shore, enabling the crew to run the boat down to the water. Although the surf was heavy, it was decided to attempt the rescue with the surfboat rather than by means of the breeches buoy because the buoy required considerable time to rig. A launch was made about 400 yards north of the *Halsted,* the only available place since a small breakwater had to be cleared to reach her. The seas were dashing in from both the northeast and southeast, almost at right angles with each other, and the surfboat was thrown on its beam-ends. The keeper was flung over the side and the boat passed over him, but as he came up he grabbed one of the surfmen's oars and was pulled aboard. So much water had been shipped by this time that the crew pulled back to shore to bail out.

The second launch was safely made, but just as the boat crossed the bar in the heaviest of breakers the steering oar broke. The keeper quickly grabbed the oar from the nearest man and by skillful management rounded the bow of the *Halsted* to drop in under her lee quarter. Since there was no immediate danger of the schooner's breaking up, the half-drowned and frozen sailors were taken ashore five at a time, the boat being backed up to the narrow strip of beach on each trip. They were furnished with a good dinner by the people of Glencoe and then left for Chicago by rail. Two of the surfmen subsequently assisted a wrecking party to float the badly damaged *Halsted,* which was released on November 29 without any loss of cargo and towed to Chicago. The schooner was valued at $25,000 and the cargo at $6,000.

The *Halsted* was rebuilt in 1888 for Annie Halsted and sold to the Soper Lumber Co. of Chicago in 1892. Like many Great Lakes schooners, she was cut down to a schooner-barge with only two masts to be towed by a steam barge in the winter of 1900–01. While in the lumber trade for the Soper Lumber Co., the *Halsted and the Middlesex*[24] were towed by the steam barge *James H. Prentice.*[25] The *Halsted* sank in the Peavey Slip, Duluth, Minnesota, on May 2, 1910, while in tow of the *Prentice.* The barge was pumped out by the Union Towing & Wrecking Co. and raised on May 7.

The *Halsted* was one of the many victims of the great storm that swept the lakes from November 8 to 12, 1913. The *James H. Prentice,* with the *Halsted* in tow, sought shelter in Washington Harbor, Washington Island, Lake Michigan, from the ravages of the gale. They were en route light from Marinette, Wisconsin, to Spanish Mills, Ontario. The winds grew so strong that their anchors dragged, and the *Prentice* left the barge with a crew of seven to the mercy of the storm.

The steamer *Louisiana,*[26] Capt. Fred McDonald, also sought refuge in Washington Harbor on the northwest corner of Washington Island. The steamer had left Lorain, Ohio, on November 2 with a load of coal for Milwaukee. After arriving there and unloading her cargo, the *Louisiana* departed in ballast for the iron ore dock at Escanaba, Michigan. The east winds were moderate as she worked up the Wisconsin shore and through Porte des Morts Passage, Death's Door. After the steamer cleared the passage and turned north on the course for Escanaba, the wind suddenly shifted to the northwest, and as it turned colder, snow began falling. The winds began making high seas as the *Louisiana* labored into the wind. As they passed Washington Island, Captain McDonald decided to seek shelter in Washington Harbor because of the adverse weather.

After entering the harbor, the *Louisiana* anchored on the windward side near the *Halsted* and came around into the wind. As the gale increased in force, the steamer started to drag farther into the harbor. Because she was light

and, therefore, high in the water, much of the hull was exposed to winds that reached velocities in excess of 70 miles per hour. The *Louisiana* continued to drag anchors and nearly hit the *Halsted* several times before stranding on the beach. A few hours after going on the rocks, the crew discovered a fire between the decks of the wooden steamer, forcing them to launch the lifeboat in an attempt to make the beach. Fortunately, their lifeboat was in the lee of the burning boat, and they were carried safely ashore. The crew of the *Halsted* watched helplessly as the *Louisiana,* valued at $15,000, hit the beach and burned to a total loss.

Meanwhile, the lifesaving crew of the Plum Island Station in Death's Door had been summoned to the assistance of the *Louisiana.* On November 9, they brought their beach apparatus in the lifeboat to Detroit Harbor, where they learned of the disaster to the steamer. They were also informed that the *Halsted* was in danger in Washington Harbor, so they proceeded overland to the aid of the barge.

They found the *Halsted* about three-fourths of a mile from the head of the harbor, dragging toward the shore. The barge was too far from land at the time to be reached by a line, and no open boat could have survived the gale that was blowing with almost hurricane force. They stood helpless, waiting for the doomed vessel to come closer to shore.

The progress of the *Halsted* shoreward was exceedingly deliberate. Her anchors would fetch her up and hold for perhaps an hour at a time, when a recurring increase in the velocity of the wind would send her dragging again. This agonizing action continued for 20 hours until at 5:00 A.M. on November 10 she lay within 60 feet of the shore, hard

The *Halsted* on the beach in Washington Harbor, Washington Island, after the great storm of November 1913. The steamer *Louisiana* stranded and burned to a total loss just a short distance from the *Halsted.* Courtesy of the Wisconsin Marine Historical Society.

and fast on the rocks. The lifesavers now put a line across the barge and with the aid of her crew soon had the whip line on board. The beach apparatus was placed in position and the men on shore were about to haul off the breeches buoy when a huge sea swept in, picked up the *Halsted* as lightly as a feather, and set her down on a shelf of the rocky shore. The vessel was now so close to land that the crew dropped a ladder over the port bow and went ashore. By 3:00 P.M., the wind had moderated slightly and the barge was in no further danger. The lifesavers started back to their station and arrived at about midday on the eleventh. They had been on duty for more than three days, most of the time exposed to a 60-mile gale and snowstorm with below freezing temperatures.

Most of the accounts of the November 1913 gale in Washington Harbor only speak of the *Louisiana* and the *Halsted,* but two smaller vessels survived this great storm. The schooner *Challenge,*[27] loaded with potatoes, was at the west dock in the lee of the land. The small schooner *J. H. Stevens,*[28] also loaded with potatoes, rode out the gale on the windward side just south of the *Halsted.* The lifesavers from Plum Island who were standing by on the beach thought for sure the *Stevens* would come ashore because at times she was completely buried in breakers. According to natives on the island who were also standing by, the schooner survived because she was manned by "schooner men" who had experienced this foul weather all of their lives.

The Soper Lumber Co. made no effort to recover the *Halsted* from the beach but instead offered her for sale. There was 9 feet of water a short distance from her starboard over a gravel bottom. The Leathem & Smith Tow-

A drawing of the schooner *Challenge*, one of the first clipper-type schooners built on the Great Lakes at Manitowoc, Wisconsin, in 1852 by William Bates. Courtesy of the Wisconsin Marine Historical Society.

The schooner *J. H. Stevens* in tow of the tug *Satisfaction* in the Sheboygan River about 1907. The wreck on the shore over the bow of the *Stevens* is the schooner *Graham Brothers*. Courtesy of the Wisconsin Marine Historical Society.

ing & Wrecking Co. made several offers to release the barge, but none was accepted. In the spring of 1914, Greiling Bros. Co. of Green Bay purchased the *Halsted* and sent their dredge to Washington Harbor while it was en route to Thompson, Michigan. A channel was dug through the sand and gravel to the stranded vessel, and after everything was in readiness, the barge was rolled into the ditch and pulled out into the harbor.

The steam barge *Albert Soper*[29] towed the *Halsted* to the shipyard at Sturgeon Bay, where she was put on the boxes for an examination and repairs. Some of the planks on the bottom of the hull, which had been broken or pretty badly chewed up by the pounding she received during the terrific storm, were replaced. In 1916, the schooner-barge became the property of the National Pole Co. of Escanaba and in 1917, the National Transit Co. of Gary, Indiana. The last owner of official record was the Smeed Box Co. of Cleveland, Ohio, Wm. J. Ellenberger of Cleveland, secretary and treasurer. The last enrollment of

the schooner-barge *Halsted* was surrendered at Cleveland on December 29, 1930; cause of surrender: abandoned sold for junk. The old vessel received a temporary reprieve when acquired by Leathem and Smith of Sturgeon Bay for use as a stone barge. She was sent to the boneyard in 1933 after 60 years of service on the inland seas. The old lady had returned home to die at "Big" Sturgeon Bay, just a few miles from Little Sturgeon Bay where she was born.

The construction of a second large schooner at Little Sturgeon began before the *Halsted* was completed. With Thomas Spear superintending the *Halsted*, Albert Marshall, his son, became the master builder of the next vessel. She was christened the *Ellen Spry* at the launching on September 6, 1873, for Gardner. She followed the lines of the *Halsted* but was just a bit longer, leaner, and deeper. The steamer *Ozaukee* brought the Sturgeon Bay Silver Band and others to Little Sturgeon for the festivities. Gardner sold the *Ellen Spry* to John Spry of Chicago before the season of 1874, and H. H. Gardner of Chicago purchased the schooner in the fall of 1883 for $15,000. According to Inland Lloyds Vessel Register of 1882, the *Spry* was valued at $21,000 and classified A 2 for insurance purposes.

The life of the schooner, only 13 years, was short when compared with her immediate predecessor the *Halsted*. While en route to Chicago with 1,200 tons of coal, the *Ellen Spry* sprung a leak off the Manitou Islands and foundered in deep water on November 6, 1886. The crew escaped in the yawl boat, which was picked up by the schooner *H. M Scove*.[30] The loss of the vessel and cargo was estimated at $28,000. The last owners of the *Ellen Spry* were William G. Keith (12/24), John G. Keith (6/24), Angus McLean (3/24), and Donald McLean (3/24), all of Chicago, with Fred Ahlstrom, master, as recorded on the enrollment issued at Chicago in the spring of 1886. Capt. John G. Keith was also master of the schooner *Halsted* in her earlier years.

An unusual depression in the lumber business caused the suspension of F. B. Gardner & Co. in August 1873. Once before, in the crash of 1857 and after the loss of the sawmill at Little Sturgeon by fire, Gardner had found himself in a similar position, but his creditors had come to his relief and he soon paid dollar for dollar. In 1873, the committee of examination found the liabilities of F. B. Gardner & Co. to be $255,759.71, with assets of $742,350.00. With this favorable showing and the known integrity of Gardner, the creditors granted a sufficient extension of time for him to overcome his difficulties.

While the *Ellen Spry* was being completed, preparations were made to build another large schooner at Little Sturgeon. The keel and timbers were gotten out and prepared, and the frame was erected in the latter part of September 1873. She was to be 10 feet longer than the *Spry*, making the length of keel 180 feet, with essentially the same breadth and depth as the *Spry* and the *Halsted*. This greater length resulted in a significant increase in capacity, somewhere in the neighborhood of 45,000 bushels of grain or 600,000 feet of lumber, compared with 38,000 bushels and 500,000 feet for the *Halsted*. The new vessel would be the largest and last built at Little Sturgeon Bay.

Work on the vessel progressed rapidly with Thomas and Albert Marshall Spear as the builders (A. M. Spear is given as the master builder on the first enrollment). Thomas Spear hoped to launch her about the middle of November and immediately lay the keel of still another vessel, the timbers of which were gotten out and made ready. Plans were also made to build a tug during the winter and install the machinery of the tug *S. G. Chase*,[31]

which had been employed in towing on the Sturgeon Bay Ship Canal in earlier seasons.

However, on November 1, 1873, Gardner suffered another financial loss. He had purchased the propeller *City of Madison*[32] in April 1873 from the Spencer Line for $16,000 to carry lumber from Pensaukee to Chicago. She went ashore on the southwest side of Washington Island during a violent gale and snowstorm. A vessel in tow of the *Madison* was let go when the storm struck to find a safe anchorage on the west shore. The *Madison,* loaded with lumber, labored heavily in the sea but reached smoother water where she hoped to anchor. Finally, the vessel struck a rock within about 165 feet of South Bay. She was broadside about 150 feet from the beach, with 5 feet of water on the inside and 10 feet on the outside. A steam pump was delivered by the Chicago & Northwestern Rail Road and taken to the wreck by the tug *Ozaukee*. The *City of Madison* was reported breaking up and a total loss on November 12, 1873.[33]

All the carpenters in the shipyard at Little Sturgeon were discharged, and only about 15 men remained during the winter of 1873–74 to finish the new vessel. No other work was done in the yard during the winter, and only enough logs were cut to keep the company's teams employed. The gristmill was the most lively operation in Little Sturgeon, having more work than it could do.

The schooner *J. W. Doane* was launched on April 28, 1874. Her measurement was 617.02 tons. Gardner sold nine-tenths of the vessel to G. Kent of Chicago for $36,000 in July 1874. The life of the *Doane* was the shortest of all vessels built at Little Sturgeon Bay. Wiley M. Egan of Chicago officially became the sole and last owner of the schooner on February 17, 1880, with R. H. Long as master. In November 1882, the schooner was bound for Buffalo from Erie, Pennsylvania, in ballast with a crew of 10 men under the command of Captain Long. At about 8:30 P.M. of the twenty-third, during a violent southwesterly gale and snowstorm, the *Doane* missed the entrance between the piers at Buffalo Harbor. The anchors were immediately let go, but the schooner dragged on to the end of the old stone breakwater before she could be checked.

The accident was witnessed by the pierhead lookout from the Buffalo Station, and as soon as he gave the alarm, the livesaving crew turned out with their surfboat to her assistance. The tugs *Orient*[34] and *R. F. Goodman*[35] were already at the scene, and the station crew attempted to establish communication between the tugs and the schooner so they could try to haul her off. The sea, however, was very high and broke against the *Doane* with such force that it was impossible to go near the vessel to take the end of her line for fear of dashing the surfboat to pieces. Therefore, they pulled around into the Erie basin where the water was smoother, landed on the inner side of the breakwater, and got hold of the schooner's towline and passed it to the tugs. They pulled on the vessel for about an hour until the line parted, and as the *Doane* failed to budge in the least, the tugs reluctantly abandoned the attempt to release her and returned into the harbor.

The lifesaving crew offered to take the men off the wreck, but they all declined with the exception of a Buffalo resident named Brown, whom they assisted onto the breakwater from the end of the jibboom and then ashore. After the station crew had gone, Captain Long and his men concluded that the breakwater would be the safest place for them to spend the night. They climbed down onto it and stayed there until the lifesaving crew went off to them at daylight and brought them ashore. The *J. W. Doane* became a total wreck at a loss of $38,000. Thus ended the life of the last and largest vessel built at Little Sturgeon Bay.

In the spring of 1874, lumber prices reached the lowest figure for some time, but since the demand was good, it was thought that prices would soon rise. Gardner's mill was cutting an average of 75,000 to 80,000 feet of lumber per 12-hour day with two circular saws. Vessels were loading all of the time but were unable to keep the dock clear of lumber. Because of low freight rates, there was no prospect of building another vessel at Little Sturgeon. One of the patent limekilns was running, and the lime was shipped on the steamer *Union* to Green Bay, Escanaba, and other points. Lumbering prospects did not improve by the fall of 1874. Nevertheless, a large number of logs were cut in the winter of 1874–75.

The business at Little Sturgeon was only a diversion for Gardner, who had larger projects at Pensaukee and in Chicago. In 1875, lumber and timber were almost unsaleable, and many lumber companies failed in business. The flour mill at Little Sturgeon was in operation, but all other activities had ceased. A new tug, the *Pensaukee,*[36] was built by Thomas Spear at Pensaukee rather than at Little Sturgeon. The tug's machinery had been taken out of the tug *S. G. Chase.* Gardner sold the Little Sturgeon Bay property to A. M. Spear for $26,000, and he took possession of it on November 19, 1875. J. R. Mann was retained as manager of the gristmill, and George O. Spear became manager of the store. The tug *Ozaukee,* which was part of the sale, was repaired and refitted throughout under the supervision of Thomas Spear.

A. M. Spear energetically pushed the business, sawing vast quantities of lumber and shingles, much of which was shipped directly to Europe. However, disasters continued to dog Gardner and Little Sturgeon. Late in November 1876, Gardner's barque *Hans Crocker*[37] left Little Sturgeon for Chicago with a cargo of shingles, hardwood lumber, vessel knees, and the like belonging to A. M. Spear. The barque sprung a leak while off Kenosha, Wisconsin, on the night of the twenty-ninth. While attempting to make that harbor, she struck a sunken crib and went ashore just south of the harbor piers. The *Crocker* rapidly went to pieces, and although the crew succeeded in reaching the shore in safety, the greater part of the valuable cargo proved a total loss.

The golden age of Little Sturgeon Bay came to a disastrous end on February 22, 1877. Just as it had destroyed Peshtigo, Williamsonville, and many other early lumber settlements, fire brought one of the best business institutions in the county to a standstill. Soon after dark, smoke was seen issuing from the blacksmith shop, situated about 650 feet to the north of the mill. When the alarm was given, the fire had already made such headway inside of the shop, which by this time was one blaze, that all attempts to save the structure proved useless. The entire building was quickly wrapped in flames. A strong wind blowing from the north quickly spread the fire by means of connecting slab piles to the mill, which was directly in its path. In a few minutes, the mill was one mass of flame and smoke. Although every effort was made to save the heart of Little Sturgeon, the fierce gale of wind and intense heat made such attempts useless. The long shed for storing shingles, which extended some 200 feet on the east of the mill, shared the same fate. On the west side of the mill at a distance of some 800 feet, was the store. Another slab pile extended between these two buildings, and but for the exertion and vigilance of those present, who worked amid flame and smoke, this establishment would also have been consumed by fire. The stand made at the store probably saved the remaining buildings in the village from destruction.

The further progress of the fire was checked by the waters of the bay on the south. Little of the contents of the mill was saved from destruction; consequently, the toll of property was heavy. The loss, which amounted to $30,000, with insurance coverage of only $15,000, proved too great for A. M. Spear. He sold his interest to William Anger, who in turn sold the property to A. S. Piper & Co. for their ice business.

The village of Little Sturgeon, which had been one of

the most prosperous points on the whole bay shore, began to decay. The *Door County Advocate* of March 22, 1882, describes Little Sturgeon as follows: "The mill buildings all have the appearance of neglect and unless something is done to revive some of the old time life into the place, it will go where the woodbine twineth in a few years. Nothing but a heap of stones and a few pieces of iron remain to mark the site of the mill, which was destroyed by fire five years ago this winter; and in a short time this old familiar land mark will be entirely obliterated."

The only major activity which flourished at Little Sturgeon in later years was the cutting and shipping of ice, mainly to Chicago. This activity began in the fall of 1879, when the common council of Chicago passed an ordinance prohibiting the use of any ice cut from ponds and streams in that vicinity except by brewers, meat dealers, and similiar establishments. As a result of this restriction, the ice companies at Little Sturgeon and Sturgeon Bay built permanent storehouses and had hundreds of men engaged in harvesting ice every winter.

During the winter of 1881–82, A. S. Piper & Co. put up 60,000 tons of good quality ice in good condition by the middle of March. Some of the men and teams employed for the harvest returned to their homes in Chicago after the work was completed. The schooner *Mediator*,[38] Capt. Oliver Swanson, made three trips to Chicago at the start of the season, taking a hold full of ice and a deck load of cedar for A. S. Piper & Co. at $600 per trip. As soon as the warmer weather set in, two more schooners were placed in this profitable trade. The men employed in loading were paid $2.00 per day for every day, work or no work. The ice stacked in heaps on the dock was shipped first on account of the lack of suitable buildings at Little Sturgeon. The last cargo of ice was shipped to market in September. All the mammoth buildings on the dock had been cleared, with only those on the point containing ice.

The law of supply and demand determines the production of all products, and the ice trade was no exception. In the winter of 1889–90, the ice crop was a failure around Chicago and Milwaukee, and the companies in Door County responded to the demand. A. S. Piper & Co. filled the old buildings at Little Sturgeon with ice and purchased about $1,500 worth of lumber to be used in erecting new sheds. Since they had an interest in the schooner *Ellen Williams*,[39] Capt. O. Swanson, they shipped the first cargo of ice from Little Sturgeon Bay on that schooner in the spring of 1890. The *Williams* and other schooners continued to carry ice to Chicago in the spring and summer, and lumber in the fall, well into the nineties. In 1898, Pip-

The schooner *Ellen Williams* in dry dock. She served in the "ice fleet" that carried this natural refrigerant from Little Sturgeon Bay to Chicago for A. S. Piper & Co. Courtesy of the Wisconsin Marine Historical Society.

er & Co. was absorbed by the Knickerbocker Co., and the ice age came to an end in Little Sturgeon.

The facilities at Little Sturgeon either crumbled or were moved to Sturgeon Bay. The depletion of good quality timber along the shores of Green Bay and northern Lake Michigan, and the opening of the Sturgeon Bay Ship Canal in 1879, which made Sturgeon Bay a reference point on all the shipping lanes in Lake Michigan, were underlying causes for the demise of Little Sturgeon Bay as a community.

When the Spears left Little Sturgeon, they settled in Sturgeon Bay, where they owned and operated the old island mill until it closed on September 19, 1883. This sawmill was built by Lyman Bradley and David S. Crandall of Lockport, New York, in 1853, and led to the founding of Sturgeon Bay. A. M. Spear moved back to Maine with his family in September 1884, where he made his home near

Portland at a place called Ferry Village, now South Portland. George O. entered the banking and brokerage business with C. L. Nelson in 1885 at Sturgeon Bay, and transferred to Green Bay in 1891. After the mill was sold in September 1887, Thomas returned to Green Bay to live a retired life until his death in 1891; his wife Amanda had passed away in 1883 while they were residing at Sturgeon Bay. George O. Spear died in Green Bay on June 22, 1904, after a long illness. A. M. Spear passed away in Portland in 1923.

Freeland B. Gardner, the driving force for the development of Little Sturgeon Bay, barely survived his establishment. The business at Little Sturgeon was only one of many projects that Gardner had on the shores of Green Bay and in Chicago. On July 7, 1877, a tornado destroyed most of the buildings in Pensaukee, including the elegant Gardner Hotel, which he had built as a showplace. This disaster, in addition to a series of business reverses, was a heavy blow to Gardner, and his health began to fail. He dropped dead of a heart attack at Pensaukee on Christmas Eve 1883 while walking to the station to catch the train for Chicago. He was about 67 years of age.

The shipyard at Little Sturgeon Bay was a tribute to F. B. Gardner, Thomas Spear, his sons Albert and George, and all of the other early residents in what was a relatively remote and primitive region of Door County. From 1866 to 1874, a period of only eight years, 10 documented vessels were built or rebuilt. In addition, a number of undocumented scows and barges were built at Little Sturgeon. They ran on all of the Great Lakes, and the average length of service for the documented vessels after leaving the yard was almost 28 years. This extraordinary longevity for wooden ships exposed to the constant hazards of the lakes speaks well for the craftsmanship and care lavished on the vessels built by the Spears. The service of the seven sailing vessels was even more striking, averaging nearly 32 years.

In later years, the shipbuilding activity in Door County was concentrated in Sturgeon Bay. The May 1975 issue of the *Scanner,* the monthly news bulletin of the Toronto Marine Historical Society, presented a list of all orders on the books at the end of March for lake ships of any size. Of the 16 hulls listed, 9 were scheduled for construction in Sturgeon Bay, with the next highest being only 3. The prediction made in the *Door County Advocate* of August 16, 1862, had come true. "Big" Sturgeon Bay, a direct descendant of Little Sturgeon, had become "the first of all shipbuilding points on the Great Lakes."

CHAPTER THREE

Three of a Kind
A Story of Pilot Island

A few years ago, we were fortunate to locate a copy of *A Gleam Across the Wave, The Biography of Martin Nicolai Knudsen Lighthouse Keeper on Lake Michigan* by Arthur and Evelyn Knudsen. This booklet is a private printing published in Sturgeon Bay in 1948. On page 56, just above the title of Chapter XIII The Great Storms of 1892, the authors included a photograph of the schooners *A. P. Nichols* and *J. E. Gilmore* on the beach at Pilot Island, Door County, Wisconsin. Although we did not realize it at first, this photograph shows a *third* wreck, which the narrative identified as the "Forrest." We were fascinated by this picture of three sailing ships wrecked at virtually the same point. This chapter recounts the history of these vessels and their final rendezvous at Pilot Island.

Pilot Island is in one of the legendary graveyards of the Great Lakes — Porte des Morts Passage, which is often referred to as Death's Door.[1] The island lies between Detroit Island to the northeast and the Lake Michigan shore of Door County to the southwest. Porte des Morts Passage has a strong current setting in or out according to the direction of the wind, and it was frequently so strong that sailing vessels could not make headway against it. The coast is rock bound and many vessels were lost or severely damaged when driven ashore. A diary of Martin Knudsen, kept from 1872 to 1889, indicates that winds and roaring seas, with a shipwreck at least twice a week, were the usual course of events. In the fall of 1872, 8 large vessels stranded or wrecked in Death's Door, and in one week of the same year almost 100 vessels were lost or seriously damaged trying to make this passage. The worst storm that had occurred on Lake Michigan up to 1880 came out of the south on October 16 of that year. This storm is referred to as the Alpena Gale because of the loss of the Goodrich steamer *Alpena*.[2] About 30 vessels were driven ashore in the vicinity of Death's Door in this one storm. Therefore, it is not too surprising that the picture that is the subject of this chapter was taken at Pilot Island in Death's Door.

The first of the trio to arrive at Pilot Island was the scow schooner *Forest*, official no. 9740, built in 1857 at Newport, Michigan, by and for David Lester of Newport. Her original measurements were length 87⁶/₁₂, breadth 22³/₁₂, depth 6 feet, 102⁷⁸/₉₅ tons OM, with one deck and two masts. The *Forest* arrived in the Chicago district in 1866 and remained in the Chicago and Milwaukee districts for the rest of her days. The scow became the *Forest* "of Racine" in 1872, with Harrison Fellows of Racine as the principal owner and master. After 23 years of service, the scow schooner was rebuilt and lengthened to 115.6 feet at Racine during the winter of 1879–80. The rig was changed from two to three masts and the total tonnage increased to 113.45.

In November 1881, 10 years before she met her end on Pilot Island, the *Forest* was wrecked in Door County. The *Forest* and the scow schooner *R. H. Becker*[3] loaded with wood at a pier being constructed by Hans Johnson at Newport, Wisconsin, a newly founded lumber settlement on Lake Michigan in northeastern Door County. While waiting for a favorable wind to depart on the eleventh, a heavy gale from the east carried the vessels and the pier ashore. Both scows had their anchors with 50 or 60 fathoms of chain out, but they did not hold fast. Capt. Theodore Lane of the *Forest* went to Sturgeon Bay and telegraphed the owner, Harrison Fellows, for instructions. He was told to strip the vessel and save what he could of her. The *Forest* was thought to be a total loss, and the *Becker*, though not so badly damaged, received some serious injuries about the bottom, and some of her planking and timber were badly sprung. The loss of the pier was estimated at $500 by Hans Johnson, who also lost seven barrels of pork and beef and 2 or 3 tons of hay that were on the pier at the time.

Both vessels were left on the beach during the winter of

The lighthouse on Pilot Island in Death's Door.

The schooner *A. P. Nichols* pointing toward the dock, the schooner *J. E. Gilmore* broadside to the beach, and the scow schooner *Forest* in front of the *Gilmore* with her bow pointing toward the *Nichols*. The ladder on the side of the *Nichols* was used in the rescue of her crew and rests on the deck of the wreck of the *Forest*. This was taken at Pilot Island looking to the south from the lighthouse in October 1892, probably the day after the *Nichols* went on. Courtesy of Fr. Edward J. Dowling, S.J.

1881–82, but it was thought they could be released in the spring at much less cost than was at first anticipated. The *Forest* was offered for sale at a bargain in February 1882. The advertisement in the *Door County Advocate* read:

Vessel for Sale

Scow *Forest* now lying on the beach at Newport, 6 miles east of Ellison Bay: $3,500 expended on hull in the last 18 months. Can be got off with little expense. The whole vessel and her outfit, which is all safely stored in Hans Johnson's barn will be sold for $1,000 cash. For further information inquire of the subscriber, Harrison Fellows, Racine, Wis. The vessel has a carrying capacity for 160,000 feet of lumber.

The *R. H. Becker* was sold to Hans Johnson before the season of 1882 and released from the beach at Newport about June 1. From then until November 1882, the scow

netted about $1,000, an excellent record for a vessel of her size. Johnson did not believe in running a vessel all year and laid the *Becker* up in November.

The *Forest* remained unsold in the spring of 1882, and her enrollment no. 111 was surrendered at Milwaukee on July 1, 1882; cause of surrender: total loss. However, Capt. George Decatur Fellows, a nephew of Harrison, removed the wood from the vessel's hold and filled it with cedar. An expedition under the command of Captain Fellows left Sturgeon Bay on August 18, 1882, with the tug *John Gregory*[4] to attempt the release of the *Forest*. It took the *Gregory* only about an hour to free the *Forest* from the beach, and the scow was not damaged as much as had been supposed. The tug towed the *Forest* to Manitowoc, where she was repaired and placed in commission in October

1882, almost a year after being driven ashore at Newport.

Harrison Fellows died on April 1, 1887, at age 46. The *Forest* was sold to Henry Pottgether of Chicago (seaman) a short time later. The scow was sold for the last time during the summer of 1889 to A. G. Johnson of Chicago (wood dealer), with John Anderson as master. Just 10 years after going on the beach at Newport, the *Forest* was driven on the rocky shore of Pilot Island, just about 5 miles to the north in Death's Door.

She was bound for Garden Bay in Big Bay de Noc, Lake Michigan, from Chicago for a load of lumber with a crew of five. On the cloudy night of October 28, 1891, with a high sea running before a south-southwest wind described as "a fresh and moderate gale to fresh breeze," the *Forest* stranded on the outer reef extending southwest from Pilot Island at 9:40 P.M.

The light on Pilot Island was visible at the time of the disaster, and the keeper, Martin Knudsen, had the *Forest* in view when she struck. The next day, he landed Capt. George Petersen and four sailors and gave them board and lodging until November 5. The *Forest* was all broken up and was abandoned as a total loss. The scow was disman-

tled on November 2 and 3 and the outfit stored on Pilot Island. Captain Petersen purchased the *R. H. Becker* to replace the *Forest* in order to enable him to fulfill his contract.

The battered hull of the *Forest* lay with its stern wedged into the rocks at the shore of the island, the bow extending out over deep water. Her well-made, hardwood deck was still intact, except that the hatches were washed away, but subsequent storms tore the cabin loose, and the ice during the winter of 1891–92 shoved it up onto the island. The cabin became the prized possession of the children of the lighthouse keeper as they used it for their playhouse. Thus the *Forest,* the first of three of a kind, rested on Pilot Island, a circumstance that would prove to be fortunate for those who were yet to come.

One of these was the schooner *J. E. Gilmore,* official no. 13307, built in 1867 at Three Mile Bay, New York, for Thomas S. Mott, Asa Wilcox, and James E. Gilmore, with Wilcox as the builder. Her original dimensions were length 137.7 feet, breadth 25.4 feet, depth 11.0 feet, and total tonnage 290.89, with one deck and two masts. John Gerlach of Cleveland became the principal owner of the

The scow schooner *R. H. Becker* at Sheboygan. She was owned by Hans Johnson of Newport, a lumber settlement on Newport Bay, Lake Michigan. Courtesy of the Wisconsin Marine Historical Society.

The schooners *Honest John, Elbe,* and *Buena Vista* lying in the Menominee Slip boneyard near the Chicago, Milwaukee and St. Paul Elevator A at Milwaukee, Wisconsin, about 1888. The schooner *Lewis Ludington,* which is on the left away from the shore, was towed to the boneyard on Jones Island before 1898. Courtesy of the Wisconsin Marine Historical Society.

schooner in 1874, and her home port was Cleveland for the remainder of her service. The *J. E. Gilmore* had one brush with death in July 1875, when she sank in the harbor at Cleveland, but she was raised and returned to service.

The long journey of the barque *A. P. Nichols,* official no. 566, to Pilot Island began at Madison Dock, Ohio, in 1861. The vessel was built by A. and D. E. Bailey for James Butler of Buffalo, New York, managing owner, and W. E. Sanborn of Erie, Pennsylvania, each owning one-half. The original measurements of the *Nichols* were 146.75 x 30.03 x 11.7 feet and 476⁹⁵/₉₅ tons OM, with three masts.

The barque officially changed owners and districts on September 18, 1865, the new owner being James R. Slauson of Racine, Wisconsin, with W. Gifford as master. On the twenty-fourth of the same month, the *Nichols* collided with the schooner *William O. Brown*[5] at Bar Point, Lake Erie, and the *Brown* sank in 24 feet of water. A typical cargo for the *Nichols* in 1876 was iron ore for Green Bay

from Escanaba at $.50 per ton. The rig of the barque was altered into a three-and-after schooner at Manitowoc in the summer of 1877. The *Nichols* sailed out of Racine or Manitowoc until the season of 1883, when she was sold to Capt. David Clow and his sons: David (1/4), Oscar (1/4), Byron (1/4), and David, Jr. (1/4). The Clows all lived in Crystal Lake, McHenry County, Illinois.

This was the same Captain Clow who was well-known in Door County for his shipbuilding and many adventures on the inland seas. In 1848, he had built the scow schooner *Honest John*[6] at Oak Creek, Wisconsin, for himself and Edward Beckwith of Racine as equal owners. David Clow settled on Chambers Island in Green Bay in 1850 and built many small sailboats in partnership with Nathaniel Brooks, a ship carpenter. They built the schooner *Sea Lark*[7] in 1854 for Clow and Francis Laning as joint owners.

Another of these boats was the *Pocahontas,* a little flat-bottomed schooner that was probably never documented.

In the summer of 1857, the founder of the Moravian settlement at Ephraim, Wisconsin, the Rev. A. M. Iversen, received a gift of money for a church. With their characteristic veneration for sacred things, the people of Ephraim agreed that their little church should not be built of rough logs, such as they had used in the construction of their homes, but must be built of sawed and planed lumber of excellent quality. Accordingly, Captain Clow was summoned to go to Cedar River, Michigan, with the *Pocahontas* for a cargo of lumber. He arrived in a short time but was alone, so Reverend Iversen had to serve as deckhand and cook, as well as supercargo, on the trip. They managed to secure the lumber, and the church was enclosed in the fall of 1857.[8]

After Brooks[9] moved away, Captain Clow began the construction of the largest vessel yet built in Door County with the sole help of his wife. They both bent their entire energies to sawing out her planking by hand with a whipsaw. The two built the vessel from stem to stern and from keel to truck. They built her almost entirely without iron, pinning her together with wooden treenails, and the proud result in July 1862, after seven years of toil, was the schooner *Sarah Clow*, named in honor of the wife and helpmate. The measurements of the *Clow*, official no. 22342, were 115$\frac{4}{12}$ x 27$\frac{2}{12}$ x 10$\frac{1}{12}$ feet and 285$\frac{53}{95}$ tons OM, with two masts.

In the spring of 1863, Captain Clow almost lost the schooner on the return trip from Buffalo, New York, where he had delivered a cargo of wheat. The *Sarah Clow* was overtaken by a furious gale off Point Belle, Lake Erie, and since the vessel was running light, the storm threw her over a sandbar and into a grassy marsh or inland pond. Since the schooner was a considerable distance from the lake, it was reported a total loss, and Captain Clow was paid the insurance. The underwriters abandoned the wreck, and Clow was able to buy it back for a small amount.

With the help of his crew, he dug a canal and heaved the vessel out to the sandbar by means of her anchors and windlass. They then cut a wide channel through the bar and waited for a wind to raise the water level and carry the *Clow* back into Lake Erie. Eventually, a favorable wind rose, and Captain Clow started a triumphant return to Chambers Island. In the fall of 1866, the schooner was sold to David Milner, Jr., of Chicago, with Captain Clow as master. The *Sarah Clow* was lost in the great storm that swept the lakes from November 16 to 19, 1869, but Captain Clow encountered this storm in the second large vessel that he built at Chambers Island to replace the *Clow*.

The *Lewis Day* was launched on July 23, 1868, and named in honor of Lewis J. Day, a merchant and shipowner of Green Bay. This vessel was also fastened with wooden pegs without the use of iron to avoid unnecessary expense and as a consequence never rated higher than B1 according to the insurance classsifications of Inland Lloyds. The measurements of the barque *Lewis Day,* official no. 15410, were 146.8 x 31.0 x 11.41 feet and 381.89 total tonnage, with three masts.

The *Door County Advocate* of December 2, 1869, published a letter from Captain Clow to Day in which he related the experiences of the *Lewis Day* in the gales of 1869 as follows:

> Detroit, Nov. 22d, 1869
>
> Lewis Day, Esq. — As we have had severe gales of wind, I suppose you would like to learn that we are safe. We left Buffalo a week ago for Saginaw, with good prospect of a profitable trip, but wind and weather had been against us. Started with a fair wind. When we got to Grand River, wind changed dead ahead, accompanied with snow. Ran back to Grand River. Next day started with a south-east wind. Wind freshened and snow so thick we could not see three lengths of the vessel ahead. Just as we reached Long Point we saw the breakers ahead. Had to haul the vessel by the wind, and in less than three seconds the jib top sail went into ten thousand pieces. Managed to clear the land and headed to Point au Pelee. Still blowing and snowing. At 3 o'clock next morning, wind hauled around to the southwest and freshened. — Headed for the beach. We made land about 30 miles from Point au Pelee. Let go anchor in 10 fathoms of water; found one anchor would not hold her; let go the other and held till next morning. — About 8 A.M. away she started for the beach, dragging. Found we could not save her that way. So we made the 11 inch hawser fast to the small chain "and gave her the hull benefit of that coil of line". — Finally brought her up, but she pitched so that her jib boom went under water, and the yawl filled. The sailors packed up their dunnage to go ashore, but were disappointed. Towards night, the next day, the wind lulled and we got up our anchors, and started for Detroit, where we arrived in due time.
> We are waiting for a chance to strip. — It looks hard to see the wrecks that come in here from all directions. The storm was most severe, and our chains and anchors would not have saved us if it had not been for the large cable. One vessel sunk near us, another lost her masts, sails and rigging, but we are safe. — I don't know as you will care for my story, but it won't cost you anything, and will let you know we are all right.
>
> I remain, yours truly,
> David Clow

Captain Clow had another unusual experience in the *Lewis Day* during a round trip from Green Bay to Chicago in June of 1876. She brought up twice on Plum Island, going and coming, but in each instance she got off without damage. The home port of the *Day* was Waukegan, Illinois, as she made frequent trips to Chicago with forest products from lumber settlements on the shore of Green Bay. On September 3, 1879, the *Day,* with a cargo of cedar posts and telegraph poles and a crew of nine bound for Chicago from Little Cedar River, Michigan, labored in a high sea off the former port. She sprung a leak and was sinking about 3 miles east of Chicago Harbor. The *Day* was seen early in the morning from the Chicago Station signaling for a tug. Receiving no response, she hauled down her flag and hoisted a distress signal. The keeper of the station immediately went to the rescue with the sailboat and five men.

It was blowing very hard, and the small boat was kept from swamping with great difficulty. Arriving at the distressed vessel, the lifesaving crew found the *Day* sinking, her steering gear carried away, and the crew exhausted from working at the pumps all night. A line from the sailboat was made fast to the stern of the *Day,* but the heavy sea made it impossible to get the boat alongside. Finally, a line from the *Day* was tied around one of the lifesavers. He then jumped into the sea and was hauled onto the deck of the *Day.* Another of the crew was hauled on board the sinking vessel in the same way, and the two men began to heave the anchor, which had been dragging. This action let the *Day* swing broadside, in imminent danger of foundering. Meanwhile, a tug came up and held the *Day* while the anchor was being raised. The craft was then towed into the harbor, the two surfmen constantly working at the pumps to the great relief of the crew. The *Day* had 2 feet of water in her hold when she arrived in port. After she was pumped out, the cargo was discharged and she was repaired.

The repeated round trips of the *Day* through Death's Door challenged the reputation of this narrow passage. After 13 years, the *Day* finally succumbed to the perils of Porte des Morts.

On Saturday afternoon October 15, 1881, the barque was working down Green Bay from Little Cedar River, Michigan, for Chicago with a cargo of cedar posts and telegraph poles just as she had done so many times in the past. The *Day* ran on Cedar River Reef and was compelled to jettison her deck load in order to expedite her release. Shortly after getting off, the vessel began to leak, but not enough to warrant Captain Clow to run back. When beating out of the bay to the east at a fair rate of speed through Death's Door, the barque missed stays in tacking and went ashore on the southeast point or reef of Plum Island at 10:30 P.M. Sunday.

The wind was not blowing hard, but Monday morning it swung around to the northeast and blew heavily all day. A big sea set in, and the *Day* pounded on the rocks and filled with water. The crew were taken off by the schooner *G. D. Norris*[10] bound from Green Bay to Milwaukee. When news of the disaster reached Milwaukee, it was generally conceded in marine circles that the *Day* would go to pieces if any rough weather set in because of the lack of iron in her hull. Although no hopes of releasing the vessel were entertained, Captain Clow secured the services of the wrecking tug *Leviathan,* Captain Anderson, to assist his stranded craft. By the time they returned on the eighteenth, the *Day* was already pretty well broken up. The *Leviathan* tried to get her off but failed, and the *Day,* which had been reduced to a semblance of a vessel, had to be abandoned. On the twenty-fourth, the crew cut down the masts, stripped the craft of everything worthwhile, and took what they could salvage to Detroit Harbor on the scow schooner *Quickstep.*[11]

The estimated loss of the *Lewis Day* was $10,000 with no insurance, and the services of the *Leviathan* cost Captain Clow an additional $400. In hopes of recovering some of this loss, the *Day* was burned on November 10 to save what little iron was in the remains. Captain Clow then went into a brief retirement down on the farm at Crystal Lake, Illinois, but this attempt at a separation from the lakes proved futile.

After only one full season on the beach, the adventures of Captain Clow continued, this time in the *A. P. Nichols.* On August 22, 1883, the *Nichols* dragged anchors at Mackinac during a heavy southwest gale, lost her small anchor and chain, pounded heavily on Mission Point, broke her stearing gear, and sprung a bad leak. The schooner was towed to Cheboygan by the propeller *Messenger,*[12] and temporary repairs were made by a diver before she returned to Chicago. A part new keel, a new rudder post, and recaulking were required at the Chicago Company before the vessel could be returned to service. The *A. P. Nichols* continued to sail out of Chicago under the command of the Clows, David Sr. and Jr., until 1892.

The fall of 1892 was a particularly boistrous one even for northern Lake Michigan, which had already experienced some of the worst storms in the recorded history of the Great Lakes. The schooner *J. E. Gilmore,* Capt. D. B. Smith, was en route to Elk Rapids, Michigan, from Chicago without cargo. On October 17, 1892, she was running before the wind through Death's Door in a heavy gale with only a split foresail, staysail, and jib. When the schooner was abreast of Pilot Island, the wind shifted

The schooner *Quickstep*, ex-*S. Anderson*, ran down the second *Ebenezer* north of Port Washington, Wisconsin, on June 14, 1879. Courtesy of Fr. Edward J. Dowling, S.J.

ahead to the southwest, driving her from her course and right for the island. Because the *Gilmore* was light, she did not carry sufficient sail to be able to tack or clear and did not have time to put it on before striking on the southwest reef about 11:00 P.M. She was tossed up onto a submerged shelf of rock in about 3 feet of water just a short distance from the wreck of the *Forest* to make a pair of schooners on Pilot Island.

The *Gilmore's* keel was crushed, and she was solidly settled on the rocky shelf. Although there was no possibility of getting the schooner off, Martin Knudsen, the lighthouse keeper, managed to communicate with the crew. A breeches buoy was rigged up in case of an emergency, but the crew stayed aboard since the cabins were safe and there were enough provisions to last for several weeks. They were to be sailed over to the mainland in the light-

house sailboat when the seas calmed down, but the storm continued to rage and they were still there when the climax was reached 11 days later.

October 28, 1892, was a dull gray day, and the great waves were leaden in color. Martin Knudsen had been watching the barometer going lower and lower, and the wind increased in velocity with every passing hour. It reminded him of the Alpena Gale of 1880, and he and his assistant, Hans Hansen, prepared for what seemed inevitable. As if to keep step with the falling barometer, the temperature was steadily going down. By afternoon it was sleeting and snowing, the wind shrieking and wailing around the lighthouse like a banshee. The men took advantage of every moment of visibility to look out into the lake to see whether there were any vessels near the island. With the wind blowing from the west and gradually shift-

Another view of the *Quickstep* in the north branch of the Chicago River. She was sold to Mobile, Alabama, in 1915 and went into the lumber trade between Cuba and Mobile. Courtesy of the Wisconsin Marine Historical Society.

ing to the northwest, four or five schooners were trying to anchor in the lee of Plum Island but were experiencing great difficulty in making their anchors hold.

The schooners *George L. Wren*[13] and *Harrison*[14] were being dragged toward the rocks near Pilot Island in spite of their anchors. They saved themselves by cutting their anchor ropes and sailing out into the lake. The schooner *Walhalla*[15] had three anchors out, but before they caught and held her, she had dragged to within less than a mile of Pilot. The two anchors with which the schooner *Democrat*[16] was trying to grip bottom did not take hold until she was about half a mile east-northeast of Pilot.

It was close to 2:00 P.M. when the men on Pilot Island sighted a three-masted schooner with reefed sails coming from the southeast, evidently intending to pass through Death's Door into Green Bay. Through the spyglass they learned that she was the *A. P. Nichols*. The *Nichols* was bound from Chicago to Masonville, Delta County, Michigan, without cargo and with a crew of eight. She missed stays while trying to tack through the passage during the afternoon and let go the larger anchor to prevent stranding on the southerly side of Plum Island. With the wind reaching hurricane proportions, the foreboom and main gaff

were broken and the mizzen topsail and raffee sail carried away. The *Nichols* slipped or lost her anchor and struggled to precarious refuge in the lee of Plum Island. She dropped her 1,400-pound anchor in the usual anchorage, but the force of the storm was such that even though she paid out the entire length of chain—over 600 feet—she was unable to anchor and was being driven toward Pilot Island.

At the lighthouse, the atmosphere was tense. Darkness had come with the fate of the *Nichols* still hanging in the balance. The light was sending out its beams, and once in a while the snow and sleet squalls would abate enough for the men to see the schooner getting closer to the island. Martin Knudsen knew that they were going to have another wreck.

At 8:00 P.M., the men dressed in oilskins and high rubber boots and stopped in the warm kitchen for a hasty cup of hot coffee before going out again into the gale. Suddenly, there was a terrific crash that sounded above the storm from the west side of the island. For a moment they all stood rooted to the spot, then they put down their coffee cups and rushed out of the door. When the next flash of the beam came around, it looked to them as though a large vessel had run up onto the shore, with its jibboom extending over the land. The *Nichols* was actually a short distance off shore but quite close to the bow of the deck of the wrecked *Forest*. The *Nichols* was rolling from side to side like a creature in agony, and when she rolled toward the *Forest*, her starboard came in contact with the deck and bore it down so that it sloped toward the deep water at a dangerous angle. The rocky shore of Pilot Island had made "Three of a Kind".

Martin Knudsen and Hans Hansen tried to get as close to the *Nichols* as they could by going out on the deck of the *Forest*. They had formulated their plans for attempting to rescue the people on the *A. P. Nichols*. They both knew every inch of the deck of the *Forest*, just where the uncovered hatches were, and what handholds they could depend on. Hans was to stand on the land side of the wreck, while Martin was to get as close as he could to the forward end of it and wrap his arm around the pawl bitt, which still stood staunch in the old deck. The plan was to have the passengers of the *Nichols* jump from her deck to where Martin stood when she rolled toward the *Forest*. He would grab them and help them back to where Hans stood, and he would guide them up over the rocks onto land.

With much shouting back and forth, an understanding was reached with those on the *Nichols* as to what was to be done. The young captain, David Clow, Jr., was the first to jump, but he missed his footing on the deck and fell into the surging waters between the two wrecks. Just as the flash came round, Martin saw his disappearing head, grabbed him by the hair, and dragged him to safety just in time to escape the next downward roll of the *Nichols*. Captain Clow, Jr., told Martin that a woman and his father, Captain Clow, Sr., were on board. He was particularly concerned about his old father, who weighed 320 pounds and was not very mobile.

The most difficult of the rescues was that of the old man, who could do very little to help himself. It was thought best to rig up a rope harness or swing for the old master, the ropes to be held by those still on the *Nichols* until he was safely on the deck of the *Forest*. A stout ladder was lowered over the side of the stranded vessel, and Cap-

tain Clow was started down, supported and helped by the rope harness. The first attempt was ill-timed, and the *Nichols* rolled away from the *Forest* with the ladder, two sailors, and the old captain high up in the air. However, when it rolled back again, it looked as though they could make it, and the sailors let go of the swing. Captain Clow tried to step off the ladder onto the *Forest*, but he was a little too slow and was grabbed by his son, Martin, and Hans. They snatched him from the jaws of death in the angry seas.

One by one, those on board were rescued and guided over the hazards of the old deck, across the half-submerged rock, up onto the island, and to the warm kitchen of the lighthouse for first aid. The old captain looked up as he revived under a hot drink. "Who is the

The schooner *George L. Wren* at South Haven, Michigan. She had a large cabin and was intended for the ocean trade. The *Wren* was dismantled and burned during the winter of 1912–13 in the north branch of the Chicago River, headed north, south of Belmont Avenue Bridge, on the west bank of the river. Courtesy of the Wisconsin Marine Historical Society.

keeper of this lighthouse now?" he asked. Martin Knudsen smiled, "I am – Martin Knudsen." It was then that Captain Clow remembered he had come to Plum Island when the *Lewis Day* was wrecked. He nodded as tears filled his tired old eyes and said, "To think that I should be wrecked near this place a second time! But this is the end of my sailing; my son will have to sail for me now." Captain Clow, Sr., returned to his 200-acre farm in McHenry County, Illinois, which was run by one of his sons.

In the morning, the *A. P. Nichols* lay tossing on the rocks, a pitiful sight. Her sails were in rags, her jibboom broken off, her spars splintered and broken. The cabin roof had been torn loose and was hanging by one corner, most of it jutting over the water. Some of the sailors scrambled aboard and salvaged what bedding, clothing, and provisions they could. These things were welcome additions at the lighthouse, where the crew of the *J. E. Gilmore* had joined the crew of the *Nichols,* making 16 persons to feed and shelter.

After they had been there about a week, the seas had subsided. Knudsen fitted up his little sailboat and took Captain Clow, Jr., out to the steamer *J. H. Outhwaite*[17] bound for Escanaba. In this way, Captain Clow informed his family and the underwriters of the loss of the *A. P. Nichols.* The crew of the *Nichols* reached Chicago on November 9, almost two weeks after the loss of the vessel.

The *J. E. Gilmore* and the *A. P. Nichols* were abandoned to the underwriters shortly after the disasters. The last enrollment of the *Nichols* was surrendered at Chicago on November 17, 1892; cause of surrender: vessel lost. The last enrollment of the *Gilmore* was not surrendered at Cleveland until April 25, 1893; cause of surrender: loss of vessel. The official record of the three schooners wrecked at virtually the same point on Pilot Island ends here. However, it is quite possible that two of these vessels survived, at least in part, these disasters in Death's Door.

We now have a second photograph to explain. The photograph is said to show the hulls of the *Gilmore* and the *Nichols* anchored out in Porte des Morts Passage, a short distance from the lighthouse. In the *Door County Advocate* of December 31, 1892, it was reported that F. H. VanCleve, a member of the Escanaba Towing & Wrecking Co., had purchased the *A. P. Nichols,* ashore on Pilot Island, from the underwriters to whom the wreck had been abandoned. Were the hulls of the *Gilmore* and the *Nichols* towed to Escanaba or some other harbor for use as docks, lighters, or river barges? Or were they broken for salvage by the wrecking company? Perhaps one of the readers of this story can shed some light on the ultimate end of two of the "Three of a Kind" that came to Pilot Island.

CHAPTER FOUR

The Long Journey of the
Windsor to Cana Island

In the beginning it was called South Detroit, then the "Ferry," and later, Windsor.[1] The growth of this small settlement on the Canadian side of the Detroit River was related to the necessity for adequate communication between the people on the two sides. Passenger and stock traffic across the river increased to such proportions by 1806 that Detroit built a ferry-house near the foot of Woodward Avenue and issued several licenses permitting commercial transport to and from Windsor. Many of these early ferries were nothing more than a combination rowboat and sailboat.

Realizing the growing importance of the ferry business, John Burtis of Detroit decided to venture into it on a larger scale. He acquired the scow *Olive Branch*,[2] took out a license, and placed the following advertisement in the *Detroit Gazette*, September 22, 1822:

> "Horse-Boat Ferry"
> The subscribers have recently acquired a large and commodious Horse Boat
> for the purpose of transporting across the Detroit River, passengers, wagons, horses and cattle, etc. The boat is so constructed that wagons and carriages can be driven on it with ease and safety. It will leave McKinstry's wharf (adjoining that of Dow & Jones) for the Canada shore, and will land passengers, etc. at the wharf lately built on that shore by McKinstry & Burtis. The ferry wharves are directly opposite.
> Mr. Burtis resides on the Canada shore and will pay every attention to those who may desire to cross the river.
> D.C. McKinstry – J. Burtis.

The *Olive Branch* was a fair-sized scow with two immense paddle wheels admidships connected to a large circular table on rollers with radiating, spokelike ridges. Two horses were harnessed on this table directly opposite each other, and as the horses walked the table revolved, turning the paddle wheels. The *Olive Branch* was not a financial success, and Captain Burtis replaced it with the steam sloop *Argo*, built in 1830 at Detroit. The measurements of the first steam ferry at Detroit were length $42\frac{1}{12}$, breadth 9, depth $2\frac{7}{12}$ feet, and $8\frac{70}{95}$ tons OM.[3] The *Argo* was in service on the Detroit River until 1834 and abandoned about 1836.[4] By this time, there was a demand for larger vessels, and the *Lady of the Lake*,[5] $26\frac{16}{95}$ tons OM, and the *United*,[6] $37\frac{48}{95}$ tons OM, were used to satisfy this need. In 1849, a second *Argo*[7] appeared, and in 1856 the *Windsor*, the subject of this chapter, entered the competition for this lucrative link between the United States and Canada.

The *Windsor*, official no. 26366, was built in 1856 at Detroit by J. S. Jenkins for George B. Russell of Detroit, a previous owner of ferryboats, as a side-wheel ferry with one deck and no mast. The measurements of the *Windsor* were length 104, breadth 30, depth $10\frac{1}{12}$ feet, and $223\frac{8}{95}$ tons OM.[8] In 1858, the steamboat was acquired by the Detroit & Milwaukee Railway Co., C. C. Trowbridge secretary. Ownership was changed to the Lake Michigan Transit Co. of Milwaukee in 1863, George Jerome of Detroit agent and attorney. The *Windsor* was enrolled in Milwaukee on November 1, 1865, as the property of the Lake Michigan Transit Co. of Wisconsin, N. J. Emmons of Milwaukee secretary.[9] The ferry was chartered in 1866 to operate as the connecting link across the river for the Detroit & Milwaukee Railway, carrying both freight and passengers to and from the Great Western Railway docks in Windsor.

The *Windsor* was involved in one of the most appalling fires in the history of Detroit.[10] The ferry was unloading cargo at the dock of the Brush Street depot just before 10:00 P.M. on April 26, 1866, while a gang of freight handlers was loading a car with 25 barrels of naphtha. Beside the freight car stood a passenger train full of people, which was scheduled to depart at 10:00 P.M. A barrel of naphtha was observed to be leaking badly, and a man started to examine it with an open lantern. There was a violent explosion, which scattered blazing naphtha in all directions. The volatile solvent in the car caught instantly, and the barrels began exploding, spreading the fire to the passenger train, the *Windsor*, and the adjoining buildings.

Several of the men plunged into the river to extinguish their saturated clothing, and about 35 took refuge on the ferry as their only avenue of escape. The flames were so fierce that the people on the *Windsor* were unable to cast off the mooring line. By the time it had burned in two, the boat itself was ablaze. It drifted down the river, coming into contact with boats docked at the Woodward Avenue wharf, and only the prompt arrival of several tugs saved these steamboats from a fiery death. Men and women

43

leaped over the *Windsor's* rail into the river, where they were rescued by the U.S. revenue cutter *John Sherman,* lifeboats from the city ferry *Detroit,* [11] and several people who had put out in rowboats. Despite these efforts, 17 persons who had fled to the hold were burned to death.

The quick action of Captain Innes of the ferry *Detroit* kept the burning *Windsor* from spreading the fire to the whole waterfront as it moved down the river. A graphic account of the catastrophe is given by the captain himself.

> You see it was this way. 'Long about eleven o'clock one night an explosion of oil occurred aboard the steamer *Windsor*, while she was tied to her wharf at the foot of Brush Street. I was captain of the old city ferry, the *Detroit,* at the time, and we had just landed at the foot of Woodward Avenue, with passengers from Windsor. I was standing at the signal ropes on the bridge leading to the pilot house when the *Windsor* took fire. In less than two minutes after the explosion, she was a mass of flames from stem to stern. She had perhaps fifty people aboard, as I found out afterwards – passengers and deck hands. In about another minute I saw her lines ablazin' – saw 'em part and saw the *Windsor* startin' to drift down in our direction. By this time the freight sheds on the wharf had caught fire, and I saw men and women leaping over the *Windsor's* rail into the water. I signalled our boys to man the life-boats, and shouted to 'em to make a line fast to her stern. This they did in short order. Then I sends a signal below to back her hard – runs into the pilot house, throws over the helm, and out and away we goes toward the middle grounds. I saw the men in our life-boats trying to rescue those people in the river – and they were surely doing their best. All at once, like the report of a gun, our tow line parted. The *Windsor* was a roaring furnace. We were then off the foot of Wayne Street, on the middle ground where the cross-current runs strong, and I knew unless we could do something to keep the *Windsor* off shore, that when she struck, the whole river front would soon be ablaze, in consequence of her drifting down with the current. But how to keep her out in the channel was sure enough a puzzler. First, I decided to ram her down the river. No, this plan wouldn't do. The *Detroit* would catch fire and then – what of my passengers – more than a score of 'em. On the other hand, the *Windsor* was drifting fast toward shore. We would have to ram her – and quick, too.
>
> My men being out in the life-boats left us short-handed – only myself, the wheelsman, engineer, and fireman, and the latter two would have to stay below. Lifeboats or no lifeboats, we must run the risk. I gave orders to send her full speed ahead – shouted to the passengers and the men to wet down the decks and stand ready with the buckets. Well, in a couple of minutes we struck her. There was a crash of fallin', blazin' timbers. The sparks fell on our decks in a shower, and we were ablaze in a dozen places. But we held on to the *Windsor,* stuck to her, pushed her out into the river, fought the flames on board our boat and headed for Sandwich Point. All told, we

must have been two hours gettin' her beached, where she burned to the water's edge.

> Next day a dozen or so Detroit citizens came aboard and offered me a purse of one thousand dollars in gold. Said I had to take it – that I had saved the river front. I refused and laughed 'em out of the notion. Why, anybody who was half a man would have done his best that night of the fire of '66.

The passenger train in the station was blocked by a freight ahead of it and some of the passengers were already in their berths, but a heroic porter dragged them out and rushed them off the train. All but one passenger, D. M. Gardner of Cascade, Kent County, were saved, although many of them were badly burned. The depot, warehouse, several cars, and all the buildings on the riverfront between Brush and Hastings streets were destroyed, at a loss of about $1,000,000. The *Windsor* was declared a total loss, and its charred wreck was nosed into the marine boneyard below Sandwich. The final account of the *Detroit* provides an ironic twist to this story, as she also burned at Sandwich, a few miles below the city on the Canadian side, in September 1875.

The resurrection of the *Windsor* occurred in 1871 when she was dragged from the boneyard and rebuilt at Detroit as a barge, official no. 62523. The owners were James Dean (2/4), W. Macguire (1/4), and John Miller (1/4), all of Detroit. The measurements of the barge were length 115.0, breadth 30.4, depth 9.2 feet, and 237.84 total tonnage, with one deck and no mast. [12] This was but the beginning of a new life for the old ferryboat, because in 1876 she was rigged as a schooner barge with two masts. She was owned by T. S. Ruddock of Chicago and under the command of Capt. L. Hermann. [13] The *Windsor* was classified A 2 with a value of $9,000 after she was rebuilt as a barge, B 1 with a value of $6,000 in 1875. She had the same rating in 1879 but with a value of only $4,000. The *Windsor* served in the lumber trade out of Chicago for almost 20 years with no major mishaps.

In May of 1883, she was involved in a minor disaster with the schooner *Lookout* [14] of Milwaukee off Manitowoc, Wisconsin. [15] The *Lookout* had run on the reef near Rock Island on Wednesday evening the second, and after throwing overboard her deck load of ties, succeeded in getting off and proceeded up the lake. Her keel and stern post were damaged in the grounding, making the rudder unmanageable. The *Lookout* anchored off Manitowoc on Friday morning and waited until evening to run into the bay. While entering the bay, the *Lookout* collided with the *Windsor,* which was at anchor. The *Windsor's* jibboom and bobstays were carried away, while the

Lookout was leaking and had suffered considerable damage to her mizzen sail. A tug was telegraphed for to tow the *Lookout* to Chicago, and the *Windsor* was compelled to run into Manitowoc for repairs.

Repairs in 1887 raised the *Windsor's* rating to B 1½, and a thorough rebuild in 1892 resulted in an A 2½ classification at $4,500. The *Windsor* of Chicago continued in the lumber trade, including a number of sailings from Sturgeon Bay to Chicago, until the end of her second life in 1893.

The *Windsor,* with a crew of six, loaded cedar posts and telegraph poles at Snow Island for Chicago late in September 1893. [16] After working her way south to a point nearly abreast of Ahnapee (Algoma), she encountered tremendous seas from the southeast early Saturday morning, September 30. Realizing the hopelessness of continuing the unequal contest with the lake, Capt. David Williams ordered the vessel put about and headed for North Bay, the harbor of refuge on the Lake Michigan side of northern Door County. About this time, the information was conveyed aft to the captain that the schooner had sprung a leak. As the water steadily gained on the pumps, the *Windsor* became difficult to handle, though steerageway was maintained until the vicinity of Cana Island. She became helpless and shortly after struck bottom on the southeast end of the reef at 2:00 A.M. that same morning.

As soon as the schooner became fast, she broached to, and the great seas ran over the deck, sweeping one member of the crew overboard with part of the deck load. Since it was evident that the *Windsor* would go to pieces, Captain Williams set about devising some means of reaching shore. The yawl boat was judged unable to stand up in the rolling seas, so a message was written on a box and thrown overboard by the crew. It read, "Send for the Sturgeon Bay life-saving crew to come at once; we will not stand much longer; the schooner is going to pieces." Fortunately, the disaster and the launching of the message, which was swept northward by the current, had been observed by Capt. Jesse T. Brown from the Cana Island Lighthouse and others who had gathered along the shore.

Cana Island is a stony mass of 9 acres located just offshore about 4 miles north of Baileys Harbor and 2 miles south of North Bay. The lighthouse was built in 1869 to protect vessels from the shallow rock shelf that extends into Lake Michigan almost half a mile and to guide them into the safety of well-protected North Bay. This bay acquired its name by virtue of being the northernmost enclosed bay on the lake side of Door County, and it had a reputation as a harbor of refuge. When the Alpena Gale swept over Lake Michigan in October of 1880, a fleet of nearly 30

vessels sought refuge from the storm in North Bay. Although about 90 vessels were wrecked or badly damaged and 118 lives lost as a result of this storm, not a single vessel or life was lost in North Bay. The last vessel to be released was the *Two Friends,* a 319-ton barque that had dragged ashore on the north side of the bay. [17] Despite the fact that the *Windsor* had not reached the safety of North Bay, it had entered its sphere of influence and was under the watchful eye of Keeper Brown at the Cana Island Lighthouse.

Captain Brown and the people who had gathered followed the box along the beach and finally captured it about 2 miles from where it had been sent afloat. The message informed them of the true condition on board the *Windsor,* and they hurriedly dispatched a messenger to Baileys Harbor. The news of the disaster was wired to Sturgeon Bay on Saturday afternoon and then relayed to Capt. T. F. Boutin at the U.S. Life-Saving Service Station on the ship canal.

Since there was too big a sea running on the lake for even a lifeboat to venture out, it was decided to make the trip of over 30 miles by land. The wagons the lifesavers had for just such an emergency and other paraphernalia were loaded onto the government tug *Dionne,* which was tending the dredge at the canal, and Captain Boutin brought his crew and outfit down to Sturgeon Bay, leaving only one man at the station. Horses were secured in the city, and shortly after 5:00 P.M., the men set out on their humane mission.

To appreciate their efforts, it must be realized that the "roads" of the time were really only wagon tracks with planks laid across the ruts in the low, swampy areas. To add to the crew's difficulties, darkness and rain began to fall, but they made good progress until the caravan passed through Jacksonport. For 2 or 3 miles north of this village, thick woods delayed their journey. The wagons were 2 or 3 inches wider than ordinary vehicles, making it difficult to clear the trees. They made a brief stop at Baileys Harbor to water the steaming horses as well as to refresh the men. Captain Boutin pushed on again, and after a good deal of delay caused by the breaking down of the lifeboat wagon, finally reached the scene of the disaster at about 12:30 A.M. on October 1, over seven hours after leaving Sturgeon Bay.

Violent seas were sweeping over the *Windsor,* and the vessel was in danger of collapse. Preparations were made immediately to get a line out to the wreck, which was lying 1,200 feet from the shore in a southeasterly direction. The mortar was brought into position and a line fired out to the *Windsor,* but because of the darkness the aim was poor

The schooner *D. A. Wells* was built at Sac Bay south of Fayette, Michigan, on the Garden Peninsula. In 1879, she went ashore on the shoal called Mile Ground between St. Martin's Island and Fisherman's Shoal. Her misfortune proved benefical to the fishermen of St. Martin's because it was necessary to immediately remove 5,000 bushels of dry grain from her hold to save the *Wells* from becoming a total wreck. Courtesy of the Wisconsin Marine Historical Society.

and the heavy current swept it out. The lifesavers had to cut the rope to keep the reel from following. After several more trials, this attempt to rescue the crew was abandoned due to the swift prevailing current, and attention was turned to the lifeboat.

It was discovered that the boat had a hole in one of its sides as a result of striking a tree during the journey through the swamps and thickets north of Baileys Harbor. Temporary repairs were made with canvas and zinc, and the boat was launched into the heaving seas. It swamped several times, but after a hard pull against the terrific wind and immense waves, the wreck was reached in safety and the five survivors were transferred aboard and then to shore. They were taken to the keeper's house and given every care by Captain Brown and his family. The lifesavers left the beach at daylight and returned to their station, arriving about 6:00 P.M. Sunday evening exhaust-

ed by a journey of nearly 70 miles and over 24 hours of continuous duty. But for the timely arrival of the lifesavers, there is no question that several other members of the crew would have drowned or died from exposure. As it was, the cook, an old man of more than 60 years, was nearly dead when brought ashore. He was unconscious, and the gallant crew had to carry him out of the boat to the house, where he was revived.

The long journey of the *Windsor* had come to an end. The protracted windstorms of early October had played havoc with the schooner, and she was stripped and abandoned by her owners. The vessel was valued at $5,000 and insured for $3,000; the cargo was valued at $1,800. The last certificate of enrollment for the ferryboat-barge-schooner-barge was surrendered at Chicago on October 12, 1893, with the terse note "Vessel lost" entered into the official record. [18]

EPILOGUE

It is a well-known fact that any disaster has the capacity to trigger subsequent events sometimes equally disastrous as sure as night will follow day. Such was the case in the weeks following the end of the *Windsor*.

The schooner *E. P. Royce,* official no. 8912, was built in 1873 at Sac Bay, Michigan, by Samuel Elliott for attorney Eli P. Royce of Escanaba, Michigan. Sac Bay was a small settlement south of Fayette on the Garden Peninsula, which juts into the northern end of Lake Michigan. As late as 1975, descendants of Samuel Elliott still lived in the homestead near Sac Bay. The only other documented schooner built at that point was the *D. A. Wells* [19] by Eli T. Hazen in 1874 for owners in Saugatuck, Michigan.

The measurements of the *Royce* were 124.0 x 29.1 x 8.8 feet, and 249.29 gross, 236.83 net tons, with three masts. She was in the lumber trade with cargoes of cedar posts, slabs, sawed timber, and poles for telegraph or telephone lines. In September of 1876, the schooner, bound from Escanaba to Cleveland with a load of telegraph poles, went ashore on Canadian Point Au Sable, Lake Huron, in 4 feet of water, leaking badly. The tug *James H. Martin* [20] of Escanaba released the *Royce* by dredging a channel 30 feet wide and 400 feet long. Part of the deck load was thrown over, but the schooner suffered no material damage.

When the *Windsor* was lost, the *Royce* was owned by Martin McNulty of Chicago, with Capt. Harry Worfel as master. [21] The cargo of the wreck of the *Windsor* proved to be a magnet for the *Royce,* and on November 26, 1893, she was salvaging telephone poles off Cana Island. [22] After the hold was filled and her decks were covered with cedar as far as the top of the rail, a storm set in and the heavily loaded schooner was unable to get away from the shore. She was driven on the beach in Little Harbor just south of Cana Island, where the crew managed to reach the shore in safety without assistance. Because of the surplus of sailing vessels at the time, the *Royce* was uninsured, and no attempt was made to release the schooner. The vessel and cargo were valued at $4,000, and the wreck was officially abandoned as a total loss on June 30, 1894. [23] Even the cargo of the *Royce,* the much sought after telephone poles originally carried by the *Windsor,* was abandoned to Lake Michigan and allowed to wash out with each offshore wind.

CHAPTER FIVE

The *William Aldrich*
She Outlived Her Time

There were a number of sailing vessels in service on the inland seas for 60 years or more, but in some respects the *William Aldrich* was unique. Her life-span, 1856 to 1916, matched the era of the schooner-rigged sailing vessel on the Great Lakes.

Little is known about the early Great Lakes schooners, with the exception of a few men-of-war, but from contemporary references they appear to have been shoal vessels somewhat on the model of the Baltimore Clipper.[1] The introduction of the centerboard may have taken place as early as 1828, but this is doubtful. One of the first distinctive lake schooners of which much is known was the centerboard clipper type introduced in 1852 by William W. Bates of Manitowoc, Wisconsin, in the form of the *Challenge*.[2] She was a shoal, rather flat-floored, sharp-ended schooner whose model raised much discussion while she was on the stocks. After the *Challenge* was launched, she became a great success and was noted for dependability and the ease with which she could reach a speed of 13 knots.

Literally thousands of schooners followed the *Challenge* down the ways of hundreds of shipyards on the Great Lakes until the decline of the schooner era began in the early 1880s and was long gone by 1916. Most of the great white-winged fleet had been degraded to barges that were dragged over the lakes by steam barges, relegated to shore and island routes, or simply abandoned. The *William Aldrich,* built only four years after the *Challenge,* was one of the fortunate few early schooners that carried sail until the end.

In the summer of 1836, Judge John Lawe and Robert M. Eberts of Green Bay purchased a large section of timberland at the confluence of the Twin and Neshoto rivers that embraced almost all of the land on which the city of Two Rivers is now located.[3] They immediately erected a small sawmill on the north side of the Neshoto River west of the Washington Street Bridge. In 1840, Andrew J. Vieau of Green Bay took possession of the mill and operated it until 1847, when it was sold to Hesikiah H. Smith, who was to be identified with many of the city's early enterprises.

In 1848, immense tracts of timber consisting principally of pine and hemlock were standing in all directions.

Logging operations were carried on quite close to the settlement, and the logs were rafted down the rivers in the summer and hauled down on the ice in the winter. There were no piers at the time, so timber had to be loaded on scows and towed out into the lake, where it was transferred to other vessels.

H. H. Smith & Co. built the first pier out into Lake Michigan and erected a second steam sawmill across the river in 1851. James F. Aldrich, William Aldrich, H. H. (Deacon) Smith, Martin B. Medberry, and John W. Medberry formed the firm of Aldrich, Smith & Co. in 1852. The two mills within a few hundred feet of each other manufactured sufficient lumber to keep a small fleet of vessels in constant employ, and Aldrich, Smith & Co. commissioned James Harbridge to build schooners to serve their interests.

The schooner *William Aldrich* on the Menominee side of the Menominee River, with the car-ferry slip in the background. Courtesy of Fr. Edward J. Dowling, S.J.

The schooner *William Aldrich* (1856 to 1916) from a painting done in 1945 by George Cuthbertson for Canada Steamship Lines Ltd. Courtesy of the State Historical Society of Wisconsin.

Arni Wegner, a grandson of Capt. Albert C. Poppe of the *Aldrich*, builds models of schooners in his shop, The Boat House, at Institute, Wisconsin.

James Harbridge, a ship carpenter from New England, and Green S. Rand had been building vessels in Manitowoc but dissolved their partnership when Harbridge went to Two Rivers to start a small shipyard.[4] He took a partner named Mayer and hired a crew of four to work in the yard, which was located on the West Twin River. They specialized in smaller craft such as canal boats and scows at first but soon undertook the construction of larger schooners. The first of these were the *Stella*[5] and the *Triumph*,[6] built for Aldrich, Smith, & Co. in 1854. Harbridge completed the *Gertrude*[7] for R. W. Jones and Richard Kingholtz of Manitowoc in 1856 and later in the same year launched the *William Aldrich*,[8] the subject of this chapter, for H. H. Smith. In 1857, the schooner *Eleanor*[9] was built for Aldrich, Smith & Co, and about 1862 James Harbridge ceased operations in his yard, dissolved his business, and moved to Manitowoc.

The enrollments of the *Aldrich* record the early history of Two Rivers. The original measurements of the schooner were length 100, breadth 25, depth 8¾ feet and 195⁶³⁄₉₅ tons OM, with one deck and two masts. While she was on the stocks, a chair factory was built by the New England Manufacturing Co. composed of Aldrich, Smith & Co., William Honey, Thomas Burns, Charles Jennison, and probably Alanson Hall of Massachusetts. The year 1857 saw further expansion of industry in Two Rivers with the construction of a pail factory by Henry C. Hamilton & Co. consisting of Aldrich, Smith & Co., Henry C. Hamilton of Two Rivers, and William Metcalf, a brother-in-law of Hamilton, of Lockport, New York.

The financial crash of 1857 caused the demise of these firms, and they were assigned to S. H. Seaman & Co., which was owned by Seaman and Conrad Baetz. William Aldrich retired, and ownership of the *William Aldrich* was transferred to S. H. Seaman, James F. Aldrich, and H. H. Smith on August 13, 1859. S. H. Seaman & Co. operated the business of Aldrich, Smith & Co., which included the two mills, the pail factory, and other properties in Manitowoc and Brown counties. In the winter of 1860–61, Joseph Mann of Mann Bros., Milwaukee, came to Two Rivers and purchased an interest in these properties. H. H. Smith retained an interest, but S. H. Seaman retired from the management, which was assumed by Joseph Mann, who became sole owner of the *William Aldrich* on April 11, 1861, with L. Simpson as master.

The schooner was recorded as the property of Mann or his brother Herman for the next eight years, and her measurements in 1867 are given as length 99.1, breadth 25.6, depth 8.6 feet and 153.87 total tons. According to enrollment no. 50, issued at the Port of Milwaukee on March 29, 1869, the schooner was sold to Peter Pastors (2/3) of

Barton, Washington County, Wisconsin, and Capt. Albert C. Poppe (1/3) of Milwaukee, who was the master of the *Aldrich* for over 20 years. Since the number system had been enacted, the *William Aldrich* was assigned the official no. 26362. In the spring of 1872, the *Aldrich* was rebuilt and lengthened about 20 feet to measurements of 120 x 26 x 7.9 feet by Allan, McClelland & Co. of Milwaukee. The capacity was increased from 153.87 to 191.89 total tonnage, and a third mast was added to provide more sail area.

In the 1870s, the schooner continued to serve in the lumber and cordwood trade between ports in Door County, Green Bay, and Milwaukee. The steam barge *Annie Laura*[10] found the *Aldrich* on the rocks at Egg Harbor late in June 1876 and pulled her off with no serious damage. An incident on the night of May 14, 1879, proved to be a portent of the future for the schooner. She left Milwaukee and was caught in a squall that forced the crew to take in nearly all of her canvas. Just after the squall, when the *Aldrich* was in an almost helpless condition, a tow of light barges crossed her bow. But by putting the wheel hard over she swung clear of all except the last barge, which shoved the jibboom inboard and broke the bowsprit. The *Aldrich* returned to Milwaukee for shelter and repairs before resuming her trip.

In October 1886, the schooner grounded on a shoal off Oconto in a sheltered position and was easily released. In

A Bible and pay log from the schooner *William Aldrich*. The Bible was published in 1857 by the American Bible Society, New York. The pay log is for the period 1882 through November 6, 1891, just five days after the collision off Cana Island. Courtesy of Arni Wegner.

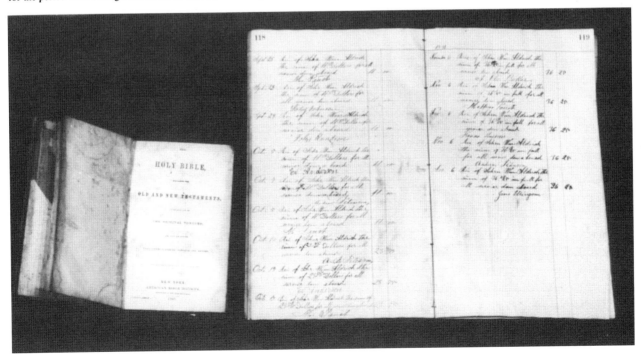

The tug *John Leathem*, with the steamer *Thistle* of the Hart Transportation Co. on the right, at Sturgeon Bay. The *Leathem* was christened after one of the members of Scofield & Co. Together with Thomas H. Smith, he founded numerous enterprises in Sturgeon Bay, including a towing and wrecking company, a lumber company, and a shipyard. Courtesy of Fr. Edward J. Dowling, S.J.

attempting to sail up to an anchorage opposite Sturgeon Bay on Thursday afternoon November 23, 1886, the schooner ran aground on the shoal off the Spear Mill and remained until Friday evening, when she was released by the combined power of the tugs *John Leathem*[11] and *George Nelson*.[12] Owing to her sheltered position, no damage was inflicted on the vessel, which was loaded with lumber from Oconto. Captain Poppe complained of the scarcity of good lumbershovers at Sturgeon Bay when he took a cargo of lumber at the upper mill in June 1887. He said he would rather pay $.35 an hour to men who were used to handling this kind of freight than $.25 to the crew he was compelled to employ.

The schooner *Aldrich* and Captain Poppe did not return to Sturgeon Bay until August 21, 1889, almost two years later, bound for Milwaukee with a cargo of lumber. Captain Poppe said he had been running to east shore ports because Oconto was played out and they had to go elsewhere for a freight.

The *William Aldrich* was already being referred to as the oldest or one of the oldest active schooners on the lakes in 1891 when she was involved in a major disaster that nearly ended her career. On November 1, the vessel was off Door County en route to Milwaukee from Nahma, Michigan, loaded with lumber above and below deck.[13] Capt. Ole M. Oleson had been given command of the *Aldrich* in July 1890, and the crew consisted of Jens Ellingsen, mate; A. Christ Baker; Mathias Paust; Erik Anderson; and Andrew B. Pedersen. Between 5:00 and 6:00 A.M., the schooner sighted a steamer with two consorts coming down the lake about 6 miles off Cana Island. Since the schooner had the right of way, Captain Oleson assumed that the steam barge would shear off and give the

Aldrich a wide berth. This was a fatal mistake because the steamer kept right on coming, and a few minutes later the last barge of the tow struck the bow of the *Aldrich* full force just forward of the foremast.

The barkentine *Parana,* Capt. John Fitzgerald, below the East Water Street Bridge, Milwaukee, in December 1871, after returning home in a heavy northwest blizzard. Courtesy of Wisconsin Marine Historical Society.

The schooner barge *S. M. Stephenson* on the stocks in the shipyard of Rand & Burger just before the launch in 1880. Courtesy of the Wisconsin Marine Historical Society.

The collision tore off the entire bow of the schooner, including the stem, jibs, and much of the rigging. A deluge of water poured into the hold of the stricken vessel, and she became waterlogged in a short time. Not only was the *Aldrich* reduced to a helpless wreck but Erik Anderson of Milwaukee, who was asleep in the forecastle, was either killed outright or drowned as the schooner filled. The steam barge proved to be the *Robert Holland* and the tow barge the *Parana*. The other consort was the *S. M. Stephenson*.[14]

The *Robert Holland* escorted her consorts into Baileys Harbor, the *Parana* being slightly injured, and returned to tow the *Aldrich* inside the harbor. A telegram was sent to Sturgeon Bay for assistance, and the new tug *Ivy M. Leathem*[15] dragged the remains of the schooner into the Sturgeon Bay Ship Canal later in the day.

Both of the other principals in this disaster, the *Holland* and the *Parana,* has already led interesting lives. The single-screw, wooden *Robert Holland,* official no. 110043, was built at Marine City, Michigan, in 1872 by John J. Hill for Henry Butteroni (1/3), Robert Holland (1/3), and David Gallagher (1/3), all of Marine City, as a steam barge with measurements of length 149.6, breadth

28.2, depth 11.8 feet and 339.71 tons. Like many early propellers, the *Holland* was designed with arches to strengthen the length of the hull and a long top deck cabin to accommodate passengers. The vessel was rebuilt for passengers and package freight and remeasured at 553.33 tons in 1875 for the Michigan Transportation Co. of Star Island, St. Clair County, Michigan, Robert Holland, secretary. In 1878, she was sold Canadian to the Great Northern Transit Co. of Collingwood, Ontario, and renamed *Northern Queen*. She was chartered to Capt. John Balmer Fairgrieve of the New England Transportation Co. in the spring of 1881 for the Collingwood and Chicago run.[16]

The New England Transportation Co. was a unique venture in Great Lakes maritime history. The company was never officially incorporated in the United States or Canada, but by 1881 a fleet of propellers was operating under its name with uniform passenger and freight rates. Its origin can be traced to the construction of the wooden propeller *Canada*[17] in 1872 at Hamilton, Ontario, by A. M. Robertson for J. B. Fairgrieve and Hugh Fairgrieve, shippers of Hamilton; Daniel Butters, merchant and shipper; and T. Howard, both of Montreal. Her ordinary route

The *Robert Holland* at Sault Ste. Marie after conversion to a steam barge in 1882. Courtesy of the Wisconsin Marine Historical Society.

The tug *Violet H. Raber*, ex-*Ivy M. Leathem*, in the Sault Locks. She was built in 1891 for John Leathem and Thomas H. Smith of Sturgeon Bay. Courtesy of Fr. Edward J. Dowling, S.J.

was between Montreal and Chicago to bring cargoes of barreled salt pork and bulk corn to Canadian ports. The venture proved sufficiently profitable for the four shareholders to buy a controlling interest in other canallers, including the *Columbia*[18] and *Lake Erie*.[19]

In 1878, Captain Fairgrieve suggested that the propellers be operated on a cooperative basis, and when an agreement was reached, the N.E.T. Line, Collingwood and Chicago, was born. With the addition of the *Northern Queen* (ex-*Robert Holland*) in 1881, on charter, the stage was set for a series of disasters that nearly decimated this fleet.

The *Columbia* cleared Chicago for Collingwood on September 10, 1881, with a cargo of bulk corn, two passengers, and a crew of 20. After sunset, she encountered a rising northwest gale that shifted the entire cargo to starboard. The *Columbia* foundered about 6 miles west of Frankfort. Although two lifeboats were lowered, only one reached the shore at Frankfort, and 14 lives were lost.

Just a few months later, an unusual disaster befell the N.E.T. Line when the *Lake Erie* and *Northern Queen* left Chicago together for Collingwood in order to assist each other in case of distress on the last trip of the season.[20] They proceeded along the west shore of Lake Michigan and ran into a blinding snowstorm off Poverty Island on Thanksgiving evening, November 24, 1881. Despite the poor visibility, the vessels began maneuvering to gain the lee of the island. During this course of action, the bow of the *Northern Queen* struck the *Lake Erie* near the after

gangway, cutting her down to the waterline. The *Northern Queen* backed off as the *Lake Erie* began to fill, took off the crew of the stricken vessel, and steamed off for Manistique, Michigan.

While attempting to enter the mouth of the Manistique River on Friday night, the *Northern Queen* struck the bar and broached to across the channel. A heavy sea was running from the south against her exposed side and she began to break up, but the crews of the *Northern Queen* and *Lake Erie* escaped to shore in the lifeboats. The hull of the propeller came to rest about 100 feet inside the ends of the harbor piers in 16 feet of water, with 4 feet over one end and 6 feet over the other. This position of the wreck reduced the effective width of the channel to only 26 feet and created a menace to navigation that would have been dynamited by government engineers. However, in 1882, the *Northern Queen* was raised and rebuilt again as a steam barge at Port Huron, with measurements of 156.0 x 29.1 x 11.6 feet and 295.10 total tons. She was returned to American registry under her original name, *Robert Holland*, and number as the property of an original owner, Robert Holland of Marine City. She was sold to A. A. Bigelow of Chicago in 1887 to serve in his lumber fleet. The *Parana* and *S. M. Stephenson* were among her consorts on runs down the lake in search of the ever-dwindling supply of forest products.

The barque *Parana*, official no. 19765, was built in 1862 at Cleveland by Quayle and Martin for Robert P. and John Fitzgerald as equal owners, with John as her first

The steam barge *Robert Holland* is behind the tug *Leathem D. Smith* at Sturgeon Bay after the fire on May 11, 1915. The burned-out stern section of the *Holland* is covered with a tarpaulin. In May 1919, the hull of the *Holland,* which had been partly submerged north of the Universal Ship Yard, was raised and towed to where Leathem and Smith were building a new dock. The old hull of the schooner *Libbie Nau,* which had been submerged in the Old Island Mill dock slip for several years, was raised and placed across the end of the *Holland.* The vessels were sunk and filling dumped in to make an excellent and permanent dock, part of which was used as a coal dock. Courtesy of the Wisconsin Marine Historical Society.

The propeller *Lake Erie* of the N.E.T. Line, Collingwood and Chicago, was lost in a collision with the *Northern Queen* off Poverty Island in November 1881. Courtesy of Fr. Edward J. Dowling, S.J.

master. She was a large first-class vessel in the grain trade and earned a place in the history of the Great Lakes because of a voyage late in the season of 1871. In December, a great blizzard out of the northwest blanketed the upper lakes, and most of the upbound sailing vesels caught in this storm sought refuge under the Manitou Islands. The *Parana* was en route to Milwaukee, and nothing was heard from her for some time after she was due to arrive in port. Finally, the vessel struggled into Milwaukee harbor looking like an iceberg, loaded down with tons of ice. Captain Fitzgerald had to go the masthead to navigate in order to see over the steam that was rising from the ice.

The *Parana* was sold to William H. Wolf (Wolf & Davidson) of Milwaukee in 1872 and like the *Robert Holland* became the property of Anson A. Bigelow of Chicago in 1887. Thus, as a consort in the Chicago lumber fleet, she struck the *William Aldrich* off Cana Island in November 1891.

Even though the *Aldrich* lay a total wreck at a dock in Sturgeon Bay, her injuries were to continue. On Tuesday night, November 3, only two days after the disaster, the steam barge *John Schroeder*[21] arrived in Sturgeon Bay to remove the lumber from the wreck. The deck load of the

disabled schooner was taken off, but the crew of the *Aldrich* refused to permit the lumber in her hold to be removed until they were paid. The *Schroeder* attempted to tow the wreck to Milwaukee, but the *Aldrich* would not steer and the undertaking was abandoned.

A pay log and a Bible from the *William Aldrich* are in the possession of Arni Wegner of Institute, Door County, a grandson of Captain Poppe. The log is for the period 1882 through November 6, 1891, just five days after the collision off Cana Island. This log was signed by each member of the crew when he received his pay for the previous period. Ole Olson, as the mate in 1883, earned $1.50 per day for labor before the opening of the season and $2.00 per day when at sea. Eight years later, his daily rate in the spring was the same, but there is some variation within the season. Later in the season, rates as high as $2.25 to $2.50 were recorded. However, these rates are low, because as early as 1872, John Treiber as mate on the schooner *Mary Booth* was getting $70.00 per month, and sailors were already getting $2.00 per day.[22]

On the last last page of the log, "Hanno Anderson" signed for the sum of $36.25 received of the schooner *William Aldrich* in full for all service done on board from October 19 to November 6 by Erik Anderson, the sailor killed in the collision.

An inscription on the inside front cover of the Bible says, in part, "Presented by the Western Seamans Friend Society, Chicago Seamans Bethel, November 17th, 1857." This Bible was probably given to the *Aldrich* on her first visit to Chicago. The society provided for the spiritual and physical needs of sailors on the Great Lakes through their bethel homes in the major ports. These homes were essentially "safehouses" where seamen could meet and stay with their loved ones. These establishments afforded all of the advantages of a Christian household to young men and provided daily religious services and meals. The pages of the Bible reserved for the family record contain the following signatures and information about some of her crew: "John Parker, Steward, March 15–1858; John Dunn, Mate; Rufus Batchelole, Captain; John Parker, Born Whickham, Canterbury, County Kent England, Milwaukee, Feb. 29, 1864." Rufus Bachelde is given as master on enrollment no. 4 issued at Michilimackinac on August 13, 1859.

Later in November, the scow schooner *J. U. Porter,*[23] owned by John H. Pauly of Milwaukee, took the lumber out of the wrecked schooner and carried it to Milwaukee. There were about 110,000 feet in the hold, and the *Porter* was paid $350 for delivery at Milwaukee. The work of taking the cargo out of the hold was one of the most difficult and unpleasant tasks imaginable, as the water was almost up to the decks and the men were compelled to work in this from the time they started until the job was finished. They were paid $14 for the round trip between Sturgeon Bay and Milwaukee and $.40 an hour while at work on the *Aldrich*.

The crew of the *Porter* chopped holes into the decks of the *Aldrich* while taking the lumber out of the hold. Captain Poppe said that the chopping of the decks would seriously interfere with his arrangements as no survey of damages had been held since the collision. After the survey, Captain Poppe and associates libeled Anson A. Bigelow to recover damages for the collision.

The libel by Captain Poppe and others against Bigelow finally came to trial in the District Court at Milwaukee, Eastern District Wisconsin, November 27, 1893.[24] Van Dyke & Van Dyke represented the libelants and Charles E. Kremer of Chicago the respondent. The faults charged against the schooner by the respondent were as follows: (1) the failure of a sailing vessel meeting a steamer to show a torch, (2) the want of a proper lookout on the sailing vessel, and (3) the change in the course of the sailing vessel. Regarding these faults, Judge Seaman found as follows:

1. It is undisputed that the schooner exhibited no torchlight, and this is claimed to be in violation of a regulation. The lights of the schooner were burning, and distinctly seen, and it is not apparent how observations could have been helped by a torch. The morning was clear, and there were no conditions to obscure the lights, and the absence of a torch was immaterial.

2. The alleged want of a proper lookout on the schooner is contrary to the testimony. The lights appear to have been observed and duly reported by him, and I do not think the testimony warrants the inference argued by counsel for respondent, that he then paid no further heed to the light until the reported change of course by the steamer.

3. The only proof as to any change in the course of the schooner relates to a situation after she had passed the steamer, when it is alleged by the witnesses for respondent that she swung up into the wind, and thus drove onto the towlines and into the barge. This view is corroborated by the fact that the schooner was struck by the barge on her port bow at the cathead. At this moment there was peril and confusion, and it is not surprising that the testimony is conflicting. The wheelsman of the schooner says that he put the wheel hard to port when collision was inevitable, to save the blow as much as possible. He may be mistaken, and, in panic, may have put the wheel the other way, or it may be, as suggested in the respondent's brief, that because of the condition of her centerboard, or other cause, the schooner did not mind her helm. In either view, this occurred in such proximity and such situation of imminent danger, produced by the wrong maneuvers of the steamer, that it must be regarded in extremis, and not taken as a fault to defeat recovery.

A decree was entered in favor of the libelants. Poppe et al. were to be compensated for damages incurred in the collision between the *Aldrich* and the tow barge *Parana* off Cana Island. The administrator of the estate of seaman Erik Anderson brought a separate suit to recover the sum of $5,000 for his loss, and the court granted $4,000. The *Aldrich* was Captain Poppe's last command, as he became the harbor master of the Port of Milwaukee.

Leathem & Smith Towing & Wrecking Co. of Sturgeon Bay operated a number of tugs for towing and wrecking purposes. They also repaired vessels recovered by their tugs and occasionally purchased them from the underwriters after they had been abandoned by their owners. The ship carpenter for John Leathem and Thomas H. Smith was Harry Johnson, who also had an interest in a number of vessels.

In the winter of 1891–92, the *William Aldrich* was reconstructed by Johnson at Sturgeon Bay, with measurements of length 120, breadth 26, depth 7.9 feet and 191.89 gross, 182.31 net tons, with three masts. The previous enrollment, no. 109, issued at the Port of Milwaukee on May 13, 1879, was surrendered at Milwaukee on May 21, 1892; cause of surrender: vessel total loss. The schooner was resurrected and the owner changed to the Leathem & Smith Towing & Wrecking Co., as recorded on July 26, 1892. Leathem and Smith had expanded their enterprises to include lumber and were in need of transportation to carry their products to market. The *Aldrich* was placed in the lumber trade between points along the Green Bay shore and Chicago, and she was often towed by the steam barge *Thomas H. Smith.*

The wooden steam barge *Thomas H. Smith,* official no. 145284, was built in 1881 at Manitowoc by Rand & Burger Shipyard for John Leathem and Thomas H. Smith, with measurements of 130.5 x 27.6 x 11.1 feet and 281.11 gross, 198.10 net tons. She looked more like a tug than a steam barge and was used for towing barges or schooners loaded with lumber from Sturgeon Bay and returning with freight for the county.

The *Aldrich* was permitted another glimpse into her future on Sunday morning November 13, 1892. The schooner was in tow of the *Smith,* coming into Sturgeon Bay from the south, when a little above the Merchant's Dock the steamer dropped her tow, which then attempted to come up into the wind, blowing heavily from the south. The *Aldrich* refused to mind the helm, however, and the only thing that averted a disaster was the dropping of both anchors in the nick of time.

It is the old ones who have been to many places and seen all things, and the *William Aldrich* was no exception. In the fall of 1893, the schooner was witness to an accident similar to the one off Cana Island two years earlier. The *Aldrich* was in tow of the steam barge *Thomas H. Smith,* Capt. Thomas O. Oleson of Sturgeon Bay, First Mate John Colwell of Marinette, and Chief Engineer Henry Machia of Sturgeon Bay, bound light for Sturgeon Bay and Menominee from Chicago early Saturday morning November 11, 1893.

A dense fog that had hung over the lake for several days shrouded the *Arthur Orr*[25] as she pounded south from Milwaukee to Chicago in the vessel track off Racine, Wisconsin, under the command of Capt. Charles Z. Montague. The *Orr* was a new steel boat that had been carrying passengers to the Chicago World's Fair from the time she came out until the close of the big show and had been chartered to run in place of a disabled freighter. The captains heard the fog signals from the other vessel, but there was no visual contact until they were within 300 feet of each other. Cross-passing signals were blown and engines reversed, but it was too late to avert a collision.

The *Orr* hit the *Smith* amidships, cutting into her port side about 3 feet at 3:00 A.M. about 5 miles east of Racine

North Point. A steam pipe was severed by the blow, and the escaping steam added to the fog and confusion. Captain Oleson ordered his men to launch a boat, and they made their escape from the sinking *Smith.* At the same time, a yawl was lowered from the *Orr* to search in the fog for the *Smith's* lifeboat. The two yawls passed each other in the fog, with the boat from the *Smith* reaching the *Orr* first. The *Smith* remained afloat for about an hour before plunging stern first into 100 feet of water.

After the collision, the *Aldrich* threw off the towline but stood by to render assistance. When the crew of the *Smith* were aboard the *Orr,* the schooner squared away and sailed to Sturgeon Bay, where she was picked up outside by a tug and towed into the canal on Sunday morning. The crew of the *Smith* was landed in Chicago by the *Orr.*

The owners of the *Smith* took the necessary legal steps to recover the value of their vessel. On Monday, they caused the *Orr* to be libeled while the latter was lying at Milwaukee; the amount of damage claimed was $25,000. On the basis of this complaint the *Orr* would have been tied up, but David Vance & Co. signed a bond for $25,000 and the *Orr* was allowed to go on her trip.

An investigation into the facts regarding the collision was conducted by the U.S. local inspectors of steam vessels, William Fitzgerald and Daniel W. Chipman, at Milwaukee, and their findings were reported on December 30. The testimony in the case was so conflicting that they were unable to decide which steamer was in the fault, but they did conclude that the pilot rules for lakes and seaboard had been violated by the officers of both vessels. They suspended the master and pilot licenses of Captain Montague of the *Orr,* Captain Oleson of the *Smith,* and John Colwell, mate of the *Smith,* for a period of 60 days.

The libel by the Leathem & Smith Towing & Wrecking Co. against the steamer *Arthur Orr* came to the District Court at Milwaukee, Eastern District Wisconsin, on July 15, 1895, Geo. G. Greene and M. C. Krause for the libelant, Geo. C. Markham and Chas. E. Kremer for the claimant. Judge Seaman ruled that there was mutual contributory negligence and that the damages must be equally divided.[26]

One-fourth of the *William Aldrich* was sold to Harry Johnson, shipbuilder and mariner, of Sturgeon Bay for $625. This change of ownership was recorded on May 28, 1895, with Johnson as master. Many sailing vessels were completely dismasted by the severe storms that frequent the Great Lakes, but only a few suffered this indignity at the hands of a principal competitor, a railroad bridge. The *Aldrich* arrived from Menominee on August 12, 1895, with a cargo of hardwood lumber for William Beidler, Stetson's Slip, in the south branch of the Chicago River, and was taken in tow by the Dunham Line tug, *James McGordon*,[27] Capt. E. B. Bowman. They proceeded up the river until the Jackson Street Bridge, where the customary signals were blown for this bridge and it was swung open.

The Metropolitan Railroad Bridge was located between Jackson and Van Buren streets and usually opened when either bridge was opened. When the bridgetender tried to start the railroad bridge, the electrical controls failed and the bridge did not move. The tender rushed onto the bridge and hailed for the tug to stop the *Aldrich*. The *McGordon* was already alongside the *Aldrich*, but Captain Bowman realized it would be impossible to stop the schooner in time and steamed out of the way. The head stays of the schooner struck the steel arch first, halting the vessel for a moment, but then the bowsprit broke off. In a second the foremast was pressed against the bridge and snapped off close to the deck load. It fell to the deck in a direct line with the keel, with the mainmast following it a second later. The crew on deck began jumping into the river, but the sailor at the wheel, Henry Stevenson of Sturgeon Bay, waited until the mizzenmast began to shake before he jumped, just as the spar tumbled over the stern. His son Claud, who was standing beside him at the wheel, and two young men who were making passage on the *Aldrich*, Arthur Washburn and John Masse, Jr., of Sturgeon Bay, escaped injury by dodging into the cabin.

The momentum of the schooner was so great that after carrying away all the spars, she slid under the bridge and out the other side, a sheer hulk. The only stick left intact was the mizzen-topmast. The *McGordon* landed the *Aldrich* at a convenient dock and took Captain Johnson down the river to report the accident to Capt. James S. Dunham, owner of the towing company. He surveyed the wreck and questioned the men on the bridge, who admitted the accident was the fault of the bridge and not due to any negligence of the tug or schooner. There were no trains near the bridge at the time since all signals and targets had been turned to warn trains to stop and one just starting from the station had been held. The Van Buren Street Bridge was opening when the collision occurred, and the accident would not have happened if only the Metropolitan Bridge had opened.

The rigging remaining on the deck of the *Aldrich* was cut away, and she was unloaded and towed back to Sturgeon Bay. The *Aldrich* made at least one round trip to Chicago in tow of the steam barge *I. N. Foster*[28] before

the spars and canvas were put back in. The rate on lumber from Menominee to Chicago in fall 1895 was only $1.12½, and as the schooner paid $.50 an hour for loading and $50 for towing there was little profit for the owners.

In the summer of 1897, Harry Johnson became the sole owner of the *Aldrich*, and in September he sold her to Frank Krones of Milwaukee, with Herman Krones[29] as master. Like many ancient schooners, her life was now sustained in part by the U.S. Life-Saving Service. The *Aldrich*, Captain Krones, stranded on a shoal 2⅛ miles south of Plum Island Station[30] while bound to Milwaukee from Hedgehog Harbor, Door County, with a cargo of wood and a crew of six on June 7, 1899. The lifesaving crew boarded her to shift about 25 cords of firewood from forward to aft, and then a fishing tug pulled on but failed to release the schooner. The surfmen refused to abandon the *Aldrich* and threw about 50 cords of wood overboard to lighten the vessel. Since the wind was fair, they ran out a kedge anchor, set the foresail and headsails, and hauled her off by heaving in on the line to the kedge. They sailed the schooner to a safe anchorage but returned the next day to recover the kedge for the *Aldrich*.

At 47 years of age (1903), the *William Aldrich* was rebuilt a second time at Milwaukee and remeasured to be 123.7 x 25.2 x 7.9 feet and 177.37 gross, 167.79 net tons, with two masts. She was converted into a deck-staysail schooner with a Grand Haven, or jackass, rig consisting of only two masts, a foremast and a mizzenmast. This rig was employed on many schooners in the twilight of the sailing ships as an economy measure to permit smaller crews and provide spare outfit for maintaining the vessels.

Reports of the U.S. Life-Saving Service[31] record three more incidents involving the *Aldrich*. In 1911, lifesavers from the Frankfort Station assisted the schooner on two occasions: 20 miles west of Frankfort while en route to Kenosha, Wisconsin, from Sturgeon Bay, Michigan, with lumber and a crew of seven on June 25, and ½ mile west of the station while in light trim from Milwaukee to Beaver Island with a crew of six on September 14. The estimated value of the vessel given in these reports is $1,000. On July 15, 1912, the *Aldrich* was assisted by the lifesavers ⅛ mile east of Manistee while bound for Charlevoix, Michigan, from Milwaukee with a cargo of grain. The estimated value of the cargo was $4,000, but the value of the vessel was only $1,600.

The *Aldrich* was sold to George W. Cota (1/2) and Christian Petersen (1/2) of Menominee, Michigan, in the spring of 1914, with Cota as master. He became the sole owner of the oldest schooner on the lakes in the fall of

1915. The *Aldrich* of Menominee continued in the lumber trade between Menominee and Georgian Bay for the Huebel Cedar Co. On June 7, 1916, the schooner was anchored off the west point at Davenport, Michigan, loading cedar posts when a terrific storm broke from the southeast shortly after midnight. When the wind hit the schooner, the anchor chain broke about 40 feet from the hawsepipe, parting as if it were a half-inch rope. The crew immediately got the small anchor out, but this was useless, since the *Aldrich*, which was driven along at an eight-mile-an-hour gait, merely dragged the hook with her. Owing to the velocity and direction of the wind, it was impossible to make sail and clear the shore into deep water. With a reef off the starboard bow, it was evident to Captain Cota and the five-man crew that the fate of the schooner was sealed. She went up on the reef off Point Epoufette with a crash, and they were obliged to remain on the vessel for four hours before being taken off by the gasoline boat *Violette* of Epoufette. As the crew abandoned the *Aldrich*, she was already going to pieces rapidly, the big seas washing over her from stem to stern, racking her old bones. The *William Aldrich* and half the cargo of cedar posts became a total loss.

Thus, almost 60 years of service (1856 to 1916) under sail had come to an end for a vessel built only 4 years after the launch of one of the first distinctive Great Lakes schooners. This record of active service exceeds those of the legendary *Our Son* (1875 to 1930), the *Lucia A. Simpson* (1875 to 1929), and the *Mary Ellen Cook* (1875 to 1923), all known for their longevity into the twentieth century.[32]

But what of the *Parana* and *Robert Holland*, which were responsible for the near fatal damage to the *Aldrich*

in the collision off *Cana* Island in 1891? The *Parana* remained in the lumber trade out of Chicago as a tow barge, and her last document was surrendered at Chicago on March 21, 1904; cause of surrender: abandoned. In 1936, she was towed out to Lake Michigan and scuttled.

In the fall of 1914, the steam barge *Robert Holland* was acquired by Capt. Walter D. Hamilton, shore captain of the Hines Lumber Co. fleet of Chicago. The *Holland* had not been in commission, and she was towed to Sturgeon Bay by the steam barge *L. L. Barth*[33] for an overhauling in the spring of 1915. They arrived on May 6, and the *Holland* was moored at the Pankratz Dock north of the shipyard. A few minutes before 12:00 midnight on May 11, 1915, a young man at the C. Greisen residence noticed flames at the dock from his bedroom window about half a mile away and turned in the alarm. When the firemen arrived, the watchman was asleep in a forward compartment and could give little information as to how the fire started. The steam pump was stationed near the fire well at the foot of Rieboldt Street and the hose was laid across the shipyard to the former Pankratz Mill property, a distance of about 1,600 feet. Because there was no light in the vicinity and the *Holland* was about 10 feet from the slab dock, it was a difficult and dangerous job to place a hose on board. A ladder was hung over the side of the boat and a plank laid from the dock to the ladder, forming a shaky link to the steam barge and threatening to dump the firemen into the bay.

By this time, the after end of the *Holland* was a mass of flames, but the firemen were able to confine the conflagration to the stern. All the light work above deck in the after end was entirely consumed as the fire charred and scorched the decks and rails and ate through the deck in

In this photograph, the schooner *Lucia A. Simpson* is on the left and the burned out hull of the steamer *E. G. Crosby* (2nd) on the right after the great fire at the yard of the Sturgeon Bay Shipbuilding and Dry Dock Company on the night of December 3, 1935. Courtesy of the Wisconsin Marine Historical Society.

The *Mary Ellen Cook* is fitting out in April 1911, probably at Chicago.

the stern. The firemen got a hose under the decks to keep the frames, hull, and considerable amount of coal in the bunkers from igniting, but the engine was well overheated and the stack tumbled over. The *Robert Holland* was not rebuilt, and her career ended with the surrender of the last document on May 24, 1915, at Chicago, well before the loss of the *William Aldrich*.

So in terms of her active service under sail and the events of her life, it can truly be said of the *William Aldrich* that she outlived her time.

CHAPTER SIX

The Reign of the *Ebenezer*s
A Tale of Three Schooners

Although the name *Ebenezer* is not heard frequently today, it was a common first name during the last century. In the marine history of the Great Lakes, there were only three documented schooners named *Ebenezer*, but they all sailed the waters of Door County. What is more surprising is that two of the three *Ebenezer*s were lost in Door County, and the third nearly met her fate at Baileys Harbor.

The first *Ebenezer* was built as the *Watts Sherman*, official no. 26168, at Buffalo, New York, in 1846 by Frederick N. Jones for Ansel R. Cobb of Buffalo and John Palmer of Whites Town, New York. Her original measurements were 103 ft. x 22 ft. 10 in. x 9 ft. 3 in. and 198 $^{51}/_{95}$ tons OM, with two masts. The schooner sailed out of Buffalo for only two seasons before going to Cleveland, where she spent a schooner lifetime – about 20 years. On July 10, 1866, the *Watts Sherman* returned to Buffalo as the property of Edward Madden of Buffalo, with John Powers as master. After 20 years of buffeting about the Great Lakes, wooden schooners were usually in need of extensive repairs or a thorough rebuild. The *Watts Sherman* had been repaired in 1864 and in 1866 carried an Inland Lloyds rating of B 2 with a value of $3,500.

Buffalo was the home port of the *Watts Sherman* from 1866 to 1881 under various ownership. The schooner was repaired in 1871 and 1872, and still maintained a B 2 rating with a value of $2,500 in 1875 but by 1879 was not insurable. Schooners were often rebuilt after 10 years of service and usually before 20 years. After 33 years of service on the Great Lakes without a rebuild, the *Watts Sherman* should have been retired because she was a "floating coffin," but the shortage of vessels after the Alpena Gale in the fall of 1880 and general growth in bulk trades probably extended her career.

Joseph J. Bennett of Vermillion, Ohio, became the sole owner and master of the *Sherman* for the season of 1881. She was rebuilt and a third mast added to the rig, raising her classification to B 1 with a value of $4,000 but insured for coarse freight only. In the spring of 1882, the vessel was sold to Aldin Chamberlin, trader, of Charlevoix, Michigan. During the summer of 1883, the schooner was acquired by Halvor Michelson (2/3) ("Vessel Owner") and Joab Gruda (1/3), both of Chicago.

Captain Michelson had about 30 feet of plank on the

Sherman's starboard side removed but could not find a sound frame. He decided to give her a $1,300 rebuild at Miller Brother's Shipyard in Chicago. However, the schooner was so rotten that an extensive rebuild was required at a cost upwards of $5,000. New timbers forward and aft were put in as well as an entire new stern, new ceiling and keelsons, new centerboard box, new deck and deck frames, several new stanchions, part new rail, and a large amount of new outside planking. Her breadth of beam was increased from 22.5 to 24.1 feet.

When the *Watts Sherman* left the dry dock on the night of August 10, she was hard to recognize as a craft built in 1846. On August 11, 1883, the *Watts Sherman* officially became the *Ebenezer* of Chicago as per authority of the secretary of treasury dated August 7, 1883, and the revitalized schooner embarked on a second life, this time in the lumber trade on the western lakes, with a capacity of 200,000 feet at age 37. The *Ebenezer* was given a rating of A 2½ with a value of $5,500 for the season of 1884.

At 3:00 A.M. on October 3, 1887, during a westerly gale and high sea, the lookout of the U.S. Life-Saving Service Station at Holland, Michigan, sighted a schooner off the harbor that seemed to be in difficulty and immediately gave the alarm. The crew manned the breeches-buoy apparatus while the watch ran out on the pier and fired a Coston signal to notify the vessel of her position. In attempting to enter the harbor, she struck the end of the south breakwater and the seas swept her outside, where she stranded closer to shore but not more than 6 feet from the pier. The lifesavers hove a line aboard the schooner to assist the crew of seven men to safety on the pier.

The vessel proved to be the *Ebenezer* of Chicago, which had sprung a leak and had become unmanageable while bound for Chicago from Muskegon with a cargo of shingles. Later in the morning, she listed to starboard and was in danger of going to pieces. At the request of Capt. William Johnson, the lifesaving crew then stripped the *Ebenezer* to reduce the forces of the wind on the hull. On the sixth, the surfmen assisted the owners in lightering the cargo to the scow schooner *Rockaway*,[1] and when this transfer was completed on the seventh, they helped to rig a steam pump on board the *Ebenezer*. After the schooner was floated, she was towed inside the harbor and then into

63

The first *Ebenezer*, ex-*Watts Sherman*, probably in Sturgeon Bay. Courtesy of the Wisconsin Marine Historical Society.

shoal water in Black Lake to wait for favorable weather before being taken to Grand Haven for repairs. Owner Michelson returned to Chicago on October 8 and reported that the vessel was badly damaged—the stern had been worked down to the transom by the heavy seas before the schooner could be released. The estimated loss in this minor disaster was $2,200.

In 1889, when the *Ebenezer* was 43 years old and large schooners were no longer being built on the lakes, she still rated A 2½ with an approximate value of $5,000. This classification recognized that the bottom planking had been refastened and recaulked in 1887 and the bottom caulked again in 1888. These extensive repairs enabled the *Ebenezer* to remain in service far beyond the usual lifetime of a wooden schooner.

The legendary gales of November did not fail to take their toll in 1891. Two schooners of interest here became victims of these severe storms in a period of less than 10 days. By the middle of November, the weather had turned unusually cold, with temperatures dropping to 10 degrees above zero, and this bitter cold added to the suffering of the schooners' crews. The *Rockaway*, loaded with lumber for Benton Harbor from Manistee, waterlogged and sank

8 miles northwest of South Haven on November 18. The five persons on board were rescued by lifesavers from the station at South Haven, but the loss of vessel and cargo was estimated at $5,000.

About a week later, the *Ebenezer* also left Manistee with a cargo of shingles for Chicago but was driven north by the high winds and waterlogged in the heavy seas. After 36 hours of exposure to severe cold and hunger, the crew of five men abandoned the schooner about 5 miles west of Point Betsey in a small boat that would have swamped coming through the breakers. They were rescued by the lifesaving crew from Point Betsey on the twenty-seventh and taken to the station, where all were fed and clothed, and those suffering from frostbite were given medical attention. A tug with two surfmen was dispatched to tow the *Ebenezer* into port before she foundered. The schooner was pumped out and after a day of rest departed for Chicago.

The *Ebenezer* was enrolled in the Chicago district until 1893, when she was sold to Michael Hilty of Milwaukee, where she would spend most of her remaining days. Anthony Bolster (3/4) and Jorgen Jorgenson (1/4) of Milwaukee purchased the schooner in the fall of 1896. The

Door County Advocate published an accurate resume for the *Ebenezer* on April 10, 1897, under the heading "An Old Timer."

The oldest vessel on the lakes hails from Milwaukee. It is the schooner *Ebenezer*, and her launching dates back to 1846, the year Milwaukee became a city. The old schooner therefore celebrated her semi-centennial anniversary at the same time as the city, and bears her honors with modesty and dignity. When the schooner first came out from the Buffalo shipyards where she was built her name was the *Watts Sherman*. At that time she was a smart schooner of good carrying capacity for those days. Now, and for many years, she has fallen from her high estate and has been numbered among the coarse freight carriers which trade between the west and east shores of Lake Michigan. In 1883 the schooner was given a rebuild which made her good for many more years. All that remained of the *Watts Sherman* was that part of the hull below the water line which was in need of nothing but a little calking thus testifying to the honesty and good workmanship of the early lake ship-builders. For a long time the schooner was in the grain and lumber trade between the upper and lower lakes. This was in the days when the vessels going down with grain came back with lumber long before the great lumber deposits of the pine wood forests of Northern Wisconsin and Michigan took the contract of supplying the country with its lumber. Just when the old schooner was brought up to this lake as a fixture cannot be ascertained, but it was many years ago. She is now owned by Anthony Bolster, and will be in commission with the first this spring as usual.

The near disasters at Baileys Harbor occurred in April 1899 after Gustav Theodore Clauson of 583 Hanover Street, Milwaukee, bought Bolster's three-quarter interest in the *Ebenezer* and became master, while Captain Bolster went into the schooner *Lomie A. Burton*. Captain Clauson was born on July 23, 1876, in Christiansand, Norway. In 1893, at age 17, he became a sailor on the Great Lakes, and the *Ebenezer* was his first command at age 23. The *Ebenezer* had the distinction of being the first sail craft to leave Milwaukee for the season when she got away for Baileys Harbor on Monday, April 10, 1899, for wood to be delivered in Milwaukee. She arrived Wednesday and subsequently took a cargo of wood at Brann's Pier. On Thursday, the schooner sent a signal of distress while anchored near the beach during a strong southeast wind.

Baileys Harbor affords excellent protection to winds from the north, east, and west but is open to the south and southeast; weather from these directions has been responsible for the loss of about a dozen sailing vessels since the Civil War. A U.S. Life-Saving Service station had been established on the east shore of the harbor in 1896, and the lookout sighted the *Ebenezer*'s signal immediately. The

crew of the station pulled to her and found that she was striking bottom in the rough sea because she was heavily loaded with wood. The surfmen took a 1,600-pound anchor into their boat, ran out 150 fathoms of hawser from the *Ebenezer*, and then hove in on the hawser to haul the schooner into deeper water. After four hours of hard work, they succeeded in anchoring the vessel in a safe berth. A change of wind that night enabled the *Ebenezer* to obtain a good run up the lake to Milwaukee.

The scene described above was repeated thousands of times on the Great Lakes during the era of sail. Although schooners handled well off the wind, they could not sail into the wind, particularly when leaving an anchorage in an onshore breeze. Frequently, they were unable to clear the beach and became victims of rocky shoals that jutted out from the shore. Sometimes they dragged their anchors into shallow water and pounded out their bottoms to become a total loss.

On April 20, the *Ebenezer* loaded wood at Brann's Pier in Baileys Harbor and then began pounding on the bottom at her anchorage 1½ miles west of the station during a fresh northeast wind, with rough seas and rain. She hoist-

Capt. Halvor Michelson of Chicago owned the first *Ebenezer* in 1883.

The schooner *Lomie A. Burton* loading lumber at Boyne City, Michigan. The schooner *Libbie Nau* of Chicago is to the left. The *Nau* was used as a breakwater on the south side of the Leathem and Smith Dock in Sturgeon Bay. It caught fire during the burning of the Door County Produce Co. warehouse in 1922 and was burned to the water's edge. Courtesy of the Wisconsin Marine Historical Society.

ed a signal of distress, and the lifesaving crew went on board. The schooner was anchored with enough line out, 200 fathoms of rope and 75 fathoms of chain, but her crew of only five men could not start her off the beach without risking a disaster. The lifesavers manned the windlass and after four hours of hard work succeeded in heaving the schooner out to her anchor. They helped make sail, and the *Ebenezer* started for Milwaukee.

Gundervald Gunderson of Milwaukee became a three-fourths owner and the master during the season of 1899, with Jorgen Jorgenson keeping his one-fourth interest. On the night of September 3, 1901, the *Ebenezer* broke away from a pier at North Unity, Michigan, while taking on a cargo of wood or lumber and was driven ashore on a bad bottom. She was pulled off in good condition by tugs on Saturday, September 7, and taken to Charlevoix, where she was sold to residents of that city.

According to enrollment no. 32, issued at the Port of

Grand Haven, Michigan, on October 4, 1901, the last owner of the first *Ebenezer* was Carry Geiken, "Vessel Owner," of Charlevoix, Michigan. The schooner sank in Pine Lake between Boyne City and Charlevoix in 1903, and the last document was surrendered at Grand Haven on February 27, 1904; cause of surrender: sunk and abandoned. The longevity of the *Ebenezer*, ex-*Watts Sherman*, was remarkable and was exceeded only by the schooner *William Aldrich*[2] (1856 to 1916) and the schooner *Edward E. Skeele*, ex-*John Mee*, ex-*Pauline* (1856 to 1921).[3]

The second *Ebenezer*, official no. 7518, was built at Fort Howard (Green Bay) in 1863 by E. Sorenson for Ole Jorgenson, G. Gunderson, and S. Anderson. Her original measurements were 97 ft. 6 in. x 22 ft. x 8 ft. 10 in. and 172 42/95 tons OM, with two masts. In 1867, the schooner was sold to William H. Horn (3/4) and Homer Hill (1/4) of Manitowoc, with Hill as master. The *Ebenezer* collided with the small schooner *Hattie*[4] of Sheboygan on Monday

May 17, 1869, at Chicago. The jibboom of the taller *Ebenezer* raked through the rigging of the smaller craft, sweeping away nearly everything above deck—jibboom, bowsprit, foremast, mainmast, rail, and the like. The *Hattie* had to be completely rerigged, but the *Ebenezer* lost only her offensive jibboom. Robert A. Goss replaced Hill as master and part owner of the *Ebenezer* when he acquired a one-third interest in the schooner in the spring of 1870.

Although Horn was involved in a number of enterprises and held considerable real estate in Manitowoc, he moved to the town of Clay Banks, Door County, in 1871 to build a new pier and settlement about 80 rods south of the Sturgeon Bay town line (Hornspier Road). By March 1871, the pier had been extended 150 feet into the lake, and Horn was pushing the work rapidly in order to complete it before the opening of the sailing season. About 720 feet were completed by May, leaving 80 feet to be finished to carry it out to the desired depth of water. The work on the new pier was completed during the first week in June, and it reached 800 feet into Lake Michigan to 18 feet of water at the outer end. Vessels drawing 9 feet of water could load at this pier to within 150 feet of the beach.

Horn's Pier was typical of the many settlements that dotted the shores of the Great Lakes when they were the "freeways" of a growing nation. A store and a saloon were also erected, and the first advertisement for this new pier appeared in the *Door County Advocate* on May 25, 1871. Forest products were principal exports over this pier on schooners that returned loaded with cargos of general merchandise for sale to the settlers in the surrounding area. Many of these pier owners had their own schooners, and the *Ebenezer* provided transportation for Horn.

The fall of 1871 saw great fires ravaging Door and Kewaunee counties and the west shore of Green Bay. These included the infamous Peshtigo Fire that wiped out that community on October 8, the same night as the great Chicago Fire. In September, fires burned with fearful violence in the town of Clay Banks, and on Saturday afternoon of the twenty-third, all of the main building belonging to Horn, including the new store and saloon, were destroyed with most of their contents. A few dry goods were saved from the store, and a small log shanty escaped the inferno.

Fortunately for his neighbors, Horn was not easily discouraged and could raise the financial resources in Manitowoc, where he was well-known and respected, to rebuild his establishment. The *Kewaunee Enterprise* published the week after the fire gives Horn's version of the disaster at Clay Banks.

From all accounts, Door County has also passed through an ordeal of fire. Mr. W. H. Horn of Clay Banks who passed through here on Monday on his way to Manitowoc tells us that he has been cleaned out of everything except his pier. He states his losses as follows: Store and goods, $8,000; two barns and grain, $400; saloon and stock, $800; black-smith and wagon shop, $300; six dwelling houses, $1,200. The occupants of these houses, who were in employ, lost all of their household goods, worth about $1,200. No insurance on anything. Mr. Horn intends to rebuild at once, and continue his business.

Horn began immediately to repair the damages and put up buildings to replace those burned, with the intention of being back in full operation before the start of the holiday season. He went to Manitowoc with the *Ebenezer*, and the merchants and produce men loaded her with flour, pork, beef, household goods—in fact, with everything he wanted—and told Horn to build up again and pay for them as soon as it was convenient. A full column advertisement in the *Door County Advocate* on December 7, 1871, attests to his success in "rebuilding the ruins of the late disastrous fire at our place" in a period of only two months.

The *Ebenezer* was sold to Henry Hafer, Charles C. Harder, and Robert A. Goss, all of Chicago, as equal owners for the season of 1872, and Hafer and Harder bought out Goss before the season of 1878. A schooner could be libeled on a claim by a debtor, and if it was not settled, the vessel would be sold at public auction by a sheriff or United States marshal. Marshal Henry Fink seized the *Ebenezer* at Milwaukee in the fall of 1878 on a claim of $710.87 for seamen's wages. She was sold by the marshal on October 17 at the foot of Biddle Street (East Kilbourn Avenue) in Milwaukee to Daniel W. Chipman for $1,000.

Chipman was engaged in the tug business in Milwaukee from 1871 to 1876, when he entered the lumber commission business. In 1878, he formed a partnership with Christopher S. Raesser under the firm name of Chipman and Raesser, which was established in the spring of 1879. They were commission merchants, dealers in wood, hardwood and pine lumber, bark, telegraph poles, posts, ties, and the like. They were located at 102 Ferry Street, Milwaukee. Chipman probably purchased the *Ebenezer* for this trade but for some unknown reason decided to dispose of her. John Saveland of Milwaukee, another commission merchant dealing in forest products, and Edward Austin of the town of Lake, Wisconsin, purchased the *Ebenezer* as equal owners in the spring of 1879, with C. Johnson as master. The Inland Lloyds Register of 1879 rated the schooner B 2 with a value of $1,800.

On Saturday night, June 14, 1879, the *Ebenezer,* with

owner Saveland on board, was run into by the schooner *S. Anderson*,[5] ore laden for Chicago, about 15 to 20 miles below (north) of Port Washington. The *Anderson* lost her bowsprit, jibboom, and the like, but the *Ebenezer* was severely damaged, with her mainmast gone at the head and about 25 feet of rail, stanchions, and plank-sheer on the port side broken. While the vessels were locked together, Saveland threw his satchel on the deck of the *Anderson* and had to wait for its return from Chicago. It was even a smaller world in 1879, because the *S. Anderson* was named after one of the original owners of this *Ebenezer*.

The last document of the *Ebenezer*, issued May 6, 1880, at Grand Haven, records J. A. Buckley and E. J. Wing of Manistee as equal owners, with Charles Otto as master. The measurements on this enrollment no. 147 are 91.6 x 22.3 x 8.0 feet and 119.67 total tons, with two masts. As early as the spring of 1871, Messrs. Buckley and Wing had a large force of men quarrying limestone at Mud Bay (Moonlight Bay) just north of Baileys Harbor. A portion of the stone was sent to Manistee to be converted into lime, and the remainder was shipped to harbors where the government was building piers to fill cribs. A small pier had already been built at Mud Bay, and it was the intention of the owners to extend it to meet the requirements of their increasing business. This establishment was on the south side of Mud Bay, known today as the Toft Estate and held by the University of Wisconsin.

The quarry operated for many years, with schooners transporting stone to Michigan and returning with lumber that was used in the construction of buildings at this establishment. This exchange of stone for timber explains the preservation of the unique stand of virgin pine that exists on the Toft Estate to this day. In October 1880, the schooner *Ebenezer* was engaged in this trade between Mud Bay and Manistee.

On Friday evening, October 15, the *Ebenezer* was at anchor off Mud Bay loaded with stone when the Alpena Gale set in from the northwest. About 2:00 A.M. Saturday morning, the wind suddenly changed to the southeast, blowing heavy and increasing in severity all day, surpassing anything known in the area for 16 years. On Saturday night, the *Ebenezer* dragged ashore and was thrown on the rocks inside of the quarry dock. Although all hands were saved, the schooner was pounded on the outside by the seas and on the inside by her cargo of stone to a total wreck. Capt. E. Swinton was offered $150 for what was left of the *Ebenezer* and thought that was all the wreck was worth, but there is no record of such a transaction taking place. The last document of the second *Ebenezer* was sur-

Capt. Fordel Hogenson, 1849 to 1927, was the builder and master of the last *Ebenezer*. From *Early Days in Ephraim*, edited by H. R. Holand, Door County Historical Society, Sturgeon Bay, Wisconsin, 1929.

rendered at Grand Haven on August 25, 1881; cause of surrender: reported lost.

Fordel Hogenson was born at Rödö, Norway, on April 12, 1849, a son of Haagen and Dorothea M. (Fordelson) Johnson, who came to Door County with their family in August 1873. In the early years, they lived in Ephraim, but then they purchased land near Sister Bay, which Haagen, a farmer by occupation, began to develop and improve with characteristic energy. Fordel Hogenson farmed in the county and also worked as a carpenter, a trade which he had learned as a youth in Norway. On April 23, 1875, he married Miss Lene Gersine Reinartsen, and they became the parents of seven children: Herrman David, Reinart Martin, Nils Benjamin, Fredida Leonore, Samuel Mathias, Elisa Marie, and Lene. His first wife passed away April 25, 1887, and he married Tonnette Amalie Tonneson on June 30, 1888.[6]

About this time, Hogenson decided to build a scow schooner for the coasting trade in the waters surrounding Door County. Together with his sons, he constructed the last *Ebenezer*, official no. 136136, on the beach just to the north of their home in Ephraim. The scow schooner was launched in June 1890, with measurements of 57.0 x 15.5 x 5.0 feet and 39.20 gross, 37.24 net tons, with three masts, which was somewhat unusual for such a small vessel. The *Ebenezer* became the workhorse of Ephraim, transporting food and other necessities to the people on the west side of northern Door County. In preparation for the long winter months, when Green Bay was frozen over and the few trails on land were impassable, the *Ebenezer* would deliver fish, cordwood, and cedar posts to Green Bay and return with food and other provisions needed to survive the winter. After the last run of the season, the *Ebenezer* would usually winter in Ephraim with other trading schooners.

It was common practice for small schooners to winter on their master's beach. The only danger was the great masses of ice that drifted in and out of the harbors with the prevailing winds at the time of the spring breakup. In the winter of 1892–93, the small trading schooner *J. K. Stack,* [7] owned by Henry Amundson of Ephraim; the scow schooner *Jenny,* [8] owned by Sam Neilson; and the *Ebenezer* were hibernating in Eagle Harbor. On April 12, during a westerly gale, floating ice was driven into Eagle Harbor and crushed the *Stack,* leaving her a total wreck. The *Jenny* was crowded against the beach at about the same time but was not so badly injured that she could not be readily repaired. The *Ebenezer* escaped the effects of the ice without suffering any damage whatsoever and was ready to sail in the spring. However, for the *Jenny,* this escape was only a temporary reprieve because she became a "Total Loss, Crushed in Ice" during the winter of 1895–96 as the property of Conrad L. Tonneson [9] (1/2) and Peter E. Knudson (1/2), both of Ephraim.

By 1896, Captain Hogenson began to seek new directions for earning a livelihood. He turned the *Ebenezer* over to Ole M. Olson of Ephraim and worked as a carpenter on the Moravian Church then being completely remodeled in Ephraim. The *Door County Advocate* of August 8, 1896, noted, "Quite a number of tourists have been here thus far and more have wanted to come, if only accommodations were to be had. Ephraim wants a good hotel, and guests would be plenty." Captain Hogenson decided to provide this service just as he had served the residents of Door County in the coasting trade. He began to take these visitors into his home, but soon had to enlarge his quarters to accommodate a growing number of patrons. He named his establishment the Evergreen Beach Hotel, and it is still a popular resort in Ephraim today.

Olson purchased a third interest in the *Ebenezer* for $175 in the spring of 1897 and sailed the craft in the wood trade from Anderson's Pier to Green Bay and other points. In the early days of the tourist trade, the summer season ended with the advent of Labor Day, and Captain Hogenson found himself with little to do in the fall. In the lumber business, the cutting of timber was done in the winter months when teams could pull wagons and sleighs over the frozen swamps to a mill or port for shipment. Captain Hogenson saw another opportunity to supplement his income; this time he would supply the lumber camps on the western and northern shores of Green Bay with hay and other merchandise. To this end, he acquired a second schooner, the *Active,* [10] from E. Christensen of Manitowoc in the fall of 1897.

On Thursday September 29, 1898, the *Active* was bound for Ford River, Michigan, with about 40 tons of hay. She reached the west shore that night in a strong southerly wind, a heavy sea, and a hazey atmosphere, and Captain Hogenson picked up a bright white light that he took for the light on the pier at Ford River. The light proved to be in a house near the shore at a considerable distance to the south, but he saw his mistake before he got in too close. He carried 3 fathoms of water out until about 100 feet from the reef a mile due south of the pier when it shoaled up suddenly, and the *Active* struck the reef with great force. The momentum caused her to rise up about 2 feet all around the hull, and she rested on the bottom in a perfectly upright position. Two tugs attempted to pull her off, but they could not budge the schooner. Captain Hogenson removed the sails and running rigging from the *Active* and then abandoned the hull after transferring 30 tons of hay to the shore. He estimated his loss at $300 for the vessel and $50 for the cargo.

Captains Hogenson and Olson sailed the *Ebenezer* into the twentieth century, with Hogenson listed as master in 1899, Olson in 1900, and Hogenson in 1901. The schooner usually wintered in Eagle Harbor, where repairs were always necessary in anticipation of a new season, and spent the summers at the old wood dock across Eagle Bay from Ephraim. Captain Hogenson hauled the vessel out at Anderson's landing in the winter of 1899–1900 and put quite a lot of timbers and planking into her. Despite this constant attention, the *Ebenezer,* like all of the wooden schooners, was losing her struggle with the elements. In 1905, the last *Ebenezer* was grounded for good because of a badly leaking bottom in the inner harbor at Ephraim where she was born. The slanting deck of the old schooner became a playground for the children of Ephraim in all seasons until the ice of winter and the waves of summer

The last certificate of enrollment of the schooner *Ebenezer,* built at Ephraim, Wisconsin, in 1890. From Record Group No. 41, the National Archives, Washington, D.C.

scattered her bones over the beaches and bottom of Eagle Harbor. The last document of the scow schooner was surrendered on May 9, 1905, at Milwaukee; cause of surrender: vessel abandoned as unfit for service.

Thus, the 42-year reign of the *Ebenezers* in Door County and all of the Great Lakes came to an end.

EPILOGUE

There was a fourth *Ebenezer* in Door County! The *Door County Advocate* of June 30, 1881, reported:

> The little trading schooner *Ebenezer* recently ran ashore in Sherman Bay during a dense fog and proved to be a total loss, nothing but the sails and rigging being saved. The *Ebenezer* belonged to some parties at Ephraim and was about as old as Garbriel himself.

This *Ebenezer* was not enrolled because she was apparently quite small. It is interesting to note, however, that her home port was Ephraim, just as in the case of Captain Hogenson's *Ebenezer*, which was not built until 1890.

CHAPTER SEVEN

From Lumber to Leisure
The *Lily E.*,
ex-*Louisa McDonald*

Many of the sailing vessels of the Great Lakes fell victim to the ever-present perils of wind, waves, and ice that had to be faced in performing their services. Those that survived were often relegated to service as river barges, harbor lighters, grain warehouses, and the like or abandoned in backwaters until they too had gone to pieces. There were a few that assumed unusual duties, and this is the story of one such schooner, which survived 43 years as a commercial vessel before being converted for service of a more genteel nature. However, even in this case the natural elements that exerted their presence with such great fury were to eventually seal her doom.

Jasper Hanson came to America from Denmark and settled in Manitowoc, where he earned his livelihood as a shipbuilder. In the fall of 1868, he completed the beautiful schooner *Jessie Phillips*[1] and then commenced work on another of nearly the same size to be ready for the water the next spring. He laid the keel at the end of October in the yard near Jones Mill, where the *Fleetwing*[2] and the *Phillips* were built. The new schooner was designed for the lumber or grain trade to have a carrying capacity of 160,000 feet or 13,000 bushels and was to be named *Louisa McDonald* after the daughter of a former resident of Manitowoc.

It was common practice in the days of sail to recycle

outfits — sails, rigging, spars, ground tackle, and the like — particularly when a vessel was lost, since these were the major items that could be salvaged. Such was the case for the *McDonald*, because as if by providence the outfit for the new schooner was delivered by disaster on almost the very day her keel was laid.

On October 30, 1868, the schooner *James Navagh*[3] of Oswego, en route to that port from Milwaukee with 15,045 bushels of wheat, struck on Two Rivers Point. The stern was carried away, taking the yawl boat with it, and the cabin quickly filled with water. The crew of nine, including Capt. John M. Griffin, were compelled to crawl out on the bowsprit and jibboom to keep above the water, where they remained for about 10 hours before being rescued in two Mackinaw boats manned by residents of Two Rivers. Margaret Miles, a widow from Chicago who was the cook, was brought ashore, wrapped in dry clothing, placed in a wagon, and driven to Two Rivers as rapidly as possible, but she died immediately afterwards.[4]

The *Navagh* broke in two and went to pieces so that there was no prospect of saving anything beyond the outfit. Messrs. Jones and Hanson purchased the wreck from the insurance company for $1,000, and Capt. James Hughes and his sons recovered both anchors and a large

The schooner *Lily E.*, ex-*Louisa McDonald*, was stranded in North Bay during the great storm of October 1880. Courtesy of Carl A. Norberg.

The *Lily E.* in the anchorage at South Shore during the winter of 1915–16. She was towed from Sturgeon Bay by the tug *Edward E. Gillen* in July 1915. Note the broken fore-topmast and missing raffee yard, which were replaced in the spring of 1916. Courtesy of Meta Lawrie.

portion of the chains, spars, and other equipment for use in the new vessel. [5]

The construction of the two-mast, fore-and-aft schooner was so far advanced by December that planking had already begun. The *McDonald* was launched on May 22, 1869, and enrolled at the Port of Milwaukee on June 4 with the official no. 15872. Her measurements were 123.6 x 25.6 x 8.0 feet and 191.59 total tonnage. She cost the owners—Alonzo D. Jones (1/2), Jasper Hanson (1/4), and D. J. Easton (1/4)—in the neighborhood of $13,000. On her maiden trip to Chicago under the command of the veteran master Capt. Joseph Edwards of Manitowoc, she was freighted with 155,000 feet of lumber, 36,000 lath, and 100,000 shingles.

Capt. Thomas H. Howland acquired a one-eighth interest when he replaced Captain Edwards before the season of 1870, and in his hands the *McDonald* made a good account of herself. She left Manistee at 8:00 P.M. on August 1, 1870, and arrived in Chicago on the afternoon of the third to deliver 166,000 feet of joist and scantling. She then left Chicago on the evening of the fourth and arrived at Manistee again at 3:00 P.M. on the fifth, thus making the quickest round trip of the season in only three and a half days. James Quinn of Chicago became the principal owner of the *McDonald* in the fall of 1870, with Howland remaining as master. A third mast was added to the rig of the schooner before the season of 1877, and her life was uneventful until the Alpena Gale in 1880.

When the storm struck on October 15, the *McDonald* was in the fleet of nearly 30 vessels that ran for North Bay, a harbor of refuge on the Lake Michigan side of northern Door County. She was en route from Manistee to Chicago with a cargo of lumber when one of the most memorable storms on the inland seas destroyed or damaged a large number of vessels. After the schooner entered North Bay, she collided with the schooner *Floretta*, which was already at anchor. The collision sank the *Floretta*, [6] and the *McDonald* suffered damage to her rail and stanchions but stayed afloat and managed to reach Manitowoc on the twenty-third. She was repaired in the dry dock at the shipyard of Hanson and Scove and departed for Chicago, arriving there on November 7. After discharging her cargo of lumber, the *McDonald* turned around for Manistee on the twelfth.

The schooner was involved in a second collision in the waters of Door County, but in this incident she experienced the major damage. Shortly after noon on Wednesday May 10, 1882, the wind in the vicinity of the Sturgeon Bay Canal increased in force until a regular gale

prevailed in the evening and throughout the night. Among the first craft to suffer damage was the *McDonald*, which sought shelter from the storm in the canal. She came inside the harbor piers at the Lake Michigan entrance and let go her anchors because she could not get a tow into the cut. The heavy wind and sea dragged the schooner against the south harbor pier, where she pounded heavily. A short time later, the schooner *Harvey Bissell* [7] also ran into the canal and let go her anchor. The wind soon drove her against the *McDonald*, and both vessels were damaged by the collision. The damage to the *Bissell* was light, but the *McDonald* had her bulwarks stove in and canvas torn. She was unable to continue on her trip north and had to be taken to Manitowoc for repairs at a cost of about $1,000. The *Bissell* also experienced some damage by collision with a second schooner, the *John L. Green*, [8] but she was able to be repaired in the canal and continue on.

The *Louisa McDonald* was sold at the end of the 1882 season to Michael Engelmann of Manistee, a lumberman who renamed the schooner *Lily E.* after his daughter. This name change became official on June 1, 1883, but first appeared on enrollment no. 153 issued at the Port of Grand Haven on June 23, 1883.

This change in owner and district brought bad luck to the aging schooner. The *Lily E.* left Manistee at 5:00 A.M. on Sunday May 20 laden with 180,000 feet of lumber consigned to the yard of M. Engelmann & Co. of Milwaukee and arrived about 9:00 P.M. during a heavy northeast gale. Although a tremendous sea was running on the outside, Capt. Charles A. Brook undertook to sail his vessel into the harbor because no tug was available in the bay. The schooner missed the entrance and struck the south pier with the bluff of her port bow but sustained no damage outside of the loss of her bobstays and cathead. The *Lily E.* was carried to leeward past the pier, and Captain Brook, seeing that she was in danger of going on the beach, ordered the sailors to let go of both anchors. The port anchor checked the schooner somewhat, but she continued to drift toward the beach.

The plight of the *Lily E.* was discovered from the harbor by Captain Downer of the tug *Starke Brothers*. [9] The tug was run wide open to the *Lily E.*, and as the crew of the tug were about to take a towline from the schooner, the port rudder chain of the tug parted, disabling the latter so that it was with great difficulty that she was able to return to the harbor. The *Lily E.* continued to drag her anchors until she was broadside in the trough of the sea and carried on to the beach. She struck stern first and was carried about by the sea until she was head on to the wind at a posi-

The schooner *Harvey Bissell* on the St. Mary's River. Courtesy of the Wisconsin Marine Historical Society.

tion about ½ mile to the south of the south harbor pier and about ¼ mile from the beach. The stranded vessel began to pound heavily and unshipped her rudder a few minutes after she struck. [10]

The disaster was also discovered about 9:00 P.M. by the lifesaving stationmen on watch along the beach, and the keeper, Capt. John E. Evenson, ordered out the surfboat at once. They pulled down the Kinnickinnic River until they were abreast of the *Lily E.*, then they dragged their boat across Jones Island and launched it into the breakers. The sea was running so high they could not reach the schooner, and the surfboat was violently thrown back three times.

The beach apparatus was brought from the station, and on the first shot from the Lyle gun, the bight of the line caught to the windward of the mizzen rigging and was made fast to the mizzen head. The whip line and hawser were sent off and the breeches buoy rigged. The buoy went off well until it was within 50 feet of the *Lily E.*, where it snagged because the lines had twisted together

while being hauled through the surf. The lifesaving crew was unable to pull the buoy either way, but the crew of the schooner went aloft and succeeded in freeing the line and getting the buoy in working order. [11]

Soon a sailor was seen climbing into the buoy and the lines were manned and worked with a will. When the buoy came close into the beach, two of the lifesavers rushed into the water waist-deep and pushed the buoy high and dry. A crowd of fishermen and their wives surrounded the sailor, but he was rescued by Captain Evenson, who invited the sailor to his home for refreshments. In reply, the sailor expressed his determination to stay and see his comrades safe on the shore. He gave his name as Robert Cousins of Sterling, Canada, and said that there were still six men on the *Lily E.* – Captain Brook; Mate J. Morcomb, Chicago; Steward John Nichols, Ludington; Charles Matteson, Manistee; John Miller, Chicago; and Gus Franke, Chicago. One after another, the crew came safely ashore, while Captain Brook remained in the rigging until all were safe before he was rescued.

The *Lily E.* in tow of the tug *Peter Reiss* in the Sheboygan River. On the shore to the right of the *Reiss* is the scow schooner *Lynx,* and over the stern of the tug the two masts of the abandoned schooner *Graham Brothers* can be seen. Courtesy of the Wisconsin Marine Historical Society.

The *Lily E.* off Manitowoc under a heavy cargo of wood. Courtesy of the Wisconsin Marine Historical Society.

All Monday morning, the *Lily E.* lay steady, but shortly after noon a complete change in her position took place, from head to the wind when she struck to turned completely around with her bow towards the shore. In the evening of the twenty-first, her spars began to work, and it was the general opinion that she would undoubtedly prove a total loss if the severe weather continued. A contract was made by the owners of the *Lily E.,* M. Engelmann & Co., with Kirtland, Wolf & Davidson Wrecking Co. to send the powerful wrecking tug *Leviathan*[12] to her as soon as the weather would permit. The *Lily E.* was valued at $10,000 and insured for $7,500 by Crosby & Dimick's Agency at Buffalo in the Thames & Mersey Co.

Captain Blackburn, the underwriters' wrecking master, arrived from Chicago on Tuesday morning to look after the *Lily E.* The condition of the wreck was little changed from Monday except that she had careened over on her port side, working into the sand until her deck on the port side forward was under water. Her deck load of lumber had nearly all been washed overboard but had been recovered and piled on the beach. Since the storm had subsided, a number of the crew went aboard during the afternoon to recover their clothing. The schooner did not appear to be damaged to any great extent as yet, and Captain Blackburn felt confident that she could be released. Her owner, Michael Engelmann, also arrived on Tuesday and engaged the tug *William R. Crowell*[13] of Manistee, which was at Milwaukee for repairs, to assist the *Leviathan* in releasing the vessel.

On Wednesday morning, the *Leviathan* towed a lighter alongside the *Lily E.* and began to remove the cargo. After her entire deck load was removed, a steam pump was

placed on board, but it failed to lower the water in her hold, and the plan of floating the schooner by pumping her out was abandoned. It was decided to attempt to release the *Lily E.* by dredging a channel through the sand and then pulling her off, since the lumber in her hold would float her. The *Leviathan* spent the day dredging a channel to the wreck, while Charlie Peak, a diver, made an examination of her hull and found the planking an inch apart in some places.

The tugs *Leviathan* and *Crowell* dredged a channel about 300 feet long to within 100 feet of the vessel on Thursday, but shortly after 2:00 P.M., a southeast sea set in, forcing them to abandon the work and return to the harbor. Early Friday morning, the weather was pleasant as the *Leviathan* and *Crowell* left the harbor for the wreck, and the opinion among the wreckers was that they would have the *Lily E.* in the harbor before nightfall. The tugs continued dredging a channel through the sand and reached the vessel before noon. During the afternoon, the *Leviathan*'s hawser was placed on board, made fast at the mainmast, and run under the schooner's starboard quarter. Shortly after 5:00 P.M., the *Crowell* got a line from the *Leviathan* and started ahead while the hawser from the *Lily E.* was made fast on the *Leviathan*. When the first strain was put on the line, it had no effect on the stranded schooner. A second attempt was no more successful, and during a third attempt the hawser parted, which closed the work for the day. Both tugs returned to the harbor, and the wreck remained in the same position as on Monday but in far worse condition. Her decks amidships were sprung, she was slightly hogged, and her cabin had been washed off.

The *Leviathan* remained in the harbor on Saturday and left for Escanaba in the evening, but one of her pumps remained on the *Lily E.* Peak was engaged to make another examination to determine why the wreck could not be pumped out and found that the oakum had worked out of her seams and several planks had started to pull away from her hull. After he plugged the seams and patched the planks, another attempt was made to pump the wreck out, but it was no more successful than the earlier ones.

Since all efforts to pump the *Lily E.* out and pull her off had failed, it was decided to dredge all around the wreck as well, and the tug *Crowell* began this operation on Saturday afternoon. The tugs *Welcome*,[14] *Starke Brothers,* and *Crowell* dredged a channel 12 feet deep on the outside and around her bow and stern on Sunday. The *Lily E.* was stripped of her canvas and anchors on Monday for the purpose of lightening her as much as possible. The three tugs attempted to pull the wreck off but had no effect whatsoever.

The owners of the *Lily E.* abandoned her to the underwriters on Tuesday May 29, eight days after the stranding. They had made every possible attempt to rescue her but had not succeeded in changing the position of the wreck in the least. She was stripped and the steam pump was removed. The tug *Crowell* returned to Manistee, but Captain Blackburn still felt confident that the *Lily E.* could be saved as soon as a southwest sea set in so that the vessel could be worked out of the bed that she had formed in the sand.

The underwriters met with the Milwaukee Tug Boat Co. on Wednesday to formulate a new plan for the release of the *Lily E.* The plan proposed by the company was to have a diver patch the hull until she could be pumped out with their large centrifugal pump and released.

The wind swung around to the southeast on Friday June 1, and a slight swell set in, causing the *Lily E.* to work in the bed of sand. Shortly after noon, the tugs *Welcome* and *J. J. Hagerman*[15] were ordered to the wreck, and a hawser from each tug was made fast to the vessel. About 2:00 P.M., the tugs began to pull, the *Hagerman* keeping a steady strain while the *Welcome* jerked. After an hour of steady work, the wreck began to move and continued gradually until about 4:00 P.M., when she was on an even keel with her stern swung around into the channel. The tugs succeeded in getting the wreck off and into the chan-

nel shortly after 7:00 P.M. The *Lily E.* was towed into the harbor and ran into shallow water opposite Wolf & Davidson's main yard.

The schooner was placed in dry dock on June 3 for temporary repairs, towed to a dock to discharge her hold full of lumber on June 13, and again docked that evening. The survey of the *Lily E.* was completed on the next day, and she was found to be so badly damaged that it was doubtful whether the underwriters could force the owners to accept her, as the wrecking bill and the cost of the repairs would be large. She required a part new keel forward, several new planks forward and aft, entire recaulking and fastening, a new stern post and rudder, and a new cabin. It had been supposed that her centerboard was badly damaged, but the survey showed that only a new head ledge would be required. Her pocket pieces were found to be in good condition, but she had been considerably damaged on the port side from working into the sand, and several new frames amidships were required.[16]

The repair of the wreck was pushed and completed in about two weeks, but the *Lily E.* remained at Wolf & Davidson because of a disagreement between M. Engelmann & Co. and the underwriters. The cost of releasing and repairing the wreck was said to exceed $5,000, while the vessel was insured for $7,500.[17] When the owners abandoned her, they claimed that she was a total wreck, but the underwriters refused to accept the abandonment and wanted the owners to pay half of the expenses, which the owners objected to. On July 2, Chris. Hansen, John Mercurt, Leverisa Johnson, John Nichel, Andrew Nelson, and Edwin Gandlesen, who fitted out the vessel and were given a certificate of the amount due by the master, libeled the *Lily E.* for wages totaling $110, unpaid because of the disagreement between the parties involved.

Capt. James Riordan of Buffalo for the underwriters and one of the owners met on July 5, but nothing definite was decided. After Engelmann arrived from Manistee, a satisfactory settlement was agreed on between the parties, the underwriters accepting abandonment of the vessel and then selling all back to M. Engelmann & Co. The *Lily E.* left for Manistee on the evening of July 9 in charge of Captain Brook, in far better condition than when she went on the beach.[18]

Although this incident was a major disaster, the worst weather of the year was yet to come with the arrival of the equinoctial gales. From November 11 to 17, a series of gales resulted in the greatest destruction of property since the Alpena Gale of 1880, which had damaged the *Lily E.* in North Bay. The loss of life was not in proportion to the loss of property in other seasons because of the efficacy of the U.S. Life-Saving Service, which did not become well established over the lakes until the late 1870s. A recapitulation of the disasters on November 21 listed 60 vessels lost or damaged and 55 lives lost, with several vessels still to be heard from. [19]

On the morning of November 11, 1883, the *Lily E.,* Captain Brook, arrived off Manistee from Milwaukee with 2,500 bushels of oats shipped by J. A. Bryden & Co. to J. Babcock & Co. and a crew of eight on board. A strong southwest gale was blowing and a high sea running as she was picked up outside by the tug *C. Williams* [20] of Manistee and towed toward the harbor. At 11:00 A.M., the towline parted and the *Lily E.* struck the pier and stranded on the beach about ⅛ mile north of the U.S. Life-Saving Service Station. The accident was immediately discovered by the station patrol, and the lifesaving crew hauled the surfboat to the beach opposite the schooner. In 15 minutes, they were alongside the stricken schooner, although their efforts were obstructed by quantities of driftwood. Captain Brook and his crew, with their baggage, were taken into the surfboat and safely landed on the beach.

During the afternoon, Engelmann arrived and requested that Captain Brook be set on board to supervise the securing of the schooner by running lines to the shore. This service was performed, and the keeper also ordered the whip line attached to the *Lily E.* so that the breeches buoy could be used in case of need. This was a wise decision because by the time the captain was ready to return to shore, he could only be landed by this means, since it was impossible for the surfboat to be forced through the floodwood.

The station crew were employed from the eleventh to the twenty-sixth in saving sails, booms, running rigging, and the like and in trying to dredge a channel to enable a steam tug to get to the vessel. At 5:00 A.M. on the twenty-sixth, the *Lily E.* was hove off the beach into deep water, but the sea began to grow so heavy that it was impossible for the tug, which was standing by, to get to her. It became necessary to scuttle the schooner in order to save her from again stranding, leaving the keeper and five of his crew with no means of escape except the small yawl that hung from the davits at the schooner's stern. The sea became so heavy that the yawl was torn from her fastenings and swept ashore, placing those on board in a perilous position. The keeper jumped overboard at a favorable moment and succeeded in reaching the shore on some of the floodwood. He hurried to the station with two other members

The *Lily E.* in the dry dock of the south yard of the Milwaukee Dry Dock Co. in the spring of 1916. The hurricane deck has been erected, and planking in the bow is being replaced. Courtesy of Meta Lawrie.

of the crew who had been left ashore in case their services were needed and obtained a team to rush the beach apparatus to the shore opposite the schooner.

The first shot from the gun hurled the line between the fore- and main-topmasts but too high to be reached by the men on board because of the danger of going aloft while the vessel was pounding so hard. The second shot threw the line between the fore and main masts closer to the deck, where it was seized, and the apparatus was soon in working order. The crew of nine were safely landed after a thorough wetting in the breeches buoy as it was pulled through the surf.

Another attempt was made to get the *Lily E.* afloat on the twenty-seventh. The pumps were constantly kept going to free her of water, and the holes made when she was scuttled were closed. But at 2:00 P.M., the sea again became so heavy that the vessel had to be scuttled a second time. All 19 members of the vessel and station crews working on board the schooner were taken ashore in the surfboat.

On the twenty-ninth, steam pumps were placed in position on board, and on the thirtieth, the *Lily E.* was pumped out, raised, and towed into the harbor at Manistee, where she was laid up for the season. During the time the U.S. Life-Saving Service assisted the *Lily E.*, the surfboat was used 41 times and landed 27 persons without mishap, except that the keeper had one of his fingers badly injured but continued to perform his duty.[21] The estimated amount

A stern view of the *Lily E.* in dry dock showing the new raffee yard. Courtesy of Meta Lawrie.

lost of the vessel and cargo was $8,400; however, this seems too high, since the *Lily E.* was not severely damaged and the value of the cargo was only $1,200, with about three-quarters of the oats saved.

The *Lily E.* was sold to John Greilick of Traverse City, Michigan, as the principal owner for the season of 1887, and from May 26, 1888, to January 11, 1900, the enrollments record that she was owned, at least in part, or sailed by Gustav, Nels, Fred, and Louis Gunderson of Sheboygan. From this time, the record of the *Lily E.* is best related in terms of her Norwegian owners and masters, whose resourcefulness and ingenuity extended her life and the lives of many other sailing vessels well beyond their time.

James Gunderson was born on January 27, 1831, in Kragerø, Norway, and sailed on saltwater for some years before he came to America in about 1855 to make his home in Sheboygan. In 1859, he married Anne Gurine Thompson and they had six sons—Gustav, Martin, Nels, Fred, Louis, and Theodore—and one daughter, Martha Maria. The Gundersons were well-known and respected sailors who owned a number of schooners, including the *Liberty, Transit, Industry, H. D. Moore,* and *J. A. Holmes,* as well as fishing tugs and propellers. They rebuilt the *Lily E.* in 1892, which restored her Inland Lloyds rating to A 2, the rating she was given when she was only six years old.

In the winter of 1899–1900, the Gundersons sold the *Lily E.* to Claus S. Jorgenson and Samuel Jorgenson, both of Racine, as equal owners. Claus was born at Langesund, Norway, on August 14, 1866, and came to Racine in 1887. On October 9, 1906, the *Lily E.* sprang a leak off Kewaunee while bound for Milwaukee from Manistee with a load of bark and a crew of five. She managed to reach Milwaukee Harbor, where Capt. C. Jorgenson requested assistance of the lifesaving crew. They boarded the schooner and manned the pumps to keep the *Lily E.* afloat until she could be docked. The estimated value of the vessel was reported as $700 and the cargo of bark as $425.[22]

Helpful encounters with the U.S. Life-Saving Service were the rule rather than the exception for most of the old schooners during the twilight of the sailing ship on the Great Lakes. The *Lily E.*, Captain Jorgenson, delivered a cargo from Racine to South Manitou Island in April 1908. While she was lying at the dock 1 mile northwest of the station on the twenty-seventh, a shift of wind into the east started a heavy swell that pounded her against the dock with great force. The station crew boarded the vessel, manned the windlass, and assisted the crew of five to work the *Lily E.* clear of the dock and to a safe anchorage in the

The *Lily E.* in the lagoon at South Shore some time after the fall of 1916. Courtesy of the Bay View Historical Society.

harbor. [23] On May 22, 1908, surfmen at the Charlevoix station took lines from the *Lily E.*, the schooner *Major N. H. Ferry,* [24] and the steamer *J. S. Crouse* [25] and assisted them to safe moorings in the harbor. [26]

Jorgenson sailed the *Lily E.* until 1909, when he sold his one-half interest in the schooner to another Norwegian captain, Anthony Bolster of Chicago, and retired from the lakes. Bolster had been owner and master of the schooner *Ebenezer,* ex-*Watts Sherman,* for three seasons, 1896 through 1898, and the schooner *Lomie A. Burton* for the season of 1899. He then sailed the schooner *Charles E. Wyman* for the Michael Hilty Lumber Co. of Milwaukee until he supposedly retired from the lakes in 1905 to establish a grocery business in Chicago. His purchase of the *Lily E.* in the spring of 1909 represented a return to the marine scene, but it is not known whether he actually sailed the schooner.

On April 29, 1911, the Chicago Transportation Company officially became the last owner of the *Lily E.* as a commercial vessel. After the season of 1912, she was laid up for the winter in Sturgeon Bay with a broken fore-topmast and later towed to the boneyard south of the shipyard, [27] where she was to remain in the mud for several years while events in Milwaukee paved the way for a new career for the old lumber schooner.

The city of Milwaukee began to develop the lakefront on its south side from Russell Avenue to just south of Nock Street in 1913. J. E. Hathaway & Co. drove wooden pilings along the shore that curved to the east between Iron and Nock streets to form a protected anchorage intended for sailing yachts and motorboats. The weather in the fall of 1913 was typical for the season as a series of storms slowed the construction of the pilings and breached them at several points. A severe storm struck the south shore of Milwaukee Bay on November 11, damaging the construction equipment and halting the project for the season.

This development of the lakefront for recreational purposes encouraged a group of Bay View residents to form a corporation in 1913 known as the South Shore Yacht Club. The new club rented a house at 342 Beulah Avenue (South Shore Drive) owned by James R. Williams, a steelworker in the rolling mills just to the north, but vacated this property on April 23, 1915. That same evening, the membership met in the residence of Commodore William Barr at 388 Beulah Avenue to discuss a new home for their club. The commodore read a letter from Daniel B. Starkey, a member, stating that he could get a schooner free for the club. The towing would also be free of charge. The homeless yacht club quickly passed a motion to accept Starkey's offer, and the decision to convert a lumber schooner, the *Lily E.,* to a floating yacht club had been made. [28]

Starkey inspected the *Lily E.* in Sturgeon Bay and reported that it was in good condition and had better lines than the Lincoln Park Yacht Club of Chicago, the ex-schooner *Carrier.* [29] The *Lily E.* was not acquired without cost. At a special meeting held at the Bay View Public Library on May 29, 1915, which was called to consider her purchase, "a motion was made and seconded that the Board of Trustees be authorized to enter into a contract with the owners of the schooner (the Chicago Transportation Company) according to the terms of $50 down and the balance of $300 to be paid in one year and the secretary be authorized to draw a check in payment for it (Carried)." A letter from Leathem & Smith Towing & Wrecking Co. said that the schooner was still on ground but that they expected to have her released soon. [30]

The *Lily E.* was pulled from the mud of the boneyard in Sturgeon Bay and taken to the Leathem & Smith dock for temporary repairs before the trip to Milwaukee. Starkey and Edward E. Gillen arranged for the tow from Sturgeon Bay to the anchorage at the south shore, where she arrived on July 5, 1915. They were elected life members of the club at the regular meeting on July 9, 1915, in consideration of the time and money they gave for the schooner. The tug employed in the tow was the *Edward E. Gillen,* ex-*J. J. Hagerman,* [31] which together with the *Welcome* [32] had pulled the *Lily E.* from the sand off Jones Island in the spring of 1883, 32 years before.

The conversion of the schooner from lumber to leisure began almost immediately and moved rapidly throughout the fall of 1915 and the spring of 1916. A new floor was placed in the hold and it was wired for electricity. Iron work was erected to support a hurricane deck to serve as the dance floor on the *Lily E.* Even the rigging was restored, with the replacement of the broken fore-topmast and the addition of a raffee yard at a cost not to exceed $5 for the latter. Some of the renovation and repair was accomplished in the dry dock at the south yard of the American Shipbuilding Co., formerly Wolf & Davidson, located at the foot of Washington Street.

Another driving force in the conversion was the establishment of the South Shore Yacht Club Auxiliary. At a regular meeting on August 13, 1915, a letter from the wives, mothers, sisters, and daughters of yacht club members asked permission to use the name South Shore Yacht Club Auxiliary for their organization. They also asked permission to use the schooner on a certain day each week and wanted the privilege of selling lunch and refreshments on Labor Day. "A motion was made and seconded that we allow the wives, mothers, sisters and daughters of the members of the South Shore Yacht Club to use the name of South Shore Yacht Club Auxiliary (Carried)."[33] The auxiliary sold lunch and refreshments on holidays and catered the club's private parties, with the proceeds dedicated to the purchase of items for what was affectionately being called the "ship." Some of their initial donations included skylights, cups, saucers, plates, glasses, and tablecloths.

By July 4, 1916, much of the work was completed, and the *Lily E.* was triumphantly taken to the Milwaukee Yacht Club on the north side of the bay for the holiday celebration. The membership boarded the good "ship" at 8:30 A.M. and had a fine trip across the bay towed by Gillen's tug. [34] There were flags at every angle, and the whole code of flags was strung at the top of the mast. The yacht club was a colorful sight and an ideal subject for another emerging recreation, the moving picture. A movie man, Raymond D. Clifton, was busy all day, and all the members of the club took part in the film. The "ship" was also used by a motion picture company of Milwaukee in a number of marine scenes.

With the advent of World War I, the resources of the club were depleted by the call to arms, and the maintenance necessary to sustain a wooden vessel was deferred. After the war, the club began to plan for a new land-based clubhouse, and the future of the *Lily E.* became uncertain. The club considered at least one offer for the "ship" from another yacht club, but she was never sold. At a regular meeting on January 30, 1920, the commodore told of visiting the park board regarding the location of a clubhouse on park property, and the problem of repairing the main deck of the *Lily E.* was discussed with nothing definite decided. [35]

In the meantime, the development of the lakefront continued, as the city had plans to fill behind the pilings to the north, along the beach to the south, and the anchorage in

The burning of the *Lily E.* in the anchorage in midsummer 1922. Note the battered condition of the hull, the jibboom, and the masts and the remains of the hurricane deck. Courtesy of Meta Lawrie.

between the pilings in order to improve and increase the amount of park land on the shore. Andrew M. Heederik spoke on a new clubhouse site at the regular meeting of March 11, 1921, and a motion was made and seconded that "the club go on record to procure the site which is to be filled in due east of the *Lily E.* for a new club house and the Building Committee was to take up the matter with the Park Board (Carried)."[36]

In the spring of 1921, the fire insurance on the *Lily E.* was cancelled, and by the fall it was a major task just to keep her afloat. At an informal meeting following the regular meeting of September 9, the group discussed ways and means to keep the "ship" afloat after Shipkeeper H. Diederich had informed the commodore that the pumps had been working for several hours with no apparent result. But as in the case of thousands of her predecessors, the nemesis of all Great Lakes vessels, the equinoctial gale, was about to deliver the final blow.

Throughout the fall, what seemed to be a never-ending gale battered the *Lily E.* in her anchorage at South Shore. With her seams opened, the vessel rested on the bottom and worked into the sand as she had done so many years before just a short distance to the north off Jones Island. It was obvious to all who were willing to face the facts that by the winter of 1921–22, the *Lily E.* could no longer serve as a floating yacht club. The membership of South Shore Yacht Club had so many fond memories of the "ship" that they had great difficulty in thinking about disposing of her remains.

The time had come of necessity for the final surrender of the *Lily E.* The "ship" was to be consigned to a boneyard, or given over to flames at her moorings, or, as suggested by the harbor commission, relegated to the fate of many of her contemporaries—being hauled down the beach and allowed to settle as a breakwater where the currents were rapidly eating away the shoreline south of the city limits. The knowledge that the city was going to fill in Gillen's Point and the cost of releasing the vessel were deciding factors in the final choice.

On a still, cloudy day in the midsummer of 1922, there was a cremation in Milwaukee. A dozen mourners wended their way to where the funeral pyre was to flame, poured on the oil, and then stood still to watch and remember as the fiery, clutching arms reached up and wrapped their victim in hot embraces. When it was over, there was little left of the *Lily E.*, and as if to make sure that she would not become another "ghost ship of the Great Lakes," she was buried in fill by the city. In 1936, the present South Shore Yacht Club was built on the point of land over the former anchorage, and in 1976 a gate was erected over the bow of the *Lily E.*, ex-*Louisa McDonald*.

CHAPTER EIGHT

The Discovery of the
America

After four frustrating weeks of searching the waters off northern Door County, the boats headed south out of Algoma on the morning of September 3, 1977. They were the *Lake Diver,* with John Steele and Jim Brotz, and the *Challenge,* with Kent Bellrichard, Rich Zaleski, and Jim Jetzer. The fishermen had reported a wreck just off the Kewaunee Nuclear Power Plant about 6 miles south of Kewaunee or 16 miles north of Two Rivers. The early settlement on the shore corresponding to this position was Carlton, where a pier had been located in the days of sail.

As the search vessels approached the power plant, a sharp target peaked on the scanning sonar to the west, or inside, of their track. They zeroed in on the target with the recording depth sounder and succeeded in getting a hook into the unknown obstacle on the floor of Lake Michigan. The divers hurried towards the bottom and discovered the remains of a badly smashed schooner, with her bow to the east, stern to the west, and three masts and rigging lying to the south along the bottom. The jibboom was lifted from the foredeck and thrust into the sand at some distance forward of the bow. It was obvious that this vessel had been in a collision, receiving severe damage before she made her final plunge. The fishermen had been right again

about the position of a wreck, and the bones of this schooner were littered with their lures and other tackle.

The discovery of a wreck is only the first step in identifying and recording these valuable elements of our Great Lakes marine history. In subsequent dives to date, no positive evidence as to the name of this wreck has been uncovered. The ship's wheel, with the trademark "14 Federal Street, Boston, Massachusetts," the steering mechanism, and an anchor shown in the photographs have been recovered. The nut from the shaft of the wheel was found lying on the deck, and its surfaces were uniformly corroded, indicating that it had been removed by a diver at some earlier date.

Although it will be necessary to conduct further underwater exploration and photography of this wreck, its location, condition, measurements, rig, and partial disassembly of the wheel strongly suggest that the *America* has been discovered.

The schooner *America* was built in 1873 at Port Huron, Michigan, by Archibald Muir for David Muir of Chicago (1/3), and Thomas Hood of Chicago (1/3), with the master builder retaining a 1/3 interest. Her measurements were typical for a schooner of that time at 137 x 26 x 11

The wheel and steering mechanism of the schooner *America* on the dock at Kewaunee, Wisconsin, on September 4, 1977. They now reside in the Manitowoc Maritime Museum. Courtesy of James J. Jetzer.

feet and 341.67 total tons, with one deck and three masts. The *America* was temporarily enrolled at Port Huron on June 11, 1873, and received her first permanent enrollment at Chicago on October 1, 1873. A. Muir sold his interest to Colen McLachlan (3/24) and David Robeson (5/24), both of Port Huron, and this transfer was recorded on the last document of the *America* issued at Chicago on May 21, 1875, and surrendered on October 8, 1880, at Chicago; cause of surrender: "Vessel lost—September 28, 1880—10 miles north and off Two Rivers Point, Wisconsin." This location is in agreement with the location of the wreck as described above.

The *America* was unusual in that she had two official numbers: 105244 and 105337. This kind of error occurred infrequently from 1867, when the official number system was instituted, to about 1880. During this period, communications were still very slow, and occasionally a second number was assigned without taking the time to determine if a vessel already had a number. The higher number, 105337, was the second one assigned and appears on the last document.

The loss of the *America* and subsequent salvage attempts are also consistent with the condition of the wreck found off Carlton. In the fall of 1880, the tugs *A. W. Lawrence*[1] and *M. A. Gagnon*[2] were hauling stone on scows to Two Rivers from Ahnapee (Algoma) to fulfill a contract that George O. Spear[3] of Sturgeon Bay had made with the federal government. They were replacements for the tug *Thomas Spear*,[4] which had burned north of Two Rivers on September 22, 1880. On Tuesday evening September 28, the *Gagnon* was at the head of the tow with a line running to the *Lawrence,* and the stone scows were behind the latter, probably a couple hundred feet. The *America,* under the command of Capt. Fred Gunderson, was in light trim, bound north for Escanaba from Chicago to load iron ore for Michigan City. The mate on watch sighted the tugs at about 11:00 P.M. with Thomas Thomey at the wheel, and at 11:40 P.M., the *America* showed a torchlight, which flamed until the collision. The tugs did not carry the towing lights as required by the regulations—two bright lights, one above the other on the pilot houses. Captain Gunderson saw the red and green sidelights as well as sparks issuing from the smokestacks but concluded they were fishing tugs because of the absence of towing lights.

When the master of the *Lawrence* noticed the *America,* he gave two sharp whistles of warning to the schooner to keep away and altered his course so as to pass to leeward of the *America,* bringing the dummy scows directly across the bow of the schooner. There were no lights on the scows, and it was not until a seaman on the jibboom shouted that there was some object ahead, under the schooner's bow, that the possibility of a collision flashed across the minds of those aboard. Soon afterwards, at about midnight, the corner of the first deeply laden scow struck the *America,* knocking a large hole in the bow of the schooner. She sank in less than five minutes about 9 miles north of Two Rivers Lighthouse and about 4 miles from shore.

The captain and crew of the ill-fated vessel took to the yawl but lost most of their personal effects, including quite a sum of money belonging to the captain and the vessel. Two hours later, they left the scene of the disaster and pulled for shore, landing at Two Rivers Point. The *Lawrence* and *Gagnon* did not arrive in Two Rivers until 4:00 A.M. because the first scow had a large hole in her bow and was difficult to keep afloat. Captain Gunderson sent a dispatch from Two Rivers to Thomas Hood in Chicago to the effect that the *America* was run down and sunk off Two Rivers Point and requested a tug as soon as possible. Captain Hood could not understand why the master would ask for a tug if the schooner was sunk at some distance off Two Rivers Point, where deep water was known to exist. Therefore, further particulars were solicited, but the manager of the Two Rivers telegraph office replied that Captain Gunderson could not be reached, having returned to Two Rivers Point.

At 2:00 P.M. Wednesday, the captain and crew left Two Rivers Point in the yawl, towed by the *Gagnon,* and found the *America.* She was head down and stern up, with parts of the mainmast and mizzenmast out of the water and the taffrail 2 feet below the surface. It was thought that the *America's* anchors held her down and that she probably could be saved. The sea was so heavy that nothing could be done that day, and the expedition returned to Two Rivers. Captain Gunderson sent another telegram to the managing owner describing the perilous condition of the *America,* and Captain Hood decided to let the underwriters undertake the work of rescuing the craft, if possible. He also ordered a railroad pass for the survivors so that they could depart for Chicago, but Captain Gunderson had to leave his watch in payment for their board before they could leave Two Rivers.

The *America* was turned over to the insurance companies, and Capt. John Prindiville, acting for the underwriters, consummated an arrangement with Stephen B. Grummond of Detroit for the speedy rescue of the schooner. The correspondence between the parties was conducted by telegraph and, therefore, could not have been

From left to right: James Brotz, Brian Barner, James Jetzer, and Bill Kappelman with the anchor from the schooner *America*, which is now at the Rogers Street Fishing Village, Two Rivers, Wisconsin. Courtesy of James J. Jetzer.

other than brief. The plan was to drag the schooner into shoal water, send divers down to patch or jacket the break in her hull with canvas, and then pump her out. According to the agreement, Captain Grummond was to receive $3,500 on delivery of the *America* at Manitowoc but nothing in case of failure.

The powerful wrecking tug *Winslow*[5] left Detroit on Sunday October 3 to rescue the partially sunken schooner. There was concern that the heavy seas, which had prevailed, might cause the *America* to settle to the bottom, but when the *Winslow* and *Gagnon* arrived at the wreck on Wednesday morning October 6, they found her in the same condition as the night after the collision. With the help of a diver, a line was hitched to the mast, and the tugs pulled on her for some time, only succeeding in turning her stern towards shore as she settled to the bottom and breaking their line. The stern of the *America* had been kept

Capt. John Prindiville, a veteran master, was an agent for the underwriters of the schooner *America* in 1880. From *History of the Great Lakes, Volume II*, J. H. Beers and Co., Chicago, 1899.

buoyed to within a few feet of the surface, but the strain due to the pull opened the seams around the hatchway and mizzenmast or sprung the timber ports aft so that the compressed air escaped and the schooner settled on an even keel. This turn of events made the recovery of the schooner unlikely. On October 7, S. B. Grummond sent a telegram to Captain Prindiville in Chicago, stating that the *Winslow* had abandoned the *America* in deep water. Captain Prindiville remarked, "She is gone for good, there is no doubt of that," and stated that any further effort to recover the vessel would be by outside parties because the underwriters were unwilling to continue the expedition.

On the same day, at the scene of the disaster, a diver went down about 50 feet, reaching the main crosstrees, and furled the gaff-topsail. It is most likely that a diver descended to the deck of the *America* during this operation and removed the nut from the wheel in hopes of salvaging it. However, without a proper puller it was impossible to remove the wheel, and the diver abandoned the attempt. The *Winslow* returned to Manitowoc on October 9 and left for Detroit a few days later, arriving at Cheboygan on the thirteenth.

The *America* rated B 1 and was insured for $10,000 on a valuation of $12,000 by the following companies: Lloyds of New York, $2,500; Manhattan, $2,500; St. Paul Fire & Marine Insurance Co., $2,000; Union of Philadelphia, $1,000; and Great Western of New York, $2,000. The owners of the *America* received $6,000 from the insurance companies and $4,500 from the owners of the tugs *Lawrence* and *Gagnon*.

In consideration of the above evidence, it is most probable that the *America* has been discovered. The location of the wreck is in agreement with the position given at the time of the disaster, and it was obviously struck by a deeply laden vessel. The wreck has three masts; its length, although difficult to determine with accuracy, is about 140 feet; and its orientation on the bottom is with the stern to the shore as described in accounts of the rescue attempt. The jibboom is stuck in the bottom and probably broke away from the foredeck when the *Winslow* tried to drag her towards shore. The nut from the shaft of the wheel found on the deck indicates that an early diver had been on the *America*.

As Captain Prindiville stated, "Any further effort to recover the vessel would be by outside parties" — almost 100 years later.

CHAPTER NINE

Official No. 135665
The *Emma L. Nielsen*

The schooner *Emma L. Nielsen* was built at Manitowoc during the winter of 1882–83 by Hanson & Scove for Capt. Paul Nielsen of Manitowoc. She was assigned the official no. 135665 as recorded on enrollment no. 55 issued at the Port of Milwaukee on April 2, 1883. Her original dimensions were 74.7 x 20.6 x 6.2 feet and 62.37 gross, 59.26 net tons, with two masts.

The *Nielsen* met with disaster late in the fall of her maiden season. She stranded in a gale ¼ mile southwest of the U.S. Life-Saving Station at Muskegon, Michigan, on November 15 while bound for Ludington, Michigan, from Milwaukee with a cargo of hay and flour and a crew of three men. The station crew had scarcely returned from the wreck of the schooner *Trial*, [1] when they were called to the assistance of the *Nielsen*. The surfboat was launched at 3:00 P.M. and forced through floating logs to the schooner, which was completely encased in ice. Captain Nielsen and two sailors were found in a pitiable condition in the vessel's rigging. Their clothing had been wet through and was frozen so stiff that it was necessary to assist them into and out of the surfboat. They were taken to a warm room in the station, where some time was required to remove the frozen garments.

The *Nielsen's* anchors had been lost early in the day, and it was impossible for the crew to have averted the disaster under the existing conditions. The gale abated later in the day, and the station crew assisted in getting a hawser from the schooner to a tug. The *Nielsen* was not released until the twenty-fourth of November and taken into port. The estimated value of the vessel was reported as $4,500, the cargo as $5,000, and the loss in this disaster as $1,500.

The schooner was repaired in the winter of 1883–84 at a cost of $1,200. In order to finance the repairs, Captain Nielsen sold the vessel to Hugo J. Klingholz of Manitowoc, as recorded on enrollment no. 48 issued at the Port of Milwaukee on March 25, 1884. Captain Nielsen remained as master, and for the remainder of the decade the *Nielsen* served in the lumber trade from Door County and ports of Green Bay. For example, in 1887, she operated out of Whitefish Bay on Lake Michigan and Egg Harbor on the Green Bay side, carrying wood to Chicago for Henry M. Benjamin.

Because of increasing competition from larger vessels,

both sail and steam, the *Nielsen* was lengthened to 98.2 feet, which increased the tonnage to 90.21 gross and 85.70 net tons. During this rebuild in the winter of 1889–90, a third mast was added to the rig consistent with the increase in length. Captain Nielsen regained ownership of the *Nielsen* before the season of 1890, with William Drake of Milwaukee having a one-third interest.

Captain Nielsen had a lumber camp at Mud Bay (Moonlight Bay) just north of Baileys Harbor in the early 1890s where cord wood was cut during the winter and all available logs were converted into ties and posts. [2] The *Nielsen* wintered in Manitowoc, where she was fitted out each spring in preparation for the first trip to Mud Bay. When the ice went out, the schooner was called on to transport the winter harvest to ports where forest products were in demand. Capt. Alfred Salvison sailed the schoo-

The schooner *Emma L. Nielsen* in the foreground on the inside at Manitowoc about 1890. The schooner *IDA* is on the outside, with the schooner *C. Amsden*, the steam barge *Francis Hinton*, the schooner barge *May Richards*, and the steamer *F. & P. M. No. 1* in line towards the harbor entrance. Courtesy of the Wisconsin Marine Historical Society.

The *Emma L. Nielsen* at Manitowoc after she was lengthened and a third mast added. Courtesy of the Wisconsin Marine Historical Society.

ner during the season of 1893, while Nielsen tended to the many details of the business.

In the fall of 1893, George Meyer ran the camp because Nielsen was kept at home in Manitowoc by the illness of his wife. When the schooner *E. P. Royce*[3] became a total loss in Little Harbor just south of Cana Island on November 26, 1893, her master, Capt. Harry Worfel, made arrangements with Meyer to board and lodge the crew of five men at Mud Bay until they were able to return to their homes in Chicago. The men were destitute because each had about $100 due in wages, not a dollar of which had been paid. After several weeks had elapsed, they received a part of their money from Martin McNulty, the owner of the *Royce*. Meyer carried the men as far as Sturgeon Bay, where they departed for Chicago on December 10. On their arrival at their destination, they were to receive the balance of their earnings.

Capt. H. Erickson was placed in charge of matters at Mud Bay after the above incident. He was well-known in Door County as the master of the schooner *Surprise*[4] and the steam barge *Wm. Rudolph*[5] for H. M. Benjamin & Co. The *Surprise* ran to Sister Bay and other ports on the Green Bay side at the same time the *Nielsen* transported wood for Benjamin. Erickson had command of the *Rudolph* until she was sold to Theodore Plathner early in the fall of 1893.

There was a good demand for men in the northern part

of the county at this time. Although there were 20 men working in the camp, Nielsen needed a larger force because he intended to make this point one of the liveliest in the county. A half score of husky-looking Scandinavians arrived in Sturgeon Bay on December 11 on their way to Mud Bay, having been sent through by Captain Nielsen from Manitowoc. They took Dunn's stage for their destination on the following morning, but when they arrived at Jacksonport, such strong inducements were held out to them that all but one remained. This was the second time that a shipment had been waylaid en route to the camp.

The offices of H.M. Benjamin in the Ludington Building on the east side of the Milwaukee River just north of Grand (Wisconsin) Avenue.

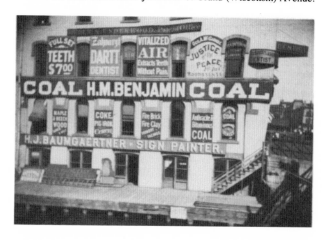

The steel steamer *Wyandotte* on May 11, 1941. Courtesy of the Wisconsin Marine Historical Society.

The *Door County Advocate* of December 16, 1893, suggested of Nielsen that "the next time he undertakes to forward laborers to his vineyard at Mud Bay he pack them into boxes or crates and send them through to their destination in the original package. That's the only way that we can see at present."

On Sunday November 19, 1895, a southerly gale accompanied by big seas drove several upbound vessels, including the *Nielsen,* from Lake Michigan into the Sturgeon Bay Ship Canal. The *Nielsen* picked up a tow outside, but her bobstays were carried away by the towline, which was on the port bitt leading to the tug on the starboard side. In backing up to effect a landing, the strain placed on the stays broke the bolts that held them to the bowsprit. This minor damage was quickly repaired, and the *Nielsen* continued on with a cargo of lumber.[6]

Charles Reynolds of Jacksonport had acquired the one-third interest in the schooner owned by Drake in the fall of 1884. He had a store in Jacksonport and intended to have the *Nielsen* transport goods and products. In the fall of 1901, Reynolds brought suit in Judge Kirwin's court at Manitowoc to compel Captain Nielsen to either buy Rey-

nolds's one-third interest in the schooner or sell the two-thirds interest he controlled. Reynolds asserted that they did not agree on the management of the vessel and that he could not get an accounting. Judge Kirwin decided that he had no jurisdiction because the matter rested solely in the United States courts.

By the turn of the century, the demand for forest products had slackened, and Captain Nielsen decided to sell his interest in the schooner. The following advertisement appeared in the *Door County Advocate* on November 23, 1901:

Schooner Nielson for Sale
The trim schooner Emma L. Nielsen is offered for sale at a bargain. She is 8 years old and her dimensions are 100 feet long, 22 feet beam and 6 foot hold, and registers 90 tons. She carries from 120,000 to 150,000 feet of lumber or 6,500 bushels of wheat. Her outfit is A-1. For further particulars call on or address,

Paul Nielsen
711 16th St., Manitowoc, Wis.

It took Captain Nielsen over a year to dispose of the vessel, as she did not change hands until 1903 to become the property of David Ferris of Alpena, Michigan, (1/3), L. Recor of Marine City, Michigan, (1/3), and Harry Recor of St. Clair, Michigan, (1/3), according to enrollment no. 3 issued at Port Huron on July 3, 1903.

The reefs along the shore to the north of the Thunder Bay area, Lake Huron, proved to be formidable obstacles for Captain Ferris and the *Nielsen* over the next three years. The schooner stranded on a reef 2 miles southeast of the Middle Island Station of the U.S. Life-Saving Service at 5:40 A.M. on June 12, 1904. The lifesaving crew reached the vessel at 7:10 A.M. to find the *Nielsen* afloat from amidships aft. They ran an anchor astern, took the cable to the windlass and hove it taut, shifted part of the cargo of cedar posts from forward to aft, then hove away on the windlass again, got the schooner afloat, and assisted the crew to make sail. The schooner proved to be uninjured and proceeded on her way.

During a fresh northwest gale on October 20, 1905, the *Nielsen* ran aground again in the same storm that claimed one of the largest schooners on the lakes—the 245-foot, four-masted *Minnedosa*[7]—and her crew of eight. The *Nielsen* dragged anchors and stranded on a point 16 miles northwest of the Middle Island Station. Surfmen were taken to the scene of the disaster in tow of a tug. On boarding the *Nielsen,* they ran a hawser to the tug, which attempted to float the schooner but was unsuccessful. The lifesavers

threw over part of her cargo of cedar posts to lighten the vessel. She was released and taken to a dry dock for repairs.

In a similar incident in the same area at the same time of the year—October 24, 1906—the *Nielsen* dragged anchors during a southeast gale and stranded on a sandbar 6 miles northwest of the station. The station crew beat down to the schooner in their surfboat under sail and boarded the stranded vessel. After jettisoning part of her cargo of cedar, they floated the schooner and brought her into the harbor, where Captain Ferris took charge.[8]

The last owners of the *Nielsen* were A. J. Young of Port Huron (1/3), L. Recor of Marine City (1/3), and Harry Recor of St. Clair (1/3), as recorded on enrollment no. 30 issued at Port Huron on June 17, 1908.

On June 25, 1911, the *Nielsen* left Port Huron upbound and light under the command of Capt. William Young. As she sailed north into dense fog, Captain Young had no reason to be aware of the presence of the large steel steamer *Wyandotte,*[9] which was downbound from Alpena to Wyandotte with a full cargo of limestone. Shortly after 3:00 A.M. Monday June 26, they collided about 11 miles off Pt. Aux Barques. The starboard side of the bow of the *Wyandotte* cut the *Nielsen* to the waterline on the port side near the bow.

The stricken schooner rapidly flooded, and the crew of

The crosstree of the mizzenmast on the *Nielsen.* Courtesy of David Trotter.

The *Nielsen's* steering wheel still in place. Courtesy of David Trotter.

five just barely escaped in the yawl when the *Nielsen* took the final plunge to the bottom of Lake Huron. The *Wyandotte* came about and picked up the crew of the schooner. She delivered them to Port Huron, where the damage to the *Wyandotte* was assessed as slight.

Although many of the vessels lost on the lakes have been located by divers in recent years, the number of schooners discovered is relatively small. In the case of the *Nielsen,* we are fortunate. This perfectly preserved time capsule was found by Larry Coplin and Dave Trotter in June 1980. According to Trotter:

> The *Nielsen* lies with a slight list to her port side and is virtually intact except for the damaged bow section. The bowsprit was pushed back in the collision and lies on the deck while the large wooden stock anchor now rests off the starboard side of the bow on the floor of Lake Huron. Both the foremast and mainmast snapped at the base and lay on the port side of the deck. The position of the anchor and the broken masts are likely the result of the *Nielsen's* collision with the bottom and not the surface accident with the *Wyandotte*. This observation is additionally supported by the fact that the bowsprit lies underneath the foremast, and that the schooner would typically settle bow first, permitting the anchor to slide off on bottom impact. The empty davits from which the yawl was launched still face outward off the stern, a remembrance of the crew's necessary rapid departure. Seventy years after sinking the two step

mizzenmast rising 75 feet above the *Nielsen's* deck, sways gently in the current as a reminder of a bygone era when many fine schooners were a part of the Great Lakes' scene. [10]

Shortly after the *Nielsen* was located, we received a call requesting the identity of a "small three-masted schooner with a wooden cross-arm anchor, having the official no. 135665 and the tonnage carved in the forward deck beams of both hatches."

Customs regulations required the marking of the tonnage and official number on these beams. [11] Article 33 says:

> Tonnage must be marked on the face of the beam on the fore side of the main hatch of seagoing and lake vessels and on the face of the beam under the after side of the starboard forward hatch of Western river steamers, on river steamers of the coast which carry passengers, both above and below the main deck; where there is no hatch to the main deck the tonnage mark should be on one of the deck beams in a conspicuous place, and as near as possible to the middle of the vessel. It should be in plain Arabic numerals, thus, 825 61–100, not less than three inches high and not less than three-eighths of an inch deep. On vessels where the main beam is of wood it should be carved or branded, and on vessels whose main beam is of iron it should be plainly marked in oil paint, white when the beam is black and black when the beam is of any light color.

With regard to the official number, chapter 1, article 10, says: "The official number but not the signal letters of a vessel must be carved or marked on her main beam, preceded by the abbreviation 'No.,' and the name and number must appear on all papers relating to her." The official numbers were assigned in blocks to custom houses for issue alphabetically according to the first letter in a vessel's name when it was registered.

In going through the many files of individual vessels, the first "135" number was the schooner *Elizabeth,* official no. 135939, issued at the Port of Milwaukee on August 24, 1887. This discovery meant that the unidentified schooner was out of Milwaukee and built in the 1880s. The next "135" in our files was 135665, and the *Emma L. Nielsen* became, to the best of our knowledge, the first missing schooner positively identified by the official number system.

CHAPTER TEN

The *Farrand H. Williams*
A Scow Schooner

The scow schooner was a type of sailing vessel distinguished by the absence of the curved lines at the bow and stern of the typical Great Lakes schooner. These vessels were simpler, more economical to build, and had good carrying capacity relative to their length. Because of their shallow draft, they could serve the small harbors that dotted the coastline of the great inland seas. Although their lines made them ideal as trading schooners, they were used in every capacity. This is the record of one such scow — the *Farrand H. Williams*.

The *Williams*, official no. 120474, was built in 1882 at Manitowoc by and for Capt. Francis Porter Williams for the wood trade and as a salvage vessel. He named the new vessel after his young son, and her measurements were 88.85 x 22.8 x 6.6 feet at 94.85 gross, 90.11 net tons, with two masts. She was the first sail to arrive in Milwaukee for the season of 1883, and her cargo of dry maple wood was sold on April 12 to H. M. Benjamin & Co. at $6.25 per cord.

On the afternoon of November 13, 1883, the schooner *J. I. Case*[1] of Racine, Wisconsin, bound down for Buffalo from Chicago with 50,000 bushels of corn, ran on Hog Island Reef, 9 miles east of Beaver Island in Lake Michigan and filled with water. Capt. A. B. Davis of the U.S. revenue cutter *Andrew Johnson*[2] discovered the wreck the next morning with her deck badly raised amidships. He brought Capt. Harry Gray and the mate to Cheboygan, Michigan, where the powerful wrecking tug *Leviathan*[3] was dispatched to the assistance of the *Case*. Captain Gray returned the following day at 9:00 A.M. with the wrecker, a gang of laborers to lighten the vessel, and the *Farrand H. Williams*, which was to lighter off the corn. The work of removing the cargo and pulling on the schooner was carried out all that day and also on the sixteenth until evening, when a gale set in from the southward and westward and the tug sought shelter in Beaver Harbor.

The *Williams* arrived at Mackinac on the seventeenth with the cargo of corn from the *Case*. Captain Williams reported that the *Leviathan* got one steam pump aboard the *Case* but had to leave because the heavy sea was breaking over her. He said that the schooner was in good condition before the southwester set in.

The tug *Henry S. Sill*[4] left Racine on Monday November-

ber 26 to relieve the *Case* but put into Manitowoc on the same night to clear herself of ice and to obtain coal. She made another start on Tuesday morning, reached the *Case,* and took her off the reef in a damaged condition. To avoid the lake as much as possible, because of the ice so late in the shipping season, the *Sill* brought the vessel through Death's Door and Green Bay. When coming up Sturgeon Bay on Tuesday afternoon, the *Case* was run aground on Hogback Reef at the spot where the schooner *Flying Cloud*[5] had stranded a few weeks before. The accident was caused by the removal of the buoys, which caused the *Sill* to mistake the channel. Fortunately, the tug was going so slowly that the schooner was not run hard aground and was pulled off by the tug after a few hours of work and passed the bay at 5:00 P.M. The *Sill* wooded up during the evening, and on Wednesday morning December 5, left for Manitowoc, where the *Case* went for repairs. Additional hands assisted the crew at the pumps on the *Case* and were able to keep the water in her hold down.

The *Case* was owned by Jerome I. Case and F. M. Knapp of Racine and was valued at $35,000. Knapp had $10,000 insurance on his interest, but Case was not insured. Much of the *Case's* cargo of corn, insured for $27,500, was lost because 20,000 bushels were wet and some was thrown overboard. The *Case* was placed in dry

The schooner *J. I. Case* was one of the larger sailing vessels of her time at 208 feet and 828 tons. She is shown here unloading coal by horse power at Racine, Wisconsin. Courtesy of Fr. Edward J. Dowling, S.J.

A Manitowoc River scene, looking east from Eighth Street Bridge, in the latter part of June 1890. The U.S. revenue cutter *Andrew Johnson* is in the foreground; astern lies the wrecking tug *Favorite* (wood) headed east; right ahead of the *Favorite* is the wooden steamer *Nevada*, with the tugs *Monarch* and *Arctic* lying next to her. A few days before, the *Nevada* stranded in Death's Door and was released and brought by the *Favorite* and *Monarch* to Manitowoc where she was repaired. Courtesy of the Wisconsin Marine Historical Society.

dock at Manitowoc, where she received a thorough re-build during the winter of 1883–84 at a cost of about $18,000.

In the fall of 1884, the wrecking schooner *Williams* was engaged by underwriters to take pig iron from the schooner *Christina Nilsson* [6] of Chicago lying on the north point to the inlet at Baileys Harbor. The *Nilsson*, Capt. N. A. Hammer of Evanston, had left Escanaba on Thursday evening October 23, loaded with 575 tons of pig iron for Chicago and a crew of eight. She had proceeded via Death's Door into the teeth of a gale and a snowstorm as far as the Sturgeon Bay Canal, where she came about and ran before the storm to seek refuge in Baileys Harbor. As the schooner approached the harbor in the blinding snow-storm and high sea, with all sails single reefed, she kept too far off (to the east) of the narrow channel. When she realized the danger, she attempted to veer eastward and

run outside of the shoal, but the schooner struck the reef hard at 8:30 A.M. on Friday and began to founder. When the anchor was dropped, the *Nilsson* swung around, strik-ing aft a second time, and sank in 2½ fathoms of water, with her rails submerged. The crew abandoned her at once and made their way to a little island on the east side of the harbor.

According to insurance records, [7] the *Nilsson* rated B 1 with a value of $8,500 in 1882 and A 2 with a value of $9,000 in 1884. New keelsons and other repairs in 1882 accounted for the higher classification and value in 1884. The vessel was insured for $8,000 with the Etna Insurance Company, and the cargo was insured for $12,000. She was abandoned to the insurance companies and was stripped by the crew on the twenty-eighth. Capt. W. H. Rounds, wrecking master for the Etna, left Chicago on the twenty-fifth for Baileys Harbor to examine the *Nilsson*.

He said that she was not out of shape and did not appear to be much damaged. She lay between two reefs, with her anchors out ahead, and was only exposed to a southeast sea. She lay partly on her bilge, with one rail about three feet under water and the other rail even with the surface of the water. However, if the stormy weather continued, it would delay operations until too late in the season to save her.

A firm in Detroit contracted with the underwriters to take the *Nilsson* off for a stipulated sum. The same party also had the job to take out the pig iron, but this job was sublet to Captain Williams. The scow *Williams* reached the wreck with three divers and all of the most improved wrecking apparatus about November 10, over two weeks after the disaster. The *Williams* was able to raise about 50 tons a day and with favorable weather would raise the entire cargo in about two weeks. She raised 250 tons in the

The schooner *Christina Nilsson* on the outside in the background with the schooner *Midnight* in the foreground. The *Midnight* was built in 1856 at Cleveland, Ohio, by Peck & Masters. On November 27, 1889, she broke away from her towing steamer *S. S. Wilhelm* in a northeast gale and snowstorm and stranded about 8 miles north of Ottawa Point, Lake Huron, near Tawas, Michigan. She had lumber from Ford River, Wisconsin, to Buffalo. Courtesy of Fr. Edward J. Dowling, S.J.

first week, which was deposited on Chipman & Raesser's Pier in Baileys Harbor, from whence it would be forwarded to market the next season. After raising another 100 tons, they expected to pull the schooner off and take her to Chicago. By the end of November, less than half of the pig iron had been removed, and it was obvious that an attempt had to be made to release the *Nilsson* from this exposed position before winter set in.

The tug *John Gregory*,[8] Captain Stubbs, engaged in the work of releasing the schooner, but to no avail. Three steam pumps were insufficient to lower the water in the vessel's hold over an inch or two after being in operation for hours at a time, which indicated that the bottom was gone out of her altogether. On Friday November 28, the pumps worked nearly all day without making the least gain on the water, and it was decided to abandon the undertaking, at least for the fall. The *Gregory* left for Manitowoc with the wrecking master at about 10:00 A.M. Saturday morning. Captain Stubbs stated that the hatches of the *Nilsson* had been battened down and every effort made to keep the water from running in from the top, but this also proved of no account, since the water came in at the bottom as fast as it was pumped out. The *Williams* was still getting up the iron from the wreck, but the curtain was rapidly coming down on the season as winter weather set in about a week later. The last document of the *Nilsson* was surrendered at Chicago on December 10, 1884; cause of surrender: vessel wrecked and a total loss.

During one of the heavy northeasterly blows early in January, the mizzenmast of the *Nilsson* was blown down, which indicated that the schooner was gradually breaking up. The wind and ice were too much for the hull even though it was under water. The spar had fallen toward the mainmast, and it was the opinion of some that the stern and cabin had been crushed in with ice, leaving nothing but the keelson, which was insufficient to hold the top weight of spar and standing rigging. The mainmast was carried away next, leaving only the foremast and bowsprit standing above water. Much of the pig iron left on deck had also been washed overboard by the ice and proved a total loss. The foremast was the last to go, carried away as the ice moved out. Then there was nothing but the badly broken hull remaining to mark the underwater grave of another victim of the equinoctial gales.

The expedition to the *Nilsson* also proved to be a disaster for Captain Williams. He had a cash-flow problem because the pig iron recovered from the wreck had not been sold. The *Williams* was libeled for seamen's wages in December for the amount of $575. In January, the *Williams* was sold at Manitowoc by the U.S. marshal to C. C.

The tug *Henry S. Sill* waiting for a tow, in the harbor of Racine, Wisconsin, with the U.S. Life-Saving Service Station at the left, in the 1880s. On May 6, 1913, she burned at Marine City, Michigan. Courtesy of the Wisconsin Marine Historical Society.

The schooner *Glen Cuyler* became one of the old-timers on the lakes. She was built in 1859 and survived to age 59 with the assistance of several rebuilds and a gasoline engine to supplement her sails in 1908. She spent her last years carrying cargoes of lumber and hay on Green Bay. Courtesy of Fr. Edward J. Dowling, S.J.

Barnes of Manitowoc for $1,500. This change of owners was not recorded until enrollment no. 89 was issued at Milwaukee on June 16, 1885, with Anton Hanson as the new master. After losing the scow *Williams,* Captain Williams owned and sailed the steamers *Grace Williams,* [9] named after his daughter, and *St. Maries,* [10] named in honor of the American and Canadian Sault Ste. Marie. He died at his home in Manitowoc on August 5, 1893.

Capt. Anton Hanson was born in Laurvig, Norway, on March 20, 1837. He came to America with his parents, Soren and Matilda Hanson, in 1853 and settled in Ephraim. Soren operated an active wood dock on the west shore of Eagle Harbor, midway between Eagle Cliff and the head of the bay, about an eighth of a mile south of the stone quarry. Anton passed his entire life on the water. He was first employed as a cook on the *Familia,* a vessel plying between England and the Scandinavian peninsula. His first shipment in America was on the schooner *Transit* [11] sailing between Manitowoc and Chicago. He served before the mast for about nine years and then as first mate for nine years before going into the schooner *Glen Cuyler* [12] in 1871 as master for Osul Torrison of Manitowoc. Captain Hanson had been united in marriage in 1864 with Lena Hanson Findahl, a sister of Mrs. Osul Torrison. In 1872, Captain Hanson acquired the schooner *Industry,* [13]

which he sailed for two years before he went into the schooner *Minnehaha* [14] in the service of Osul Torrison. He remained in the *Minnehaha* until he was placed in command of the *Williams* for the season of 1885.

Perhaps because of his sturdy ancestry, Captain Hanson was a man for all seasons and did not believe in laying up for the winter. In the first week of December 1889, when most vessels were already in port, the schooner *Arctic* [15] and the scow *Williams* were caught in Sister Bay during a terrible gale and came within a hair of going ashore and becoming total wrecks. Captain Hanson furnished the following account in the *Door County Advocate* of December 7, 1889, of the peril and final escape of the two vessels:

We had been taking on wood at Roeser's pier for James Hanson, and finished loading Wednesday afternoon. The weather looking pretty bad we pulled away from the pier and dropped anchors between Wiltse's pier and the Sister Island, expecting that the wind would come from the northeast. We had got things snug when the wind began to blow from the north, northwest and it wasn't long before the sea began to run high. As night approached, the wind increased and we soon saw that it was necessary to drop both anchors and pay out all the chain. The *Arctic* was laying a little outside of me, but as the air was thick with snow, we could see nothing of each other. In the mean-

Loading cordwood at Onekama, Michigan, in 1894. The vessels from left to right are the scow schooner *Charley J. Smith,* the schooner *Vermont* of Onekama, the schooner *Minnehaha* of Manistee, and the scow schooner *Emily and Eliza.* Many of the scows were dedicated to the wood trade. Courtesy of the Wisconsin Marine Historical Society.

time, the wind was blowing so strong that it nearly took the men off their feet, and the sea was running very high. We put in a miserable night; expecting every minute that our chains would part and that we would have to jump for our lives.

When day finally broke, we were not a little surprised to find ourselves near the bluff on the south side of the bay, having dragged our anchors for more than a mile. The *Arctic* was also close by, and as the gale seemed to increase as the day advanced the situation became desperate. In the afternoon, the *Arctic* was seen lowering her boat and the crew started for the shore, but the undertaking was a dangerous one as the big sea threatened to swamp her every moment. Our vessel had, by this time, become so covered with ice that the decks were nearly even with the water, and I made up my mind that we would try to reach the shore also. Our yawl had been lowered sometime before, so as to be in readiness in case the chains parted, and this was nearly half full of ice. I managed to board her and after a half hour's work cut the ice out. The other three of the crew then got in and we made for the shore, though how we managed to do it in the heavy sea in that small boat is more than I can tell. A big crowd of people had gathered on the shore and they did all in their power to help us make a landing.

"The two vessels held on during the remainder of the night and toward morning the wind moderated somewhat and the danger was over. We found that the scow and sails were so loaded down with ice that it would not do to try to get away without a tug, and a messenger was dispatched to Fish Creek for the *Hill*.[16] The tug happened to be at Menominee, but she put in an appearance Saturday morning and towed us to Horseshoe Island, in Eagle Harbor, where we laid until Monday getting the ice thawed out and making other repairs. The *Arctic* succeeded in getting away Friday afternoon, she being less troubled with ice than we on account of her build. She ran for the Door, and succeeded in getting to Milwaukee all right.

"Had our chains parted, both vessels would certainly have gone to pieces, and it is a question whether any one of those on board could have got off alive, as the high bluff and bold shore, together with the cold and freezing weather, would have finished us in a very few minutes. I have sailed nearly all the days of my life, but the experience of Wednesday and Thursday is the worst I ever had.

Captain Hanson remained in Sturgeon Bay for a few days until favorable weather permitted the *Williams* to continue on to Manitowoc, where she was stripped and laid up for the winter of 1889–90.

This incident did not convince Captain Hanson of the dangers of winter navigation, because he took the *Williams* on a long voyage during 1892–93. Along about Christmas 1892, the scow left Milwaukee for Jacksonport to obtain a load of wood, but near Kewaunee adverse winds induced Captain Hanson to run into that port for shelter. The weather turned pretty cold, and it was deter-

The American schooner *Burt Barnes* had two masts and hailed from Manitowoc, Wisconsin. She was sold Canadian in 1904 and rigged with three masts as shown in this photograph. Courtesy of Fr. Edward J. Dowling, S.J.

mined to hang on a while for a change. The change did not come until about the first week of April, when the *Williams* finally pulled out; her canvas had remained on all winter. The crew lived aboard during that time, and since they were all relatives of Captain Hanson, the season of inactivity was doubtlessly passed quite pleasantly.

The *Williams* was also in service during the winter of 1894–95, since she was seen passing the Sturgeon Bay Canal on December 20. Capt. Albert Fairchild of the tug *Maggie Lutz*,[17] who reported her, said she would load wood at Baileys Harbor. The scow schooner spent much of the seasons of 1895 and 1896 delivering wood at the canal to fuel the government dredges clearing the waterway. Wood remained the principal cargo of the *Williams* throughout the 1890s as she traded along the west shore of Lake Michigan, no farther north than Baileys Harbor or Jacksonsport and no farther south than Manitowoc, with intermediate stops at Sturgeon Bay.

Captain Hanson took command of the schooner *Burt Barnes*[18] for the O. Torrison Co. of Manitowoc from the spring of 1899 through the season of 1901. In the fall of 1899, the *Williams* was sold to Capt. C. O. Pedersen of Detroit Harbor to serve in the Washington Island fleet. Capt. Anton Hanson died at Manitowoc on July 15, 1902, leaving a widow and five children.

Capt. C. O. Pedersen was born in Oslo, Norway, and settled in Chicago when he arrived in America. He came to Detroit Harbor on Washington Island about 1877 and married Julia Anderson of Ephraim on August 24, 1888, at Sister Bay. Captain Pedersen owned only three sailing vessels while on the island, and they were all scow schooners. In the fall of 1876, he bought the scow *Laurel*[19] of Chicago and registered her in Milwaukee before the season of 1877. The *Laurel* was sold to Capt. Peder Hanson of Washington Island in the fall of 1884. In 1883, Captain Pedersen built the scow *Agnes Behrmann*[20] at Detroit Harbor with Henry Behrmann of Milwaukee as equal owner. The *Behrmann* was built to haul cordwood to market and return with freight for the islanders. According to enrollment no. 26 issued at the Port of Milwaukee on September 7, 1893, Captain Pedersen and the Wisconsin Chair Company of Port Washington were equal owners of the *Behrmann*. This document was surrendered at Milwaukee on June 29, 1897; cause of surrender: abandoned as unfit for service.

But this was not the end of the *Behrmann*. Captain Pedersen could not give up his trustworthy and beloved "Agnes" and resurrected her in the summer of 1898 for a short second life. The last enrollment of the *Behrmann*

was surrendered at Milwaukee on December 1, 1898; cause of surrender: stranding—vessel total loss October 10, 1898. The location was not given. However, Capt. Ralph Larson said that she went to pieces at Gills Rock in a storm out of the northwest. Thus, Captain Pedersen became the last owner of the scow *Farrand H. Williams* as a replacement for the scow *Behrmann*.

In the service of Captain Pedersen, the *Williams* remained in the wood trade but spent more time in Green Bay than on Lake Michigan. On September 16, 1900, at 18 years of age, the scow *Farrand H. Williams* stranded in Horseshoe Bay, Green Bay, and became a total loss.

Most of the scows were relatively small sailing vessels owned by their masters. They usually served particular localities or sailed limited routes on the Great Lakes. In a sense they were the poor man's schooner. The *Williams*, for example, was built by her owner and never rated higher than B 2[21] with a value of $3,000. On the larger scale they were not important to the era of sail, but without their services, many smaller, more remote communities could not have survived.

CHAPTER ELEVEN

The *Lummy*
The *Lomie A. Burton*

The schooner *Lomie A. Burton,* official no. 15958, was built in 1873 at Chicago by Samuel Kempton for Allen Burton of Chicago (3/8), John Gillard of Chicago (3/8), and W. W. Lovell of Racine (2/8), with Gillard as master. She was a vessel of the larger class, with dimensions of 131.1 x 26.0 x 9.7 feet at 215.21 total tons and three masts. [1] The men who sailed her affectionately called her the *"Lummy,"* and she carried lumber to Milwaukee and Chicago for most of her life on the lakes.

The original owners managed the *Burton* until the season of 1887, when she was acquired by Daniel W. Chipman of Milwaukee (1/8), Christopher S. Raesser of Baileys Harbor (1/8), John D. Wanvig of Milwaukee (2/8), and Augustine J. Ray of Chicago (4/8), with Wanvig as master. The firm of Chipman & Raesser had interests in Milwaukee and Baileys Harbor and employed the *Burton* to transport farm and forest products from the latter port.

Wanvig became the managing owner in the fall of 1887 and remained as master until 1890, when Anton Christensen became part owner and master. Christensen was the managing owner and master of the *Burton* for nine seasons.

John Daniel Wanvig was born at Namsos, Norway, on July 31, 1861, and came to America in 1877 after he had served on salt water for five years. He rose to the rank of captain in 1884 and married Anna Christensen of Risør, Norway, in 1885. Anton Christensen was also born at Risør in 1863 and came to America in 1881 to settle in Milwaukee. In 1888, he married Alida Regine Wanvig.

During the winter of 1898–99, the *Burton* became the property of Anthony Bolster of Milwaukee, but Capt. Peder Hanson of Washington Harbor, Washington Island, acquired one-third for $1,500 and became master before the end of the season.

Capt. Hanson, who was known as Big Peder in shipping circles, came to Door County from Norway in 1871. As a youth, he had sailed on the high seas and visited many parts of the world, but on coming to Washington Island in 1872, he turned his attention to fishing until his marriage to Caroline Jacobson in 1876. According to the *Door County Advocate* of September 7, "The Reverend Captain Bundy of the Bethel Society's little schooner *Glad Tidings*

joined in marriage Andrew Johnson and Peter Hansen to the two daughters of Anton Jacobsen, the last man fishing regularly from Rock Island."

Capt. Henry Bundy preached the gospel during the sailing season among the islands and in the out-of-the-way places along the lakes—places where the gospel had hardly been known and where it had never been preached until Captain Bundy carried it there. The *Glad Tidings* [2] had stopped at Kewaunee, Sturgeon Bay, and Baileys Harbor before Washington Island. The *Kewaunee Enterprise* reported: "A little schooner, called the *Glad Tidings* sailed by Capt. Bundy, will cruise about Lake Michigan and Green Bay, supplying destitute families with bibles, tracts, etc. She touched here Thursday morning for provisions and proceeded north. Capt. Bundy informed our reporter that he could spare no testaments or tracts for the lake shore this trip—his entire cargo being needed for that unspeakably wicked place, Sturgeon Bay."

The *Door County Advocate* of August 10, 1876, responded: "There are no destitute families in Sturgeon Bay requiring bibles, and if what is said of the *Glad Tidings* is true, the only tracts she will be asked to leave will be those of her heels. We venture the assertion that there are more well preserved bibles in this village than any other on the peninsula. The care that is taken of them is extraordinary, they are thoroughly ventilated and dusted at every house-cleaning, and will descend to future generations as monuments of the respect in which they were held by their present owners."

After his marriage, Captain Hanson purchased land and developed a farm until his wife died in 1884. In 1885, he married Caroline Anderson and returned to his original calling on the great inland seas as the master of the scow schooner *Laurel* [3] in 1885 and 1886. In the fall of 1888, Captain Hanson acquired an interest in the schooner *O. M. Nelson.* [4] He served as managing owner and master of the *Nelson* until June 4, 1899, when she stranded on the south end of Pilot Island during a southerly gale with fog. The lifesaving crew from Plum Island rescued the crew, and a wrecking tug arrived later to try to release the *Nelson* but failed. The wreck was stripped because the hull was a total loss, leaving Captain Hanson on the beach.

With the *Burton* as a replacement for the *Nelson,* Cap-

The schooner *Peoria* in a windbound fleet at Charlevoix, Michigan, about 1899. From left to right, the schooners are the *Vega*, the *Ottawa*, the *O. M. Nelson*, the *Black Hawk*, the *Linerla*, the *Peoria*, and the *Rosa Bell*. Note the unusual rig on the *Vega*—only a fore- and mizzenmast. This Grand Haven, or ketch, rig appeared on the Great Lakes in later years as a matter of economy and carrying capacity. With the mainmast removed, it was easier to handle the vessel and the cargo above and below deck. Courtesy of the Wisconsin Marine Historical Society.

tain Hanson continued in the lumber trade. The *Burton* was no stranger to Door County, having served various ports on both sides of the peninsula for over 25 years.

The Sturgeon Bay Canal had been something of a nemesis for the schooner on several occasions. In July 1882, the side-wheel steamer *Corona*[5] was going out of the cut and the *Burton* was coming into the canal under sail when they discovered each other. Fortunately, the schooner had not yet entered the canal and was able to drop anchor at the entrance to avoid a serious collision. As it was, the *Burton* had part of her headgear carried away by the *Corona*. In attempting to sail through the canal on May 18, 1883, the lumber-laden schooner was carried out of the channel and stuck fast in the mud opposite L. R. McLachlan's place, where she was pulled off by the tug *John Gregory.*[6] On November 9, 1883, she again fouled with the steamer *Corona*, which was coming into the canal while the *Burton* was sailing out. The tug *Gregory*, which was only 100

fathoms astern of the *Burton*, struck the schooner, and the schooner *Delos DeWolf*[7] in tow of the tug, came down on the *Gregory*. The *Burton's* stern on the starboard side was cut down from the taffrail to the waterline and her quarter deck sprung. The *DeWolf* lost her jibboom and bowsprit and was considerably damaged. While sailing through Sturgeon Bay on May 12, 1887, the *Burton* ran aground in the lower part of the bay and had to be pulled off by the tug *Temperance.*

Captain Hanson sailed the *Burton* in the lumber trade for 10 seasons before she was sold to the Mueller Fuel & Coal Co., Peter S. J. Strobel, secretary, in the fall of 1908. The last owner of the schooner was Herman Krones of Milwaukee as of November 12, 1910, according to enrollment no. 35 issued at the Port of Milwaukee.

Herman Krones was born in Milwaukee on March 27, 1873. His mother, Mary Krones, operated a tavern on the south side of Milwaukee and financed the purchase of his

The side-wheel steamer *Corona* of the Goodrich Transportation Co. about 1884. Courtesy of the Wisconsin Marine Historical Society.

first schooner. According to certificates of enrollment issued at Milwaukee, Herman Krones, together with his mother Mary, his wife Minnie, his brother Frank, or his wife's mother, Elizabeth Kordt, had an interest in the schooner *Willard A. Smith*[8] from August 22, 1890, to

The *Corona* in later years as an excursion boat for the Wood Lawn Beach near Buffalo, New York. Courtesy of the Wisconsin Marine Historical Society.

February 17, 1891; the schooner *Lem Higby*[9] from September 1, 1892, to May 28, 1894; the schooner *William Aldrich*[10] from September 24, 1897, to April 16, 1914; and the *Lomie A. Burton*, the last schooner sailed by Captain Krones.

Since he owned the *Aldrich* and the *Burton* at the same time, Captain Krones sailed the *Burton* while Jake Hyde sailed the *Aldrich*. In addition to Hyde, Martin Thompson and Alfred Peterson lived with the Krones family from time to time and slept in the basement in exchange for the performance of household chores or for cutting the children's hair. With his crew at hand, Captain Krones could sail "when the wind was ready." They lived at 1163 Madison Street, next door to Capt. Wilhelm Glockner, who had been master of the schooner *La Petite*[11] until she was lost on Lake Michigan south of the Sturgeon Bay Canal in 1903.

The *Burton* managed to survive the seas for over a decade into the twentieth century but struggled to her end in 1911. While en route from Cross Village, Michigan, to Milwaukee on July 24, 1911, with a cargo of lumber, she encountered a severe storm and rough sea off North Manitou Island. With winds up to 70 miles an hour, the deck load washed overboard and the vessel waterlogged. The *Burton* was sighted by the lookout at the North Manitou Station of the U.S. Life-Saving Service and was

The schooner *La Petite* in the Menominee Canal, Milwaukee, Wisconsin, in the late 1800s. The buildings in the background are believed to be the Kalamazoo Knitting Co. and, at the far right, the J.B. Johnson Soap Co. (later the Palmolive Building), which stood at North 4th Street and Fowler (St. Paul) Avenue. Courtesy of the Wisconsin Marine Historical Society.

The U.S. revenue cutter *Tuscarora*, based in Milwaukee, was a familiar sight in Door County after the turn of the century. She was sent to the coast about 1925 and reported dismantled in December 1939. Courtesy of the Wisconsin Marine Historical Society.

assisted by surfmen 5 miles south of the station. The schooner was picked up by the U.S. revenue cutter *Tuscarora* and towed to South Manitou Island, where she was pumped out and continued on to Milwaukee.

The *Burton* sailed across Lake Michigan to the vicinity of Death's Door and then on the southern track to Milwaukee. Just three days after the above incident, the lookout at the Baileys Harbor Station sighted the *Burton* at daybreak several miles out in the lake. She was making bad weather of it and began to blow distress signals. The crew put off in their power lifeboat and made a quick run through the heavy seas to the side of the vessel, about 6 miles to the southeast. She was again waterlogged, and her crew of six were utterly exhausted from hours of desperate work at the pumps. The lifesavers ran a towline from the *Burton* to their boat and with several of their number at the pumps brought her safely into the harbor, where she was freed of water some 15 hours later.

In the fall of the year, the third strike occurred, and the *Lomie A. Burton* went to the common grave of many of her contemporaries. On Thursday night November 16, 1911, the schooner sought refuge in the harbor at South Manitou Island during a snowstorm, strong wind, and rough sea. The heavy wind caused her to drag anchor, and the crew had "no chance to do anything"[12] before she went on the beach ¾ of a mile northwest of the station early Friday morning. Soon after striking the beach, the vessel began pounding, with the seas sweeping her full length. It was not long before one of her spars went out, followed soon after by another. Then the *Burton* broke in two forward, and things began to look blue for the crew who had gathered aft.

The lifesavers arrived on the scene and succeeded in getting a line over the wreck to set up the beach apparatus. The crew were hauled ashore one at a time in the breeches buoy, nearly exhausted from the cold and exposure, and soaking wet. The rescued men were Captain Krones, Sam Johnson, Carl Larson, John Nelson, Martin Thompson, and Tom Wall. The last man was brought ashore at 5:30 Friday morning, less than half an hour before the vessel went to pieces.

Although her crew was safe, the beloved *Lummy* was gone, laid to rest on the beach in South Manitou Harbor, where her remains could still be seen as late as 1928. Her nameboard was hung in the U.S. Life-Saving Service Station at South Manitou Island:

After the *Burton,* Captain Krones was in the marine salvage business with the steam barge *Helen Taylor.*[13] The *Taylor* had burned off Hessel, Michigan, on Lake Huron just east of the Straits of Mackinac in the Upper Penin-

The steam barge *Helen Taylor* at Manistee about 1895. This view gives a good indication of why she was named the Pumpkin Seed. Courtesy of the Wisconsin Marine Historical Society.

sula, with three on board, no lives lost, on October 7, 1919. Captain Krones rescued her in 1920, and she was put back on register in 1921 after being rebuilt. The *Taylor* was nicknamed the Pumpkin Seed because of her broad shape—length 56.4 feet, beam 30.2 feet, draft 3.8 feet.

In 1920, Captain Krones moved to 1176 Superior Street and in 1926 to Illinois Avenue. From these loca-

tions, he walked the beaches of Bay View, often hauling huge timbers from the beach to his backyard. He was in the marine junk business along the rivers of Milwaukee and the shores of Lake Michigan. In later years, he owned the fish tug *Freddie,*[14] bought on Jones Island. *Freddie* was abandoned at Milwaukee in 1945 to be followed by the death of Capt. Herman Krones, "mariner and junkman," on February 24, 1946.

CHAPTER TWELVE

The Perils of *Pauline,*
—and *John,*—and *Edward*

We have written about Great Lakes schooners that had extraordinary long lives, such as the *William Aldrich*[1] (1856 to 1916) and the *Halsted*[2] (1872 to 1930), and are aware of the lengendary *Our Son*[3] (1875 to 1930), the *Lucia A. Simpson*[4] (1875 to 1929), and the *Mary Ellen Cook*[5] (1875 to 1923). Much to our surprise, we recently discovered the record of the *Pauline,* a schooner built in 1856 and lost under sail in 1921, well over half a century later. The story of the *Pauline* illustrates the changing fortunes of sailing vessels, their owners, and the masters who sailed them during this era of Great Lakes history.

The schooner *Pauline* was built at Milwaukee, Wisconsin, in the year 1856, according to the certificate of George Barber, master carpenter, dated Milwaukee, July 16, 1856, on file in the collector's office of this port.[6] Her owners were Philip Lawrence (2/6), Zacharias Saveland (2/6), Tonnes Saveland (1/6), and Andre Olson (1/6), with Z. Saveland as master. Her measurements were length 105 feet, breadth 26.8 feet, and depth 8.6 feet at 214⅖₅ tons OM. The *Pauline* was described as a schooner with two masts, a square stern, poop cabin, and a figure head. The vessel was issued official no. 19674 after the official number system was established in 1867.

Since Lawrence and Saveland had interests in both Milwaukee and Green Bay, the *Pauline* frequently risked the dangers of Death's Door—Port des Mortes Passage— in her earlier years before the Sturgeon Bay Canal was constructed. The *Door County Advocate* of September 6, 1862, reported: "Shipping at Sturgeon Bay—The schooner *Pauline* arrived August 29th and sailed September 2nd loaded with shingle bolts and square timber for Mr. P. Lawrence of Green Bay and Milwaukee."

The *Pauline* became the property of William Johnson of Chicago before the season of 1865, according to enrollment no. 147 issued at the Port of Chicago on April 4, 1865. Few men had a wider experience in the lake shipping industry than Johnson, who was born in Arendal, Norway, in 1836. After serving as a sailor on the Baltic, the North Sea, and the Mediterranean, he came to Chicago in 1855 at age 19 and entered the employ of George Steele, who owned a number of vessels. Steele became so attached to the young sailor that Johnson stayed in his home and was regarded as a member of the family during his service with Steele.

Johnson owned the *Pauline* for over 15 years, and during this period, she was involved in only a few minor mishaps. Early casualty reports[7] record that the schooner was damaged by collision on Lake Michigan while bound for Milwaukee from Manistee in June 1866, with a loss of $303, and that her outfit was damaged by lightning while in port at Chicago in May 1869, at a cost of $300. In April 1871, the *Pauline* collided with the steamboat *Sarah Van Eps*[8] while en route to Green Bay from Chicago, with the loss reported as $600.

Insurance records for this period reveal that the *Pauline* was repaired and rated B 1 with a value of $4,500 in 1866. In 1869, she was rebuilt to maintain a B 1 classification, but by 1879 her classification was only B 1- with a value of $2,500. The *Pauline* was sold to William W. Chapin of Manistee in the fall of 1880 for $3,800 cash, well above her insured value, and John Anderson was given the command. After only one round trip under the new owner, the schooner was struck down by the Alpena Gale.

On Friday evening October 15, 1880, in the vicinity of Baileys Harbor, the gale arrived from the northwest but deceived the many vessels seeking shelter in the harbor by suddenly shifting to the southeast at about 2:00 Saturday morning. Since Baileys Harbor is protected to the north and east but open to the south and southeast, this shift created havoc in this small harbor, which was crowded with schooners.

The first to go on was the schooner *Josephine Lawrence*[9] of Port Washington, Capt. James A. Boyd, loaded with rubble stone from Washington Island for Chicago. She had arrived Friday night and found shelter in the anchorage, but when the wind shifted, the *Lawrence* began dragging in the heavy seas that had built up from the southeast, parted her chain at about 2:00 P.M. Saturday, and went ashore on the sand beach at the head of the bay.

The schooner *L. J. Conway*[10] of Milwaukee, Capt. Louis Larson, had loaded cordwood on Friday and gone to the anchorage, where she was protected from the northwest gale, but steadily dragged all day Saturday until she lost one anchor and went up on the beach about 3:00 P.M.

The *Lettie May,* a small trading schooner, in Ellison Bay or Sister Bay, Door County. She was built at Fort Howard, Wisconsin, in 1874 and spent most of her life in Door County. The *May* was owned by M. F. Kalmbach of Fort Howard from 1874 through 1879, by Albert Kalmbach of Baileys Harbor together with John Rank of Baileys Harbor as equal owners in 1880 and 1881, by George Trueblood of Baileys Harbor from 1887 through 1892, and by Hans Johnson of Newport, Door County, Wisconsin, with Peter Knudson as master for the season of 1893. Courtesy of the Wisconsin Marine Historical Society.

to join the *Lawrence.* The next arrival was the little trading schooner *Lettie May* [11] of Green Bay, Capt. Albert Kalmbach, loaded with sundries for Green Bay. She laid at anchor until Saturday noon, when her chain parted and she ran out into the middle of the harbor. The crew let go another anchor, but the *May* was swept ashore and washed up near the range lights, high enough for them to wade ashore.

The *Pauline,* Captain Anderson, was a late arrival at about 6:00 P.M. Saturday, loaded with lumber and shingles for South Chicago. She entered the harbor at the height of the gale, and the scene was one dreaded by all seafaring men. The harbor was already filled to capacity, with vessels of all classes struggling to hold their positions

with all anchors and chains out in the face of gale-force winds and huge seas that were sweeping everything before them into the shallow water at the head of the bay. The *Pauline* let go her anchors but carried away her chain and windlass at about 7:00 P.M. to join the *Lawrence, Conway,* and *May* already resting in the sand at the north end of the harbor. The crew took to the rigging, where they stayed all night, and were taken off in the morning by a pound net boat.

The four vessels mentioned above were not the only ones to experience hull or other serious damage in Baileys Harbor during the great storm. Other casualties included the schooner *Cascade* [12] of Chicago, Capt. John Stubbs, with corn for Buffalo; the schooner *James Platt* [13] of

Chicago, Capt. John O. Gray, with 23,000 bushels of corn for Buffalo; the schooner *Peoria*[14] of Chicago, Capt. P. Hagan, with lumber for Chicago; and the schooner barge *Brunette*[15] of Detroit, Captain Hill, with 48,000 bushels of corn for Buffalo. The latter had been in tow of the propeller *W. L. Wetmore*,[16] which let her go during the storm. When the barge went into the breakers, Captain Hill broke his leg and had to be treated by a physician from Sturgeon Bay when the storm subsided.

Within a week after the gale, the harbor had cleared, with the exception of the schooners *Josephine Lawrence*, *Peoria*, and *Pauline*. The *Lawrence* proved too old and too heavily loaded to be saved. The last enrollment of the *Lawrence* was surrendered at Milwaukee on October 16, 1880; cause of surrender: total loss. Stranded near Baileys Harbor, Wisconsin, October 16, 1880. The little *Lettie May* was quickly released, and the tug *A. W. Lawrence*[17] of Sturgeon Bay pulled off the schooner *L. J. Conway* on Tuesday. The *Wetmore* returned for the *Brunette*, which was leaking, although not enough to prevent her from go-

ing through to Buffalo in tow of the steam barge on Tuesday. The tug *Balize*[18] of Detroit was ordered to Baileys Harbor from Port Huron to tow the *James Platt* and *Cascade* to Buffalo. They departed on Sunday the twenty-fourth, and a survey of the *Platt* after she arrived in Buffalo placed her damages at $2,600. Out of the 23,000 bushels of corn on the *Platt*, only 60 were found to be wet. John Kelderhouse of Buffalo bought the *Platt* as she arrived for $6,000. She was towed for the remainder of the season but given a thorough rebuild during the winter of 1880–81.

The tug *Alfred P. Wright*[19] of Manistee was dispatched to assist the *Pauline*, which was well up on the beach in the sand about half a mile east of the range lights near the *Lawrence*, which was now buried to her rails in the sand. The hull of the *Pauline* was sound and she was in a good position for getting off, but the work was abandoned in November to be resumed the following spring.

Linc (Lincoln) Erskine and George Bennett of Baileys Harbor purchased the wreck of the *Peoria* on the reef near

The schooner barge *Buffalo* was built in 1871 as the *Brunette*. The *Brunette* was chartered for Atlantic Coast service in 1898 but came back to the Great Lakes and was renamed *Buffalo* in 1902. Courtesy of the Wisconsin Marine Historical Society.

The steamship *W. L. Wetmore* was in the coarse freight trade and towed the schooner barge *Brunette* until the *Wetmore* was totally wrecked on Rabbit Island in Georgian Bay on November 29, 1901, at a loss of $20,000. Courtesy of the Wisconsin Marine Historical Society.

the old lighthouse from her owners for $100. They sold the schooner for $600 and the cargo of 150,000 feet of lumber for $150 to Scofield & Co. of Sturgeon Bay. When Baileys Harbor opened to navigation in April 1881, the *Peoria* was lightered of half her lumber, 75,000 feet, but the tugs *John Gregory*,[20] *John Leathem*,[21] and *W. C. Tillson*[22] of Sturgeon Bay were unable to start her. John Leathem, the celebrated wrecker and submarine diver, was superintending the job of getting the *Peoria* off. He found it impossible to raise her with jackscrews, and this attempt had to be abandoned. The vessel's keel rested inside of a big rock that held her in such a position that tugs pulling from the outside could make no impression on her.

The *Peoria* was finally pulled off by the combined exertions of the tugs *Gregory, Tillson,* and the more powerful *Leviathan*[23] of Milwaukee on Saturday afternoon May 14 and towed to a pier in the harbor. She was taken in tow by the *Leathem* at 2:00 P.M. Sunday for Milwaukee, where they arrived at 9:00 A.M. Wednesday. The *Leathem* was by the side of the wreck all the way down.

The *Peoria's* decks were about 1½ feet under water even though she had 60,000 feet of lumber in her hold and 300 ties that were placed there to help float her. When she arrived, she sank in the river at the Milwaukee Shipyard Co. The *Peoria* was raised on Thursday by means of scows and placed in dry dock. A survey of the wreck showed her bottom to be in pretty bad shape. She required a new keel and other general repairs at a cost of about $1,200 in addition to the $1,000 it cost Scofield & Co. to get the vessel off. The cargo of lumber was removed from the *Peoria* on Sunday May 22, and she was again towed to the shipyard to be docked for rebuilding under the supervision of John Leathem. The rebuilt schooner was launched on June 3 and left on the night of the seventh for Red River, Green Bay, where Scofield & Co. had a sawmill.

Despite her escape from Baileys Harbor, the *Peoria* would make the harbor her permanent place of rest near the very spot where she almost left her bones in 1880. In the fall of 1901, the *Peoria* was bound to Chicago from East Jordan, Michigan, with a cargo of 140,000 feet of hardwood lumber. In crossing the lake on Sunday November 10, she encountered the full force of a southerly gale, and Capt. Mannus J. Bonner determined to seek shelter in Baileys Harbor. He succeeded in getting into that haven without much trouble and dropped anchor as far to the eastward as was consistent with good judgment to try to gain some lee position. Shortly after coming to (into the wind), it was found that the right bower was not sufficient, since she was gradually dragging toward the land. The other anchor was dropped, but the wind and sea were so furious that the two mudhooks failed to hold the schooner. It became evident that she would soon strike bottom unless the gale abated. Captain Bonner had signaled for the lifesaving crew to stand by, and Capt. Ingar Olson was not long in answering the call for help.

On account of the vessel's exposed position, 1 mile west of the station, and the very rough sea, it was impossible for the station crew to get alongside the schooner. But by use of a line from the *Peoria's* bow, the lifesavers held their boat in position under the lee, and by means of a whip line rigged from the main boom, succeeded, after four hours of hard labor, in taking off the crew of six men without mishap. The shipwrecked party was taken to the station and provided food, stimulants, and shelter, also dry clothing from the stores of the Women's National Relief Association.

After the rescue of the *Peoria* in the spring of 1881, there was only one vessel – the *Pauline* – still lying on the beach at the north end of Baileys Harbor, waiting for the return of her owner, Chapin, to save her from a fate worse than death at sea. He returned in June 1881 with the larger tug *C. Williams* [24] of Manistee to reclaim the *Pauline*. A channel was dredged through the sand from deeper water to the schooner, and after taking the hardwood lumber out of her hold and substituting cedar, the *Pauline* was pulled into open water. The masts were cut off to prevent the wreck from capsizing before the *Williams* towed the hull directly to the Milwaukee Shipyard Co., where they arrived on July 18, 1881, almost nine months to the day after the disaster.

Chapin had already spent $1,000 in the attempt to rescue the *Pauline* in the fall of 1880 and an additional $1,000 to land her in Milwaukee. The wreck was hauled out for reconstruction but proved so unsound that the work of tearing away left only two short pieces of keel and a few floor timbers forward and aft of the *Pauline,* not enough material to constitute a large wagonload. Despite this wholesale dissection at a cost of not less than another $1,000, Chapin ordered the builders to go on with the work and construct for him a craft 20 feet longer and 18 inches deeper than the *Pauline,* and as much like her as possible. The "new" vessel was launched on October 11, 1881, at a cost to Chapin that was not less than $14,000, exclusive of a considerable portion of the outfit of the old *Pauline.* Much to the surprise of everyone, Chapin renamed the schooner *John Mee* in spite of the fact that he seemed intent on preserving the *Pauline.*

The last document of the *Pauline,* enrollment no. 58, was surrendered on December 9, 1881, at Grand Haven; cause of surrender: vessel abandoned as unfit for service. The first document of the *John Mee,* temporary enrollment no. 45, was issued on October 22, 1881, at Milwaukee, with the official no. 76264. Permanent enrollment no. 67 was issued at Grand Haven on October 28, 1881, after she returned to her home port of Manistee. The dimensions of the *Mee* were length 122.9 feet (20 feet longer than the *Pauline*), breadth 26.9 feet (same as the *Pauline*), depth 9.0 feet (12 inches deeper), and 199.43 total tons compared with 135.32 total tons. A third mast was added to the rig consistent with the increase in length, and the carrying capacity was raised to 150,000 feet of lumber. The *Mee* had one deck, a plain head, and a square stern, and the builder's certificate was signed by John Fitzgerald of the Milwaukee Shipyard Co. For purposes of insurance, the *Mee* rated A 2 with a value of only $10,000 in 1882, despite Chapin's large expenditure.

Chapin owned the schooner for seven seasons until he sold her to John Thompson (4/8), Nels Olson (3/8), and Louis Olson (1/8), vessel owners of Sheboygan, before the season of 1888, with Nels Olson as master. Almost 20 years in the life of the *Mee* passed without a major incident, and she became the *John Mee* of Chicago before the season of 1898, when Nels Olson of Chicago (mariner) became the principal owner. After Captain Olson retired from the lakes in Chicago, Capt. Thorvald "Tom" Berntsen became master in 1907. As was customary, Berntsen acquired a one-quarter interest in the schooner.

Berntsen had been born in Norway on January 23, 1855, began his career on the water as a pilot boy during the Franco-Prussian war, and came to the United States in 1888. After sailing schooners on the Atlantic, he moved to the Great Lakes in 1893. Captain Berntsen kept an immaculate ship and fed his crew well. Al F. Wakefield, who sailed under Berntsen, remembered seeing nine assorted pastries on the table at breakfast one morning, a most unusual fare for a sailing vessel.

The Chicago Transportation Company, a corporation created and existing under and by virtue of the laws of the

Capt. Thorvald "Tom" Berntsen was born in Norway in 1855 and died in Milwaukee in 1936. He was put in command of the Milwaukee lightship No. 91 in 1917 after he left the *Skeele*, and retired from this service in 1925 at age 70. From *Norwegian Sailors on the Great Lakes*, Knut Gjerset, Norwegian-American Historical Association, Northfield, Minnesota, 1928.

Captain Berntsen poses at the wheel of the *Skeele* on a calm day in 1915. Courtesy of C. Patrick Labadie.

state of South Dakota, became the principal owner of the *Mee* in the spring of 1911, but Berntsen remained as master and maintained his one-fourth interest. At the end of the season, the *John Mee* was renamed *Edward E. Skeele* by authority of the commissioner of navigation on August 2, 1912. This was the second alias for the *Pauline* as she continued to roam the waters of Door County. In November 1913, the *Skeele* took on 6,500 bushels of potatoes at Ellison Bay, 3,500 at Egg Harbor, and then went to Menominee to get a deck load of slabs, which she was unable to secure. The schooner was towed over to Sturgeon Bay from Menominee by the tug *Satisfaction*[25] and lay there until favorable winds arrived on Monday evening November 3. While windbound, Captain Berntsen spent a short time with relatives in Sturgeon Bay.

From 1915 to 1920, the managing and principal owner of the *Skeele* was A. M. Chesbrough, lumberman, of Thompson, Michigan. Berntsen owned one-fourth in 1915, but his interest was acquired by Capt. Hans Pedersen of Milwaukee before the season of 1916 and Capt.

James Erickson of Milwaukee for the season, until Chesbrough became the sole owner in 1917. Chesbrough bought the schooner because there was not enough water alongside the docks at Thompson for steam barges and sometimes not enough for the *Skeele* because the harbor was filled with sawdust from the mills at Thompson and Manistique. After loading at Thompson, the help of a steam tug from Manistique was required to pull the schooner off the bottom for the start of the return trip to Traverse City. By this time, the tiny port of Thompson had gained a permanent place in Great Lakes marine history as the point of departure for the *Rouse Simmons*,[26] the "Christmas Tree Ship," on her fatal voyage in 1912.

According to enrollment no. 16 issued at Marquette, Michigan, on December 24, 1920, Lawrence A. Buck (1/2) and W. L. Kennedy (1/2) of Escanaba, Michigan, were the last owners of record of the *Skeele* of Marquette (hailing port Escanaba), with James Louis Larsen as master. An unusual sight was witnessed on Green Bay Wednesday afternoon December 1, 1920, when the schooner,

110

The schooner *Rouse Simmons* in the harbor at Sheboygan, with the schooner *Challenge* lying just ahead. The *Simmons* became known as the Christmas Tree Ship because she brought trees to Chicago to be sold for the holiday season. She foundered off Two Rivers, Wisconsin, on November 23, 1912, while bound for Chicago from Thompson, Michigan, with a cargo of trees to become one of the legends of the lakes. Courtesy of the Wisconsin Marine Historical Society.

Capt. J. Louis Larsen, sailed into Sturgeon Bay from Green Bay under a full spread of canvas and came to anchor off the Goodrich Dock. The *Skeele* was one of the few old-time schooners still operating, and it was unusual to see one of these craft in commission as late as December 1. She was loaded with potatoes bound for Chicago. The last owners of the schooner were Captain Larsen and Orin W. Angwall, who borrowed the money for the purchase from Buck, but an enrollment was not issued to record this change of ownership.

On September 25, 1921, the *Edward E. Skeele* stranded on Barrie Island, Lake Huron, in Canadian waters, and went to pieces. An eyewitness account of the end of the *Skeele* was given by Orin Angwall. [27]

> We were lying at anchor in Julia Bay, loading cedar posts, and had about 6,000 posts aboard, when this blow came on in the evening. It blew up a living gale during the night (the Coast Guard at the Soo registered 56 m.p.h.), and she

was pitching so hard that the anchor chains chewed the hawse pipes so that with every pitch a lot of water was going below. Our yawl-boat washed away, and by 6 in the morning there was four feet of water in the hold, and we were fearful that someone would be killed if the posts got to jumping around. It was getting so bad that we decided that if we were going to save our lives we would have to slip the anchors and let her go ashore. So I slipped one, and—slipped the other, and she piled ashore and broke up, and we left her. It was about the worst night that I have ever spent.

Usually, it is fortunate to find a single personal account of the loss of a sailing vessel, but in this case there is a second extensive version of the disaster. In an article in the *Milwaukee Journal* of September 6, 1934, Harold W. Pripps, a Milwaukee businessman, described the end of the *Skeele* in detail. Pripps was assistant manager of the Fidelity & Deposit Co., 208 E. Wisconsin Avenue, and lived at 7132 Hillcrest Drive, Wauwatosa, Wisconsin. In

The schooner *Edward E. Skeele* at Marinette, Wisconsin, in 1919. Courtesy of the Wisconsin Marine Historical Society.

The *Edward E. Skeele* after a squall on Lake Michigan in the summer of 1915. Captain Berntsen can be seen in the background behind the cabin. Courtesy of C. Patrick Labadie.

1921, Pripps and his wife were passengers on a cabin cruiser belonging to Capt. J. Louis Larsen of Green Bay. At Fairport, Wisconsin, while tied up to the dock, the boat caught fire, the tank exploded, and she went down.

> My wife and I had got off, luckily, and we were on the dock at the time. Capt. Larsen was aboard but escaped unhurt. We lost all our baggage and cameras and fishing tackle.
>
> We felt very badly, of course. Then Capt. Larsen told us that he was going to make a trip in a three masted schooner, up to Cook's Harbor, Manitoulin Island, Ontario, and from there to Gladstone, Michigan with a load of cedar posts. He said we could go along. I thought that would be fine and agreed. I went, but my wife decided to stay home.

The Milwaukee man boarded the schooner at Chicago on Saturday September 17, 1921. The captain of the *Skeele* on her last trip was of Capt. James Louis Larsen, who was known as Louis Larsen because his father, Capt. James Larsen, had the same first name. Here the circle closes, as James Larsen, [28] who as a young fisherman rescued the crew of the Canadian bark *Two Friends* in North Bay during the Alpena Gale of 1880, was also on the *Skeele* when she met her end in 1921. The other members of the crew were Orin W. Angwall, first mate; Orville

"Dewey" Stephenson of Marinette; John Lockland of Menominee, an old-time sailor; Eli Muller of Green Bay, Louis Larsen's brother-in-law; and Harold W. Pripps, passenger, chronicler, and photographer.

The first night was so rough that the captain had thought of turning back. Pripps kept a diary in which he described the first midnight hours aboard, hours that later seemed a fitting prelude to the ship's disastrous end.

> I went below and turned in. Shortly before midnight I woke up with the wind howling through the rigging and the boat pitched about so that the dishes rattled in the galley, and everything that wasn't set just so, crashed to the floor. Foot steps were sounding overhead as the men ran about. I thought something must be happening. Capt. Larsen came down with Orin, the mate, and they looked at the glass and the chart and when they talked about running back to Chicago I was sure something was wrong. Captain told me to go to sleep and I did after an hour or so. It seems when we got opposite Waukegan, the wind shifted to the northwest and we ran out northeast in the trough. When we came about was when the dishes crashed.

The second morning of the trip they found themselves off Racine with a clear sky and rough sea, but the sense of danger of the the night before was forgotten. The day was fine for sailing, and by Monday night they had crossed the lake to Little Point Sable. It was just the kind of weather to give an old schooner a chance to do her best. On Wednesday September 21, the lake got rough again. They were then in Canadian waters, and the captain told Pripps it was the roughest day he had ever seen. "You'll never see bigger swells on the Great Lakes unless there's a typhoon," he said.

The Milwaukee man helped the captain's father, James Larsen, as he worked on a new yawl, which he was building on deck. Friday and Saturday passed uneventfully, except for loading cedar poles after arriving in Julia Bay off Barrie Island and a little hunting while on shore.

Pripps, in his log of the trip, described being awakened Sunday morning by the howling of the wind through the rigging and the creaking of the blocks as the boat pitched about. He graphically described the hours preceeding the wreck and deserting the ship to save their lives.

> Captain awoke and ducked up the companionway to see what it was. Called the rest of his watch and they went forward to give the anchor more chain. The wind had shifted to northwest which was the worst possible for our position, but we could do nothing to improve position, and it was impossible to beat out into open water because of the darkness. You couldn't see your hand before your face and the captain wouldn't take a chance on making sail in this narrow bay with the gale howling right into it, and we lying there in the most unfavorable position.
>
> Daybreak revealed a scene which was disquieting to say the least. We swung with our stern to the beach, which was only half a mile away, with an ugly strip of black rocks and foaming breakers between. We had breakfast, standing up in the galley. After an hour or so we put out our starboard anchor which weighed 1,400 pounds and felt sure that with this and the 1,200 pounds port anchor out our position was quite secure.
>
> Sunday, September 25: Matters keep getting worse instead of improving as we hoped. We put on a kettle of stew, but this slid off the stove in spite of the guard rail, so we had another slim lunch, standing up. At 2:30 p.m., the gale having steadily increased until by this time it was difficult to make our way forward. The port anchor chain parted with a bang, which gave us something to think about.
>
> We rushed forward. We let out all the chain we had on the starboard side, 45 fathoms, but this single chain on one side caused the vessel to sway from side to side, whereas the two anchors had held her right into the wind. At one time our stern would be down in a trough and we would look up hill to the bow, and the next instant as the immense roller passed amidships we would be pitching downhill into the foaming seas, which poured over the bow and rushed aft. The rising of the bow on the next comber would then fetch us up short on the heavy anchor chain with a sickening jerk. The mate went forward and hung over the bow at the risk of his life and came aft to re-

port that the strain on the heavy chain would pull the bow out in a short time. It looked pretty black for the old *Skeele*.

> The captain ordered Eli and me below to pack up our bags. I also wrapped my new camera and films in the oil-cloth from the cabin table and tied securely, hoping to keep them dry if we went ashore. About this time I was called up on deck in time to see our new yawl boat being washed ashore. We were in a pretty pickle, because we now had nothing to go ashore with in case the schooner struck. I suggested that we swim for it, if we had to, and, as if to show us the folly of this, the mate pitched one of the cedar posts overboard. We watched its rapid progress landward. When it hit the breakers it disappeared, was caught by the undertow and came up again several hundred yards to the left. 'That's what will happen to you if you try to swim, so stick to the schooner as long as you can,' he said.
>
> Suddenly we felt our remaining anchor commence to drag, and once our hook pulled out of the mud our progress to the foaming beach was slow but irresistible. The captain ordered a raft built of cedarposts, lashed crosswise on a 15-foot ladder and Eli and I went below to bring our bags on deck. These we piled on the poop, about the wheel, and then stood and waited the inevitable outcome. Sea after sea came over us and we feared that the masts would go out of her. Everyone was calm and collected and we joshed 'Dewey' when he came out of the fo'castle with his 'Sunday' suit on. We were all soaked to the skin by the flying spray. When about 300 yards from the beach we were picked up by a mammoth roller and when we

The *Skeele* of Thompson, Michigan, in the Milwaukee River just above the Juneau Avenue Bridge. Courtesy of the Wisconsin Marine Historical Society.

The *Skeele* under full sail. Note the presence of a raffee, the triangular sail, and the absence of a topsail on the foremast. The raffee was not unique to Great Lakes schooners but was more common here. Its purpose was to increase the sail area when before or perpendicular to the wind, somewhat like a spinnaker on a yacht. The yard for the raffee sail was a carry-over from the earlier brigs and barques, which were square-rigged, that is, had square sails supported and spread by yards. It was employed in English coastal waters in the 1860s and known by the same name. Courtesy of James Allan Larsen.

Capt. James Larsen mending sail and Orin Angwall, first mate, leaning against the rail during the last trip of the *Skeele* in September 1921. As a young fisherman, age 25, James Larsen rescued the crew of the Canadian barque *Two Friends* stranded in North Bay during the Alpena Gale of 1880. Courtesy of James Allan Larsen.

dropped into the trough our stern struck with a sickening crunch.

The wheel, housing and gear were shot into the air as if popped out of a gun, because we had struck right in our rudder and disappeared over the side. The captain immediately ordered the starboard anchor cut away and the mate rushed forward, hit the pin with a sledge and the chain ran out of the hawse pipe. This caused the schooner to swing broadside to the beach and afforded a little lee to shelter the launching of the raft. Every sea broke over us now and the masts swayed like drunken sailors.

We lowered old Capt. Jim (the captain's father), Eli and old John over the side. John was too heavy and the raft sank when he got on, so we pulled him back on deck again. We got the raft up and it took us almost 30 minutes to get Jim and Eli ashore. We finally made it and after a super-human effort they succeeded in righting the heavy yawl boat which had been lodged upside down on the rocks in the tossing waters near the shore. After bailing it with their sou-westers, they fastened the middle of the long line to the yawl and we hauled it out to the schooner. They kept the other end of the line.

John, Dewey and I got into the boat for the second trip and when it got a short distance from the schooner it filled and we went ashore under water most of the way, hanging on for dear life. We were dumped out when we hit the first line of rocks and from there it was a struggle to the beach. I was picked up time and time again and dashed off my feet, each time striking my shins on the cruel rocks. I tried to keep my head up and my back to the sea, as per instructions, hence the barked shins.

The captain and mate came ashore next and we were

all mighty thankful we were all safe on the beach. It was close to dark about this time. I had put some matches in a tin box and to our joy we found these dry, as were the cameras and films. We went in a cedar thicket and started a roaring blaze, while the mate and Dewey went down an old logging road to see whether they could find any habitation on the island. They came back with lanterns in an hour, bearing the cheery news that they had struck a most sympathetic homesteader and his wife, a Mr. and Mrs. Charles Eaton. They took us in and gave us the best they had and we slept the sleep of the dead.

Monday, September 26: Mr. Eaton took Capt. Larsen and me to Gore Bay, where we sent telegrams. One of them was to the American Counsel at the Canadian Soo, notifying him of the loss of the ship. When we got back in the afternoon we went down to the beach and found that the sea had gone down and that the schooner was much farther in, laying in four feet of water.

And there she would lie until her bones rotted because there was no chance of salvaging her. The expense would have been more than the vessel was worth. The last document of the *Edward E. Skeele* of Escanaba was surrendered at Marquette on January 3, 1922; cause of surrender: total loss. Vessel wrecked on Barrie Island, North Channel, Lake Huron, on September 25, 1921. No loss of life. Seven persons on board.

She was a good schooner in her day, one of the best of the old fleet, but although the perils of the Great Lakes were overcome by the *Pauline* and by *John, Edward* went the way of most of the old ones, after 65 years of service under sail and 40 years after her reconstruction by the Milwaukee Shipyard Co.

NOTES

CHAPTER NOTES

NOTES — Chapter One

1. Arthur C. and Lucy F. Frederickson, *Ships and Shipwrecks in Door County, Wisconsin, Volume II* (Sturgeon Bay, Wisconsin: Door County Publishing Co., 1963), 61–62, 65; Dwight Boyer, *Ghost Ships of the Great Lakes* (New York: Dodd, Mead and Company, 1968), 181; Hjalmar R. Holand, *History of Door County, Wisconsin*, volume 1 (Chicago, 1917), 254–56.

2. Arthur C. and Lucy F. Frederickson, *Frederickson's Charts of Ships Wrecked in the Vicinity of Door County, Wisconsin*, Box 272, Frankfort, Michigan, 1959; Flint Enterprises, 520 W. Third St., Flint, Michigan, 1962.

3. National Board of Lake Underwriters (Buffalo: Printing House of Matthews and Warren, 1875), 120.

4. Lake Hull Register of the Association of Lake Underwriters (Detroit: Free Press Book and Job Printing House, 1879), 129.

5. John Brandt Mansfield, *History of the Great Lakes, Volume 1* (Chicago: J. H. Beers and Co., 1899), 734.

6. *Door County Advocate,* Sturgeon Bay, Wisconsin, October 21, 1880.

7. Annual Report of the U.S. Life-Saving Service, 1886, pp. 55–57.

8. Note 1, *supra.*

9. *Door County Advocate,* Sturgeon Bay, Wisconsin, November 4, 1880.

10. Probably the tug *G. W. Gardner,* built in June 1862 at Cleveland by Quayle and Martin and based in Chicago.

11. Note 1, *supra.*

12. The schooner *Guido Pfister,* official no. 85304, was built in 1873 at Manitowoc, Wisconsin, by Jasper Hanson. Her measurements were 694.27 gross tons, 661.46 net tons, and 198.2 x 33.0 x 13.2 feet with three masts. The *Pfister* stranded near Duluth in 1885, and the last enrollment was surrendered at Buffalo on October 27, 1885; cause of surrender: wrecked.

13. The tug *Champion,* official no. 5720, was built in 1868 at Detroit, Michigan, by Gordon Campbell. Her measurements were 263.36 gross tons, 147.07 nets tons, and 134.6 x 21.4 x 10.7 feet. On September 15, 1903, she burned to the water's edge while at anchor at Put-in-Bay, Lake Erie, value $18,000. The last enrollment was surrendered at Detroit on September 18, 1903; cause of surrender: vessel lost.

14. The tug *Oswego,* official no. 19063, was built in 1857 at Philadelphia, Pennsylvania, by Hillman and Shaker. Her measurements were 106.0 x 19.6 x 9.6 feet. On October 10, 1891, she burned in the Detroit River opposite Detroit, loss $16,000.

15. *Door County Advocate,* Sturgeon Bay, Wisconsin, September 8, 1881.

16. Probably the former tug *Home,* official no. 11210, built in 1861 at Buffalo, New York, and abandoned in 1881. She may have been rebuilt in 1881 at Sturgeon Bay as a steam scow used in shallow harbors to load scows with logs.

17. The tug *Leviathan,* official no. 14612, was built in 1857 at Buffalo, New York, by Buel B. Jones. She was a large and powerful wrecker with new measurements of 126.0 x 25.8 x 9.0 feet at 232.44 gross, 129.05 net, tons. On November 12, 1891, the *Leviathan* burned at Cheboygan, Michigan, and was a total loss.

18. The schooner *Nabob,* official no. 18175, was built in 1862 at Manitowoc, Wisconsin, by Green S. Rand. Her measurements were 310.38 gross tons, 294.87 net tons, and 137.6 x 26.5 x 11.6 feet with two masts.

19. The barque *E.C.L.,* official no. 7294, was built in 1855 on the bottom of the old brig *Wabash* at Chicago by Dolittle and Miller. Her measurements were 248.92 total tons and 126.5 x 26.2 x 10.0 feet with three masts. She was rerigged as a schooner in the winter of 1879–80.

20. The schooner *George H. Warmington,* official no. 85217, was built in 1872 at Vermillion, Ohio, by Isaac W. Nicholas. Her measurements were 559 gross tons, 521 net tons, and 170.3 x 31.5 x 13.5 feet with three masts. She was sold Canadian, C122015, in 1906.

21. The schooner *W. R. Taylor,* official no. 72964, was built in 1877 at South Bay, Ontario, by George Dixon. Her measurements were 322 tons and 131.2 x 25.1 x 12.5 feet with three masts. She was renamed *Stuart H. Dunn* in 1898 and sank after colliding with a pier at Port Dalhousie, Ontario, on July 4, 1920. She was recovered and may have seen further service.

22. The tug *Winslow* (1st) was built at Cleveland, Ohio, in 1862 by Quayle and Martin for H. J. and N. C. Winslow of Cleveland. She was wrecked in Cleveland Harbor on October 7, 1864, and the machinery was put into the new hull by Quayle and Martin in 1865. The measurements of the *Winslow* (2d), official no. 26243, were 129.3 x 21.9 x 10.9 feet at 210.67 total tons. She was sold Canadian, 96855, in 1902 and burned in Meldrum Bay en route to Georgian Bay on April 21, 1911.

23. The bulk freighter *Minnesota,* official no. 91272, was built in 1880 at Milwaukee by Wolf & Davidson for the Inter-Ocean Transportation Co. of Milwaukee. She burned on November 15 or 17, 1903, while hauling coal off Walpole Island, St. Clair River, abreast of Grand Point near Algonac, Michigan.

24. The tug *Jesse Spaulding,* official no. 95759, was built in 1883 as the *Henry Marshall* at Green Bay by the Thrall Brothers. Her measurements were 52.21 gross tons, 26.26 net tons, and 71.6 x 16.5 x 8.6 feet. She was renamed *Sioux* in 1900 and was dismantled and sunk in Milwaukee in 1918.

25. The tug *George Nelson,* official no. 85946, was built in 1886 at Saugatuck, Michigan, by John B. Martel. Her measurements were 45.98 gross tons, 22.99 net tons, and 65.0 x 17.4 x 8.0 feet. The last enrollment of the *Nelson* was surrendered at Port Huron on September 24, 1912; cause of surrender: abandoned.

NOTES – Chapter Two

1. Hjalmar R. Holand, *History of Door County, Wisconsin* (Chicago, 1917).

2. The brig *Fanny Gardner*, official no. 9199, was built in 1853 at Pensaukee, Wisconsin, by Alfred Gilson for F. B. Gardner. Her measurements were 327⁴²/₉₅ tons old measure, length 128⁸/₁₂ feet, breadth 27³/₁₂ feet, and depth 10²/₁₂ feet with two masts.

3. The *Parmelia Flood.*

4. The *F. B. Gardner* was built at Sheboygan.

5. The *Fanny Gardner.*

6. The prophesy that certainly has come to pass and is in evidence today in Sturgeon Bay.

7. Detailed statistics for all vessels built or rebuilt at Little Sturgeon Bay are given in the appendix. These statistics support a lengthening of only 40 feet for the *F. B. Gardner.*

8. The steam barge *D. Leuty*, official no. 157065, was built in 1882 at Lorain, Ohio, by Henry D. Root. On the night of October 31, 1911, she was blown on the rocks off Light House Point, one-half mile east of Marquette, Michigan, in a heavy snowstorm. Efforts to release the *Leuty* were unsuccessful, and she became a total loss valued at $20,000.

9. The side-wheel steamer *Queen City,* official no. 20519, was built in 1856 at Oshkosh, Wisconsin, by Pringle. The machinery was from the steamer *Vaness Barlow* built in 1851 at Neenah and condemned in 1855. The *Queen City* burned and sank off Cedar River, Michigan, on November 22, 1875.

10. The side-wheel steamer *M. C. Hawley,* official no. 91228, was named in honor of Captain Hawley's daughter. The steamer's measurements were 208.77 gross tons, 171.94 net tons, length 138.0 feet, breadth 20.0 feet, and depth 8.7 feet. She was renamed *City of Green Bay* in 1884 and converted to a propeller at Manitowoc in 1889. On August 19, 1909, the propeller burned at Whistler's Point, Michigan, while crossing Saginaw Bay, Lake Huron, to become a total loss.

11. The tug *A. W. Lawrence,* official no. 105948, was launched in May at Sturgeon Bay by John Gregory of Chicago for A. W. Lawrence & Co. of Sturgeon Bay. The boiler of the *Lawrence* exploded off Milwaukee on October 30, 1888, and she foundered, losing four lives.

12. The tug *St. Mary* of Frankfort found the abandoned *Ann Maria,* official no. 387, off Portage, and the tug *Caroline Williams* of Manistee went out and towed the derelict into South Manitou Harbor. The *Ann Maria* was almost a complete wreck, her masts, rails, bulwarks, and everything else above deck swept clean. The tug *Margaret* of Ludington towed the wreck to Milwaukee, where she was repaired by Wolf & Davidson. On October 8, 1902, the *Ann Maria* stranded at the entrance to the harbor at Kincardine, Ontario, during heavy weather and became a total loss, losing four of her crew and one volunteer lifesaver.

13. The tug *Champion,* official no. 5720, was built in 1868 at Detroit, Michigan, by Gordon Campbell for Campbell Owen & Co. and others. Her measurements were 263.36 tons, length 134.6 feet, breadth 21.4 feet, and depth 10.7 feet. On September 15, 1903, the *Champion* burned to the water's edge while at anchor at Put-in-Bay, Lake Erie, value $18,000.

14. The tug *Sweepstakes,* official no. 22383, was built in 1867 at Cleveland, Ohio, by Quayle and Martin for H. N. Strong of Detroit. Her measurements were 205.88 tons, length 130.7 feet, breadth 21.8 feet, and depth 11.8 feet. The tug was renamed *Sea King* in 1913 and was reported abandoned in 1924.

15. The barge *Walter A. Sherman,* official no. 62858, was built in 1882 at Buffalo, New York, by Robert Mills for Laban B. Fortier (2/3) and Alfred Mayer (1/3), both of Buffalo. Her measurements were 519.55 gross tons, 493.58 net tons, and 163.4 x 32.8 x 12.0 feet with three masts. She was reported abandoned in 1927.

16. The tug *William L. Proctor,* official no. 81002, was built in 1883 at Buffalo, New York, by George H. Notter for George Hall of Ogdensburg, New York. Her measurements were 117.01 gross tons, 58.51 net tons, and 104.0 x 20.0 x 10.0 feet. The *Proctor* was sold Canadian in 1916 to the Sincennes McNaughton Line, Montreal. The tug was rebuilt in 1917 at Sorel, Quebec, and renamed *Conqueror,* C138233. The *Conqueror* was last listed in 1937 and reported broken at Sorel.

17. The barge *Argosy,* official no. 29296, was built in 1868 at Buffalo, New York, by George H. Notter for H. H. Hall (2/3) and William Gardner, Jr. (1/3) of Ogdensburg, New York. Her measurements were 168.90 gross tons, 160.45 net tons, and 107.3 x 24.0 x 9.0 feet. The last enrollment of the *Argosy* was surrendered at Ogdensburg on June 27, 1911; cause of surrender: sold foreign.

18. The schooner *J. B. Kitchen,* official no. 75511, was built in 1873 at Cleveland, Ohio, by Murphy and Quayle. Her measurements were 287.31 gross tons, 272.95 net tons, and 132.8 x 26.8 x 9.5 feet with two masts. The last enrollment of the *Kitchen* was surrendered at Port Huron on April 27, 1907; cause of surrender: sold alien. She was sold Canadian, C116814.

19. The side-wheel steamer *George L. Dunlap,* official no. 10347, was built in 1864 at Fort Howard by William H. Wolf for the Green Bay Transit Co. On November 19, 1880, ice in the river at Bay City, Michigan, cut a hole in the starboard side. The leak was discovered when the *Dunlap* was 14 miles out on the way to Alpena, and the vessel barely returned to Bay City. The *George L. Dunlap* was dismantled and her engine put into the new steamer *Darius Cole,* built in 1885 at Cleveland, Ohio.

20. The propeller *St. Joseph,* official no. 23354, was built in 1867 at Buffalo, New York, by Hitchcock and Gibson for John T. Edwards & Co. of St. Joseph, Michigan, as a passenger and package freighter. In later years, the vessel was a lumber steam barge. She was sold Canadian in 1916 and became the *Frank B. Stevens,* C134517, owned by the American Transit Co., Sarnia, Ontario. The *Stevens* was dismantled at Sarnia in about 1922.

21. The barque *City of Painesville,* official no. 5394, was built in 1867 at Fairport, Ohio, by D. E. and J. E. Bailey. Her measurements were 600.81 total tons and 181.9 x 34.3 x 13.2 feet with three masts. She was rerigged as a schooner in 1873.

22. The schooner *J. Maria Scott,* official no. 75610, was built in 1874 at Oswego, New York, by Goble and McFarland. Her measurements were 348.89 total tons and 136.6 x 26.0 x 12.0 feet with three masts. Later she was converted to a steam barge, and she was renamed *White Star* in 1890. The *White Star* burned at Port Huron, Michigan, on March 9, 1901, value $7,000.

23. The tug *Crusader,* official no. 125252, was built in 1874 at Port Huron, Michigan, by Leighton and Dunford. The tug

caught fire on the morning of November 6, 1894, at Sault Ste. Marie, Michigan, and became a total loss. Two lives were lost, and the estimated loss on the vessel was $12,000.

24. The *Middlesex* was built as a steamer, official no. 91307, in 1881 at St. Clair, Michigan, by Simon Langell. On November 18, 1881, she burned at Piquamery Point, Lake Huron, while lying in the harbor. The *Middlesex* was rebuilt as a tow barge in 1883 at Algonac, Michigan, by Abram Smith. She was sold Canadian in 1918 and was renamed *Woodlands,* C138504. The barge was reported broken up in May 1929.

25. The steam barge *James H. Prentice,* official no. 76581, was built in 1885 at Trenton, Michigan, by John Craig as a schooner-barge and was later converted to steam. The vessel was converted to a sand sucker in 1920 and was abandoned in September 1934 at Toledo, Ohio.

26. The steamer *Louisiana,* official no. 140882, was built in 1887 at Marine City, Michigan, by Morley and Hill for W. B. Morley and others. Her measurements were 1753 gross tons, 1259 net tons, and 267.0 x 39.6 x 20.0 feet.

27. The schooner *Challenge,* official no. 4349, was built for Jarvis E. Platt (1/2) and O. H. Platt (1/2) of Manitowoc, Wisconsin, with measurements of 110³¹⁄₉₅ tons old measure, length 85³⁄₁₂ feet, breadth 22⁵⁄₁₂ feet, and depth 6⁵⁵⁄₁₂ feet with two masts. The *Challenge* was beached, bound from Manitowoc to Chicago with wood, 12 miles south of Sheboygan on September 10, 1910, and became a total loss—vessel $1,100, cargo $100.

28. The schooner *J.H. Stevens,* official no. 12787, was built as a sloop in 1859 at Milan, Ohio, by D. Edwards for Joseph Blair of Detroit. She was rebuilt in 1866, 1872, and 1891, with final dimensions of 94.31 gross tons, 88.19 net tons, and 100.0 x 21.3 x 6.6 feet with two masts. On June 10, 1927, she burned off Presque Isle, Michigan, Lake Huron. The last enrollment of the *Stevens,* issued at Milwaukee on April 22, 1927, was surrendered at Milwaukee on June 10, 1927; cause of surrender: vessel burned and sank, 13 miles north of Presque Isle, Michigan, total loss.

29. The steam barge *Albert Soper,* official no. 105977, was built in 1881 at Grand Haven, Michigan, by Duncan Robertson for Soper & Pond of Chicago to be used in the lumber trade. The *Soper* was sold alien on March 31, 1920, but there is no record of her going on Canadian registry.

30. The schooner *H.M. Scove,* official no. 95256, was built in 1873 at Manitowoc, Wisconsin, by Jasper Hanson. Her measurements were 305.60 gross tons, 290.32 net tons, and 130.0 x 26.0 x 10.0 feet with three masts. The *Scove* was lost between Pilot Island and Detroit Island in Death's Door in November 1891.

31. The propeller *S.G. Chase,* official no. 22365, was built in

1854 at Kensington, Pennsylvania, by Burley. She was a harbor tug of 27³³⁄₉₅ tons old measure, length 50⁶⁄₁₂ feet, breadth 12 feet, and depth 5 feet.

32. The propeller *City of Madison,* official no. 4350, was built in 1857 at Buffalo, New York, by C. A. VanSlyke for E. K. Bruce of Buffalo, New York. She was a Welland Canal–size passenger and freight steamer, with measurements of 394⁵³⁄₉₅ tons old measure, length 134³⁄₁₂ feet, breadth 26²⁄₁₂ feet, and depth 12¹⁄₁₂ feet.

33. The *City of Madison* was rescued in August 1874 by the wrecking tug *Leviathan.* The vessel was repaired by Wolf & Davidson and burned in Lake Michigan, 65 miles northeast of Chicago off Kenosha, while running light on August 17, 1877.

34. The tug *Orient,* official no. 19414, was built in 1874 at Buffalo, New York, by the Carroll Brothers. Her measurements were 37.72 gross tons, 18.86 net tons, and 62.4 x 15.8 x 7.6 feet. The *Orient* sank with all hands off Point Pelee, Lake Erie, on October 4, 1887.

35. The tug *R. F. Goodman,* official no. 110546, was built in 1882 at Buffalo, New York, by the Union Dry Dock Co. Her measurements were 22.72 gross tons, 11.36 net tons, and 51.0 x 13.8 x 6.7 feet. The *Goodman* burned at Lester Park, Duluth, Minnesota, on August 16, 1898.

36. The tug *Pensaukee,* official no. 150057, was crushed against the dock at Cleveland, Ohio, on June 5, 1902, by the barge *Aurora.* The measurements of the tug were 34.06 gross tons, 17 net tons, and 52.0 x 14.2 x 6.5 feet.

37. The barque *Hans Crocker,* official no. 11174, was built in 1856 at Milwaukee, Wisconsin, by James M. Jones for William B. Hibbard of Milwaukee. Her measurements were 473¹⁶⁄₉₅ tons old measure, length 139 feet, breadth 32⁹⁄₁₂ feet, and depth 11⁶⁄₁₂ feet with three masts.

38. The schooner *Mediator,* official no. 16345, was built in 1862 at Clayton, New York, by S. G. Johnson. Her measurements were 256.93 gross tons, 244.09 net tons, and 127.3 x 26.0 x 11.0 feet with three masts. She went ashore on Lake Superior on September 19, 1898, to become a total loss. The last enrollment of the *Mediator* was surrendered at Chicago on October 10, 1898; cause of surrender: vessel lost.

39. The schooner *Ellen Williams,* official no. 7308, was built in 1855 at Cleveland, Ohio, by Peck and Masters for A. R. Williams of Chicago. Her measurements were 321.47 gross tons, 305.40 net tons, and 130.4 x 30.1 x 10.3 feet with three masts. The *Williams* was dismantled on March 14, 1910, to serve as a stone barge on the Chicago River. After several years, she was sunk in Lake Michigan as unfit for service.

NOTES – Chapter Three

1. Conan Bryant Eaton, *"Death's Door The Pursuit of a Legend,"* The Island Series, *Door County Advocate,* Sturgeon Bay, Wisconsin: 1967.

2. The Goodrich Transportation Co. steamer *Alpena,* official no. 404, was lost between Grand Haven, Michigan, and Chicago at a cost of 60 to 86 lives.

3. The scow schooner *R.H. Becker,* official no. 56207, was

built in 1867 at Dover Bay, Ohio. Vital statistics: 140.82 gross tons, 133.78 net tons, and 108.0. x 23.0. x 7.0 feet, with two masts. The *Becker* was towed outside the harbor at Sheboygan, Wisconsin, and was beached on May 16, 1908, to be broken up by the seas. The last enrollment of the *Becker,* issued at Milwaukee on April 28, 1893, was surrendered at Milwaukee on May 15, 1908; cause of surrender: vessel lost.

4. The tug *John Gregory,* official no. 76025, was built in 1878 at Green Bay, Wisconsin, by John Gregory of Chicago. Vital statistics: 75.25 gross tons, 46.34 net tons, and 80.0 x 17.0 x 9.3 feet. On November 13, 1904, the *Gregory* capsized at the entrance to Cleveland Harbor during strong winds, drowning her captain and blocking the harbor. The last enrollment, issued at Cleveland on May 17, 1894, was surrendered at Cleveland on January 24, 1905; cause of surrender: vessel lost.

5. The schooner *William O. Brown,* official no. 26915, was built in 1862 at Buffalo, New York, by Rufus R. Johnson for William O. Brown. She measured 399⁴⁵/₉₅ tons old measure, length 139⁸/₁₂ feet, breadth 26³/₁₂ feet, and depth 11⁸/₁₂ feet with two masts. The *Brown* was lost on Lake Superior in November 1872, but the last enrollment, issued at Chicago on May 23, 1870, was not surrendered at Chicago until June 30, 1874; cause of surrender: total wreck.

6. The scow schooner *Honest John,* official no. 11180, measured 117⁸⁵/₉₅ tons old measure, length 81⁶/₁₂ feet, breadth 21¹⁰/₁₂ feet, and depth 7⁶/₁₂ feet with two masts. She was abandoned in the Menominee River slip near the Chicago, Milwaukee & St. Paul Elevator A at Milwaukee, Wisconsin, in 1883. The last enrollment, issued at Milwaukee on April 2, 1880, was surrendered at Milwaukee on March 31, 1884; cause of surrender: abandoned.

7. The schooner *Sea Lark* measured 23⁷/₉₅ tons old measure, length 43⁷/₁₂ feet, breadth 12⁷/₁₂ feet, and depth 4¹⁰/₁₂ feet with two masts.

8. From the diary of Rev. A. M. Iversen, Ephraim, Wisconsin.

9. Brooks built boats in Milwaukee until 1877, when he disposed of his yard and fixtures to Wolf & Davidson and moved his family to Kansas to farm.

10. The schooner *G.D. Norris,* official no. 10336, was built in 1856 at Cleveland, Ohio, by George W. Jones for Daniel Newhall of Milwaukee, Wisconsin. Her measurements were 262.14 gross tons, 251.70 net tons, and 128.0 x 26.4 x 11.0 feet with two masts. The last enrollment of the *Norris,* issued at Port Huron on June 6, 1887, was surrendered at Port Huron on March 31, 1888; cause of surrender: total loss.

11. The scow schooner *Quickstep,* official no. 20567, was built in 1868 at Bay de Noc, Michigan, by and for William Stevens of Green Bay, Wisconsin. She ran on a rock near the inlet to Detroit Harbor, Washington Island, Lake Michigan, on October 6, 1886, and was badly broken, becoming a total loss. The last enrollment, issued at Milwaukee on June 27, 1884, was surrendered at Milwaukee on November 12, 1888; cause of surrender: vessel wrecked on October 6, 1886, total loss.

12. The propeller *Messenger,* official no. 16654, was built in 1866 at Cleveland, Ohio, by E. M. Peck. Her measurements were 288 gross tons, 244 net tons, and 136.0 x 29.0 x 9.4 feet. The *Messenger* burned at Rogers City, Michigan, in November 1890.

13. The schooner *George L. Wren,* official no. 10816, was built in 1868 at Fort Howard, Wisconsin. The last enrollment was surrendered at Chicago on June 28, 1911; cause of surrender: abandoned. She was dismantled and burned during the winter of 1912–13 in the north branch of the Chicago River, headed north, south of the Belmont Avenue Bridge, on the west bank of the river.

14. Probably the schooner *C. Harrison,* official no. 4569, which was built in 1854 at Milwaukee, Wisconsin, for Caleb Harrison of Milwaukee. She stranded in heavy weather north of the pier in Whitefish Bay, Door County, Lake Michigan, on October 31, 1898, and was quickly converted into kindling wood. The last enrollment of the *Harrison,* issued at Milwaukee on April 16, 1897, was surrendered at Milwaukee on November 12, 1898; cause of surrender: total loss.

15. The schooner *Walhalla,* official no. 26365, was built in 1867 at DePere, Wisconsin, and the last enrollment, issued at Grand Haven on November 18, 1899, was surrendered at Grand Haven on December 1, 1902; cause of surrender: abandoned.

16. The schooner *Democrat,* official no. 6932, was built in 1877 at Au Gres, Michigan, and was in commission until 1898.

17. The steamer *J.H. Outhwaite,* official no. 76636, was built in 1886 at Cleveland, Ohio. She stranded in a heavy gale, broke in two, and burned at Little Sable Point near Cheboygan, Michigan, on November 27 and 28, 1905.

NOTES – Chapter Four

1. M. Mansfield Stimson, "From Shore to Shore," *Inland Seas,* vol. 10, no. 3, Fall 1954, p. 195.

2. Port of Detroit, 1817, register no. 11, 14 tons.

3. Port of Detroit, June 25, 1830, register no. 5.

4. *Merchant Steam Vessels of the United States 1790–1868,* "The Lytle-Holdcamper List," revised and edited by C. Bradford Mitchell with the assistance of Kenneth R. Hall (Baltimore, Maryland: The University of Baltimore Press, 1975), 12.

5. The side-wheel steamboat *Lady of the Lake* was built in 1833 at Mount Clemens, Michigan. The measurements were length 57⁶/₁₂ feet, breadth 10 feet, and depth 4⁶/₁₂ feet. (Port of Detroit, August 19, 1833, enrollment no. 13.)

6. The side-wheel steamboat *United* was built in 1836 at Detroit by S. Jenkins for Lewis Davenport of Detroit, owner and master. The measurements were length 69⁵/₁₂ feet, breadth 17 feet, and depth 3⁶/₁₂ feet. The steamboat was rebuilt in 1842 at Detroit with measurements of 56⁴⁹/₉₅ tons old measure, length 79 feet, breadth 17⁵/₁₂ feet, and depth 4⁶/₁₂ feet. The rig was changed to a barge in 1869. (Port of Huron, May 4, 1869.)

7. The side-wheel steamboat *Argo* (2d), official no. 1427, was built in 1849 at Detroit for George B. Russell of Detroit with James Clinton as master. The measurements were 111³⁹/₉₅ tons old measure, length 91 feet, breadth 19 feet, and depth 7 feet. The last enrollment was surrendered at Detroit, January 15, 1879; cause of surrender: "out of commission."

8. Port of Detroit, December 4, 1856, enrollment no. 127.

9. Port of Milwaukee, November 1, 1865, enrollment no. 128.

10. George B. Catlin, *The Story of Detroit* (Detroit: The Detroit News, 1926), 549; James Cooke Mills, *Our Inland Seas* (Chicago: A.C. McClurg & Co., 1910), 195.

11. The ferry *Detroit,* official no. 6150, was built in 1864 at

Algonac, Michigan, by Pangborn for William P. Campbell of Detroit with Thomas Chilvers as master. The measurements were 126⁵⁸/₉₅ tons old measure, length 80 feet, breadth 20⁶/₁₂ feet, and depth 8⁸/₁₂ feet. (Port of Detroit, August 19, 1864, enrollment no. 186.)

12. Port of Detroit, May 30, 1871, enrollment no. 131.

13. Port of Chicago, August 26, 1876, enrollment no. 5.

14. The schooner *Lookout*, official no. 14675, was built in 1855 at Buffalo, New York, by George Hardison for Henry A. Frink of Buffalo (3/4) and Charles P. Mowry of Ashtabula, Ohio (1/4 and master). The measurements were 312⁴⁷/₉₅ tons old measure, length 126⁶/₁₂ feet, breadth 27²/₁₂ feet, and depth 9¹¹/₁₂ feet. After over 40 years of service, the *Lookout* was wrecked five miles north of the Two Rivers Life-Saving Service Station on April 29, 1897, at a total loss of $2,000.

15. *Door County Advocate,* Sturgeon Bay, Wisconsin, May 10, 1883.

16. Annual Report of the U.S. Life-Saving Service 1894, pp. 100, 274, 364; *Door County Advocate,* Sturgeon Bay, Wisconsin, October 7 and 14, 1893.

17. "Where is the *Two Friends?* – A Story of North Bay," p. 3.

18. Port of Chicago, April 8, 1887, enrollment no. 64.

19. The schooner *D.A. Wells,* official no. 6843, measured 62.0 x 18.33 x 6.66 feet and 56.20 gross tons, 53.39 net tons, with two masts. She was reported abandoned on March 31, 1918.

20. The steam tug *James H. Martin,* official no. 75114, was built at Cleveland, Ohio, in 1869 and was abandoned on June 17, 1918.

21. Port of Chicago, April 23, 1888, enrollment no. 93.

22. *Door County Advocate,* Sturgeon Bay, Wisconsin, December 2 and 9, 1893.

23. Note 21, *supra.*

NOTES – Chapter Five

1. Howard I. Chapelle, *The History of American Sailing Ships* (New York: W. W. Norton & Company, Inc., 1935), 268.

2. The schooner *Challenge,* official no. 4349, was built for Jarvis E. Platt (1/2) and O. H. Platt (1/2) of Manitowoc with measurements of 110³¹/₉₅ tons old measure, length 85³/₁₂ feet, breadth 22⁵/₁₂ feet, and depth 6⁵⁵/₁₂ feet with two masts. The *Challenge* was beached, bound from Manitowoc to Chicago with wood, 12 miles south of Sheboygan on September 10, 1910, and became a total loss – vessel $1,100, cargo $100.

3. Arthur H. Lohman, *Early Days in Two Rivers, Wisconsin* (Milwaukee: Meyer-Rotier Printing Co., 1909), 21.

4. Evan Gagnon, *NESHOTAH, The Story of Two Rivers, Wisconsin* (Stevens Point, Wisconsin: Worzalla Publishing Company, 1969), 75.

5. The measurements of the *Stella* were 176⁷⁰/₉₅ tons old measure, length 100⁶/₁₂ feet, breadth 25⁵/₁₂ feet, and depth 7⁸/₁₂ feet with two masts. The schooner went ashore near Chicago in August 1864 while bound from Muskegon to Chicago with a cargo of lumber.

6. The measurements of the *Triumph* were 120⁵⁴/₉₅ tons old measure, length 85¹¹/₁₂ feet, breadth 21⁸/₁₂ feet, and depth 7³/₁₂ feet with two masts. She was wrecked near the north pier at Chicago in 1865.

7. The *Gertrude,* official no. 10202, measured 97¹⁴/₉₅ tons old measure, length 81 feet, breadth 19⁶/₁₂ feet, and depth 6⁵/₁₂ feet with two masts. On September 26, 1880, she foundered on Lake Michigan at the mouth of Otter Creek, Michigan. The last document was surrendered at Milwaukee, October 5, 1880, marked "Total Loss."

8. William Aldrich was born in Greenfield, New York, in January 1820 and came to Wisconsin in 1851. He was a member of the Wisconsin State Assembly in 1859, moved to Chicago and was a member of the Forty-fifth Congress, the Forty-sixth Congress, and the Forty-seventh Congress. The Honorable William Aldrich died at Fond du Lac on December 3, 1885.

9. The measurements of the *Eleanor,* official no. 7298, were 260⁷⁴/₉₅ tons old measure, length 120⁶/₁₂ feet, breadth 26 feet, and depth 9¹/₁₂ feet with two masts. She stranded on Whiskey Reef in Lake Huron three and one-half miles south of Port Austin, Michigan, on August 15, 1880.

10. The steam barge *Annie Laura,* official no. 105106, was built in 1871 at Marine City, Michigan, by Phillip Rice. She burned at the St. Clair Flats on August 10, 1922, with eleven on board, but no lives were lost. In June 1923, she was raised and blown up.

11. The tug *John Leathem,* official no. 76064, was built in 1878 at Sturgeon Bay by John Gregory of Chicago for Scofield & Co. of Sturgeon Bay with measurements of 75.25 gross tons, 38.61 net tons, and 80.0 × 17.0 × 8.5 feet. She was renamed *Holliswood* in 1921 and went to the East Coast.

12. The tug *George Nelson,* official no. 85946, was built in 1886 at Saugatuck, Michigan, by John B. Martel. Her measurements were 45.98 gross tons, 22.99 net tons, and 65.0 × 17.4 × 8.0 feet. The last enrollment of the *Nelson* was surrendered at Port Huron on September 24, 1912; cause of surrender: abandoned.

13. *Door County Advocate,* Sturgeon Bay, Wisconsin, November 7, 1891; *Milwaukee Sentinel,* Milwaukee, Wisconsin, November 2, 1891.

14. The *S.M. Stephenson,* official no. 115722, was built in 1880 at Manitowoc, Wisconsin, by Rand & Burger for the Kirby Carpenter Co. of Menominee, Michigan, as a schooner-barge. In 1887, she was sold to the A.A. Bigelow fleet of Chicago and was towed behind the *Robert Holland* or the *White & Friant.* The *Stephenson* was rebuilt as a steam barge in 1901 and was reported abandoned in January 1935 at Bay City, Michigan.

15. The tug *Ivy M. Leathem,* official no. 100509, received her first inspection on October 15, 1891. She was built by Burger and Burger of Manitowoc, Wisconsin, for John Leathem and Thomas H. Smith of Sturgeon Bay. She was renamed *Violet H. Raber* in 1894 and was reported abandoned in 1914.

16. W. R. Williams, "The New England Transportation Company," *Inland Seas,* vol. 14, no. 1, Spring 1958, pp. 50–54.

17. In October 1892, the Canadian steam barge *Canada* was

burned at Port Huron and then rebuilt as the American schooner *Schilde*, official no. 116578. The *Schilde* was renamed *Eureka* in 1896. On November 7, 1901, the barge became waterlogged and was abandoned by the crew of five, including the wife of the mate, who took to the raft on Saginaw Bay, Lake Huron, where she died from exposure.

18. The propeller *Columbia* was built in 1873 at Hamilton, Ontario, by A. M. Robertson for Daniel Butters with measurements of $137 \times 23^{6}/_{12} \times 13^{5}/_{12}$ feet and 360 tons.

19. The propeller *Lake Erie* was built at St. Catherines, Ontario, in 1873 by M. Simpson for the Lake and River Steam Navigation Co. of Hamilton with measurements of $136 \times 23^{4}/_{12} \times 7^{4}/_{12}$ feet and 347 tons.

20. *Milwaukee Sentinel*, Milwaukee, Wisconsin, November 29 and 30, 1881; *Door County Advocate*, Sturgeon Bay, Wisconsin, December 8, 1881.

21. The *John Schroeder*, official no. 76883, was built in 1890 at Sheboygan, Wisconsin, by Rieboldt and Wolter for the John Schroeder Lumber Co. of Milwaukee for trading on Lake Michigan. She was renamed *William A. Hazzard* in 1912 and was abandoned at the Jefferson Avenue plant of the Winkworth Transit Co., Detroit, in June 1934.

22. Manuscript Collection, State of Michigan Library, Lansing, Michigan.

23. The *J. U. Porter*, official no. 45092, was built as a barge at Black River, Ohio, in 1868 by W. S. Lyon and was converted to a scow schooner in 1881. The *Porter* was abandoned at Fairport, Ohio, in 1906.

24. *Federal Reporter* vol. 59, p. 202 (1893).

25. The steamer *Arthur Orr*, official no. 107005, was built at South Chicago in 1893 by the Chicago Ship Building Co. under the supervision of Charles Z. Montague for Charles W. El-phicke of Chicago with measurements of $286 \times 41.3 \times 21.3$ feet and 2329 gross, 1972 net tons. The *Orr* was hauled away from River Rouge in June or July 1947 to be scrapped by the Steel Company of Canada, Ltd., at Hamilton in 1948.

26. *Federal Reporter* vol. 69, p. 350 (1895).

27. The *James McGordon*, official no. 75867, was built by Wolf and Davidson of Milwaukee in 1876. She was rebuilt and renamed *J. C. Evans* for the Dunham Towing and Wrecking Co. in 1898. The *Evans* was junked in 1914.

28. The *I.N. Foster*, official no. 100031, was built as a schooner in 1872 at Port Huron, Michigan, by Fitzgerald & Co. for Hutchinson & Foster of Cleveland. In August 1887, the *Foster* went on Fisherman's Shoal near Rock Island, where she was abandoned to the underwriters. After purchasing her for $2,000, Leathem & Smith pulled the *Foster* off to be rebuilt in their yard. They converted her into a steam barge in 1893 with the engine from the tug *A.J. Wright* and the boiler from the wrecked steamer *Calumet*. The steam barge was also owned by the Sturgeon Bay Stone Co. and others before being abandoned in 1927 at Buffalo.

29. "The *Lummy* – The *Lomie A. Burton*," p. 99.

30. Annual Report of the U.S. Life-Saving Service 1899, pp. 187, 326.

31. Annual Reports of the U.S. Life-Saving Service 1911 p. 132; 1912, p. 140; and 1913, p. 174.

32. "The Perils of *Pauline*, – and *John*, – and *Edward*," p. 105.

33. The steam barge *L.L. Barth*, official no. 116266, was built by James Davidson at West Bay City, Michigan, as the *S.S. Wilhelm* in 1889. She was sold to the Hines Lumber Co. in 1900 and renamed in 1903. In 1927, the *L.L. Barth* was condemned and abandoned in the river at Grand Haven.

NOTES – Chapter Six

1. The scow schooner *Rockaway*, official no. 21475, was built in 1866 at Oswego, New York, by B. Morgan. Her measurements were 164 gross tons, 156 net tons, and $106.2 \times 24.2 \times 7.0$ feet with two masts.

2. "The *William Aldrich* – She Outlived Her Time," p. 49.

3. "The Perils of *Pauline*, – and *John*, – and *Edward*," p. 105.

4. The schooner *Hattie*, official no. 11989, was built in 1863 at Milwaukee for Thomas Cunningham of Sheboygan. She was only $34.0 \times 9.2 \times 4.8$ feet and 13.11 tons with two masts. The *Hattie* stranded on St. Martin's Island during a gale in the fall of 1871 and became a total wreck.

5. The schooner *S. Anderson*, official no. 115335, was built in 1874 at Green Bay by and for Soren Anderson. She was rebuilt and renamed *Quickstep* in 1887. Like many Great Lakes schooners, she left the Lakes and went into the lumber trade between Mobile, Alabama, and Cuba in May 1915. On November 9, 1917, the *Quickstep* stranded at Punta del Ubero, State of Pinar del Rio, on the north coast of the west end of Cuba. There were eight persons aboard, but no lives were lost.

6. From the Church Register 1919–64, Ephraim Moravian Church, pp. 234–35.

7. The schooner *J.K. Stack*, official no. 75805, was built in 1875 at Escanaba, Michigan, for David O'Connor of Escanaba with measurements of $32.75 \times 10.33 \times 4.0$ feet at 12.26 total tonnage.

8. The scow schooner *Jenny*, official no. 76812, was built in 1889 at Egg Harbor by Ole A. Anderson for himself (1/4) and Fred Jurgens (3/4) of Egg Harbor. Her measurements were 15.99 gross tons, 15.19 net tons, and $45.5 \times 14.5 \times 3.3$ feet with two masts.

9. Conrad L. Tonneson was a brother of Tonette A. Tonneson, the second wife of Captain Hogenson.

10. The schooner *Active*, official no. 105087, was built in 1869 at Sheboygan by Martin Olson for Henry Timmer of Sheboygan with measurements of 50.72 gross tons, 48.19 net tons, and $68.8 \times 17.2 \times 5.8$ feet with two masts.

NOTES – Chapter Seven

1. The schooner *Jessie Phillips*, official no. 75367, had two masts with measurements of 128 × 26 × 8 feet at 197.62 tons. The *Phillips* was abandoned in 1903.

2. The schooner *Fleetwing*, official no. 9883, was built at Manitowoc in 1867 by Henry B. Burger for S. Goodenow and Peter Johnson. On October 1, 1888, she stranded in Garrett Bay near Death's Door and went to pieces.

3. The schooner *James Navagh*, official no. 13304, was built in 1857 at Oswego, New York, by James Navagh. She was 275.55 tons with two masts.

4. *Manitowoc Pilot*, Manitowoc, Wisconsin, November 6, 1868; *Milwaukee Sentinel*, Milwaukee, Wisconsin, November 10, 1868.

5. *Milwaukee Sentinel*, Milwaukee, Wisconsin, December 9, 1868.

6. Temporary repairs were made on the schooner *Floretta*, official no. 9688, in North Bay, and she was towed to Chicago by the tug *J. H. Hackley*, where the repair was completed at a cost of about $2,000. On September 18, 1885, the *Floretta* foundered about 15 miles off Manitowoc while bound for Chicago from Escanaba with a cargo of iron ore. The crew took to the yawl and made the shore at Manitowoc.

7. The schooner *Harvey Bissell*, official no. 11281, was built in 1866 as a barque at Toledo, Ohio, by Little for Harvey Bissell and Lyman Miner at 496.86 total tons. She stranded in heavy weather on November 25, 1905, on False Presque Isle, Lake Huron, and became a total loss.

8. The schooner *John L. Green*, official no. 75777, was built in 1875 at Port Clinton, Ohio, and was abandoned in 1914.

9. The tug *Starke Brothers*, official no. 115226, was built in 1872 at Buffalo, New York, by George Notter with measurements of 61.4 × 15.4 × 8.0 feet at 35.96 gross tons; she was abandoned at Milwaukee in 1889.

10. *Milwaukee Sentinel*, Milwaukee, Wisconsin, May 21, 1883.

11. Annual Report of the U.S. Life-Saving Service 1883, pp. 237, 238.

12. The tug *Leviathan*, official no. 14612, was built in 1857 at Buffalo, New York, by Buel B. Jones. She was a large and powerful wrecker with new measurements of 232.44 gross tons, 129.05 net tons, and 126.0 × 25.8 × 9.0 feet. On November 12, 1891, the *Leviathan* burned at Cheboygan, Michigan, and was a total loss.

13. The tug *William R. Crowell*, official no. 80531, was built in 1875 at Buffalo, New York, with measurements of 56.94 gross tons, 29.73 net tons, and 74.0 × 17.1 × 8.9 feet. The *Crowell* foundered between Chicago and Michigan City on December 3, 1893.

14. The tug *Welcome* (1st), official no. 80582, was built in 1876 by Wolf & Davidson for the Milwaukee Tug Boat Line. Her original measurements were 56.65 gross tons, 28.33 net tons, and 82.0 × 17.5 × 8.9 feet. She was rebuilt and renamed *George T. Nelles*, official no. 202985, in 1906 and was abandoned in 1926.

15. The tug *J. J. Hagerman*, official no. 75591, was built in 1872 at Buffalo, New York, by George H. Notter for the Milwaukee Tug Boat Line with measurements of 42.81 gross tons, 21.41 net tons, and 67.4 × 16.4 × 8.6 feet. The *Hagerman* was

renamed *Edward E. Gillen* (1st) and rebuilt in 1915, was severely burned and reported abandoned in 1928, and was put in the Sturgeon Bay boneyard, where she still could be seen in 1933 or 1934.

16. *Milwaukee Sentinel*, Milwaukee, Wisconsin, June 15, 1883.

17. *Milwaukee Sentinel*, Milwaukee, Wisconsin, July 3, 1883; Annual Report of the U.S. Life-Saving Service 1883, p. 287. In the latter reference, the estimated loss is $5,300, which is in good agreement with the $5,000 given as the cost of releasing and repairing the wreck.

18. *Milwaukee Sentinel*, Milwaukee, Wisconsin, July 10, 1883.

19. *Milwaukee Sentinel*, Milwaukee, Wisconsin, November 21, 1883.

20. The tug *Caroline Williams*, official no. 5811, was built in 1868 at Buffalo, New York, by Henry Williams for John Canfield of Manistee. She burned on April 22, 1884, about 15 miles southwest of Grand Point Sable while towing the wrecked schooner *Watertown* from Manistee to Chicago.

21. Annual Report of the U.S. Life-Saving Service 1884, p. 148.

22. Annual Report of the U.S. Life-Saving Service 1907, pp. 105, 246, 247.

23. Annual Report of the U.S. Life-Saving Service 1908, pp. 139, 238, 239, 264.

24. The schooner *Major N. H. Ferry*, official no. 16631, was built in 1867 at Ferrysburg, Michigan, by H. C. Pierson for William M. and Thomas W. Ferry of Grand Haven as equal owners. She was sold Canadian in 1909 and was reported broken in June 1913.

25. The steamer *J. S. Crouse*, official no. 77313, was built in 1898 at Saugatuck, Michigan, by R. C. Brittain for his own use in the coarse freight and lumber trade. She burned on November 15, 1919, while backing away from the D.H. Day Dock, Sleeping Bear Bay, at Glen Haven, Michigan. She rests in about 12 feet of water on the west side of the remains of the dock.

26. Annual Report of the U.S. Life-Saving Service 1908, p. 152.

27. *Door County Advocate*, Sturgeon Bay, Wisconsin, October 31, 1912.

28. From the Minutes of the Regular Meetings of the South Shore Yacht Club, Bay View, Wisconsin.

29. The schooner *Carrier*, official no. 4334, was built in 1865 as a barque at Marine City, Michigan, by David Lester for himself (1/3) and Chester Adams (2/3) of Hartford, Connecticut. The Lincoln Park Yacht Club acquired this schooner for use as a clubhouse in about 1914. On September 30, 1923, the *Carrier* foundered off Evanston, Illinois, while in tow of a subchaser from Lincoln Park to Waukegan.

30. Note 28, *supra*.

31. Note 15, *supra*.

32. Note 14, *supra*.

33. Note 28, *supra*.

34. Note 15, *supra*.

35. Note 28, *supra*.

36. *Ibid*.

NOTES—Chapter Eight

1. The tug *A. W. Lawrence*, official no. 105948, was built in 1880 at Sturgeon Bay, Wisconsin, by John Gregory of Chicago for the Sturgeon Bay Lumber Company, Augustus W. Lawrence, secretary. She was lost off Milwaukee on October 30, 1888, when her boiler exploded. The last document, issued at Milwaukee on May 15, 1888, was surrendered at Milwaukee on November 7, 1888; cause of surrender: vessel wrecked on October 30, 1888, total loss.

2. The tug *M. A. Gagnon*, official no. 90728, was built at Two Rivers in 1874 by Jasper Hanson for Peter, Joseph, Jonas, and Mary Ann Gagnon of Two Rivers as equal owners. She was sold to the U.S. Corps of Engineers in 1884, was renamed *Dionne*, was returned to commerce as the *Gagnon* in 1894, and was abandoned in 1909. The last certificate of enrollment, issued at Milwaukee on January 29, 1903, was surrendered at Milwaukee on June 18, 1909; cause of surrender: vessel abandoned.

3. George O. Spear was born in Maine in 1840 to Thomas and Amanda (Preble) Spear. He came to Wisconsin with his family in 1857 and worked in the shipyards at Fort Howard (Green Bay), Peshtigo, Little Sturgeon Bay, and Pensaukee with his father, a master builder. In 1879, he moved to Sturgeon Bay, where he purchased the McMaster property, which consisted of a sawmill and about 2,000 acres of land. Spear believed that "dummies," tugs towing scows without masts, would replace the schooners for carrying lumber and stone to Chicago and other ports on Lake Michigan. Also see p. 55.

4. The tug *Thomas Spear*, official no. 145216, was built in 1880 at Sturgeon Bay by Thomas Spear of Green Bay for George O. Spear of Sturgeon Bay. The last document, issued at Milwaukee on May 15, 1880, was surrendered at Milwaukee on October 12, 1880; cause of surrender: total loss by fire on Lake Michigan, September 22, 1880.

5. The tug *Winslow* (1st) was built at Cleveland, Ohio, in 1862 by Quayle and Martin for H. J. and N. C. Winslow of Cleveland. She was wrecked in Cleveland Harbor on October 7, 1864, and the machinery was put into the new hull by Quayle and Martin in 1865. The measurements of the *Winslow* (2d), official no. 26243, were 129.3 × 21.9 × 10.9 feet at 210.67 total tons. She was sold Canadian, 96855, in 1902 and burned in Meldrum Bay en route to Georgian Bay on April 21, 1911.

NOTES—Chapter Nine

1. The schooner *Trial*, official no. 24233, was built at Manitowoc in 1857 by Green S. Rand. The last enrollment was issued at Milwaukee on March 19, 1874, and was surrendered at Milwaukee on November 15, 1883; cause of surrender: vessel wrecked.

2. *Door County Advocate*, Sturgeon Bay, Wisconsin, December 9, 1893.

3. *Door County Advocate*, Sturgeon Bay, Wisconsin, September 30, 1976.

4. The schooner *Surprise*, official no. 22581, was built at Milan, Ohio, in 1856. The last enrollment, issued at Milwaukee on June 3, 1898, was surrendered at Milwaukee on May 23, 1900; cause of surrender: abandoned.

5. The steam barge *Wm. Rudolph*, official no. 80762, was built in 1880 at Mount Clemens, Michigan, by R. J. Kandt. The last enrollment, issued at Milwaukee on June 16, 1908, was surrendered at Milwaukee on November 15, 1913; cause of surrender: abandoned.

6. *Door County Advocate*, Sturgeon Bay, Wisconsin, November 23, 1895.

7. The Canadian schooner-barge *Minnedosa*, C94884, was built in 1890 at Kingston, Ontario, for the Montreal Trans. Co.

8. Annual Report of the U.S. Life-Saving Service 1907, pp. 109, 240, 241.

9. The steel steamer *Wyandotte*, official no. 205458, was built in 1908 at Ecorse, Michigan, by the Great Lakes Engineering Works for the Wyandotte Transportation Co. She was the first vessel constructed with self-unloading equipment and was cut up for scrap in 1967.

10. "The *Nielsen* Experience," *Diving Times*, vol. 5, no. 2, April/May 1982, p. 1.

11. General Regulations Under the Customs and Navigation Laws of the United States, Government Printing Office, Washington, D.C., 1864 and 1874.

NOTES—Chapter Ten

1. The schooner *J. I. Case*, official no. 75720, was built in 1874 at Manitowoc by Rand and Burger with measurements of 827.90 gross tons, 786.41 net tons, and 208.0 × 34.5 × 14.5 feet with three masts. She was sold Canadian, C141595, in 1919 and was towed out into the St. Lawrence River and sunk by her last owners, the Sin-Mac Lines, Ltd., of Montreal in 1936.

2. The revenue cutter *Andrew Johnson* was built in 1865 at Buffalo, New York, for the U.S. Revenue Service. She was sold to the Cleveland Naval Reserve for $2,250 in 1897 and was eventually abandoned at Bois Blanc Island, Detroit River, filled in with stone blasted from the river, and used as a dock.

3. The tug *Leviathan*, official no. 14612, was built in 1857 at Buffalo, New York, by Buel B. Jones. She was a large and powerful wrecker with new measurements of 232.44 gross tons, 129.05 net tons, and 126.0 × 25.8 × 9.0 feet. On November 12, 1891, the *Leviathan* burned at Cheboygan, Michigan, and was a total loss.

4. The tug *Henry S. Sill*, official no. 95382, was built in 1875 at Buffalo, New York, with measurements of 35.41 gross tons, 17.71 net tons, and 62.8 × 15.8 × 7.5 feet. The last document of the *Sill* was surrendered at Detroit on May 24, 1913; cause of surrender: vessel lost by fire.

5. The schooner *Flying Cloud*, official no. 9196, was built in 1851 at Clayton, New York. On October 29, 1892, she stranded on rocks at Glen Arbor, Michigan; the vessel and its cargo became a total loss.

6. The schooner *Christina Nilsson*, official no. 125293, was built in 1871 at Manitowoc by Jasper Hanson for Charles M. Lindgren of Chicago. Her measurements were 311.36 gross tons, 295.79 net tons, and 139.4 × 26.0 × 11.4 feet with three masts.

7. Inland Lloyds Vessel Register, Buffalo: Printing House of Matthews, Northrup & Co., 1882, p. 69, 1884, p. 70.

8. The tug *John Gregory*, official no. 76025, was built in 1878 at Green Bay, Wisconsin, by John Gregory of Chicago with measurements of 75.25 gross tons, 46.34 net tons, and 80.0 × 17.0 × 9.3 feet. On November 13, 1904, the tug capsized at the entrance to Cleveland Harbor during strong winds, drowning her captain and blocking the harbor. The last document of the *Gregory* was surrendered at Cleveland on January 24, 1905; cause of surrender: vessel lost.

9. The steam barge *Grace Williams*, official no. 85882, was built in 1885 at Manitowoc, one block north of the harbor, by Capt. F. P. Williams. Her measurements were 22.91 gross tons, 11.66 net tons, and 48.0 × 12.2 × 5.0 feet. The *Williams* foundered in a gale near North Manitou Island, Lake Michigan, on May 28, 1896, while in tow of the tug *Temple Emery*.

10. The steamer *St. Maries*, official no. 115473, was built in 1875 at Sugar Island, Michigan, and stranded four miles south of Sturgeon Point, Michigan, Lake Huron, on August 30, 1892. The last enrollment was surrendered at Port Huron on September 5, 1892; cause of surrender: burned.

11. The schooner *Transit*, official no. 24231, was built in 1854 at Manitowoc, Wisconsin, by H. Rand. The last document of the *Transit* was surrendered at Milwaukee on September 25, 1891; cause of surrender: total loss.

12. The schooner *Glen Cuyler*, official no. 10338, was built in 1859 at Pultneyville, New York. She was rebuilt several times, received a gasoline engine in 1908, and was reported abandoned on April 19, 1918.

13. The schooner *Industry*, official no. 100023, was built in 1870 at Manitowoc, Wisconsin, by Peter Larson with measure-

ments of 55.66 gross tons, 52.88 net tons, and 73.5 × 18.5 × 6.0 feet with two masts. Her last document was surrendered at Grand Haven on March 1, 1918; cause of surrender: abandoned.

14. The schooner *Minnehaha*, official no. 90584, was built in 1872 at Manitowoc, Wisconsin, with measurements of 59.37 gross tons, 56.41 net tons, and 71.2 × 18.4 × 6.6 feet with two masts. She stranded in a high wind and sea three miles east of South Chicago at 3:00 A.M. on July 3, 1909, becoming a total loss.

15. The schooner *Arctic*, official no. 359, was built in 1853 at Ashtabula, Ohio, with measurements of $256^{61}/_{95}$ tons old measure, length 112 feet, breadth $25^{8}/_{12}$ feet, and depth $9^{10}/_{12}$ feet with two masts. She was sunk by collision with the steamer *Clyde* nine miles off Point aux Barques on September 17, 1895.

16. The fish tug *L.P. Hill*, official no. 141026, was built in 1889 at Fish Creek, Wisconsin, by W. W. Hill with measurements of 22.58 gross tons, 11.29 net tons, and 58.8 × 14.8 × 5.6 feet. Her last enrollment was surrendered at Milwaukee on February 14, 1914; cause of surrender: abandoned.

17. The fish tug *Maggie Lutz*, official no. 90582, was built in 1873 at Sheboygan, Wisconsin, by Robert Gray with measurements of 15.26 gross tons, 8.14 net tons, and 45.0 × 12.5 × 4.3 feet.

18. The schooner *Burt Barnes*, official no. 3193, was built in 1882 at Manitowoc, Wisconsin, by Green S. Rand with measurements of 134.06 gross tons, 127.36 net tons, and 95.5 × 24.5 × 7.3 feet with two masts. She was sold Canadian, C150489, in 1904 and foundered 12 miles from Picton, Ontario, near Braddock's Point, Lake Ontario, with 210 tons of coal on September 2, 1926.

19. The scow schooner *Laurel*, official no. 15409, was built in 1852 at Plaster Bend, Ohio, and was lost at the entrance to Detroit Harbor, Washington Island, in 1891.

20. The measurements of the scow schooner *Agnes Behrmann*, official no. 106189, were 110.93 gross tons, 105.39 net tons, and 91.7 × 24.9 × 6.7 feet with two masts.

21. Scows were not usually rated high because they had little dead rise and could not therefore be easily freed of water. That made them a relatively poor insurance risk.

NOTES — Chapter Eleven

1. Port of Chicago, July 5, 1873, enrollment no. 3.

2. This was the second *Glad Tidings*. The first *Glad Tidings* used by Captain Bundy measured three tons, the second measured thirty-three tons, and the third, built in 1883, measured sixty tons. The captain liked to offer these figures as some indication of the growth of Christianity on the islands of the lakes.

3. The scow schooner *Laurel*, official no. 15409, was built at Plaster Bend, Ohio, in 1852 and was lost at the entrance to Detroit Harbor, Washington Island, in 1891. The last enrollment, issued at Milwaukee on November 7, 1888, was surrendered at Milwaukee on December 21, 1891; cause of surrender: total loss.

4. The schooner *O.M. Nelson*, official no. 155066, was

built in 1882 at Suttons Bay, Michigan. Her dimensions were 167.23 gross tons, 158.87 net tons, and 107.7 × 25.3 × 8.4 feet with two masts. L. E. Bahle was the master carpenter, and O. M. Nelson and L. E. Bahle were equal owners. The last enrollment of the *Nelson*, issued at Milwaukee on June 2, 1899, was surrendered at Milwaukee on June 13, 1899; cause of surrender: total loss.

5. The side-wheel steamer *Corona*, official no. 125091, was built at Manitowoc, Wisconsin, for the Goodrich Transportation Co. by Greenleaf S. Rand in 1870. She was totally destroyed by fire at Edgewater, opposite Tonawanda, New York, where she was laid up for the season on November 17, 1898.

6. The tug *John Gregory*, official no. 76025, was built in

1878 at Green Bay, Wisconsin, by John Gregory of Chicago with measurements of 75.25 gross tons, 46.34 net tons, and 80.0 × 17.0 × 9.3 feet. On November 13, 1904, the tug capsized at the entrance to Cleveland Harbor during strong winds, drowning her captain and blocking the harbor. The last document of the *Gregory* was surrendered at Cleveland on January 24, 1905; cause of surrender: vessel lost.

7. The schooner *Delos DeWolf*, official no. 6327, was built in 1856 at Oswego, New York, and rebuilt in 1867 at 299.26 tons. She went from two to three masts in 1886 and measured 307.51 gross tons, 292.14 net tons. The last enrollment of the *DeWolf* was issued at Buffalo on April 16, 1900, and was surrendered at Buffalo on June 29, 1906; cause of surrender: abandoned.

8. The schooner *Willard A. Smith*, official no. 80587, was built in 1876 at Charlevoix, Michigan, with two masts at 20.90 tons. Her tonnage was changed to 44.22 gross tons, 42.01 net tons, in 1882 according to an enrollment issued at Grand Haven, Michigan, on June 25. The *Smith* pounded to pieces while lying at anchor near Anderson's Pier, Horseshoe Bay, Green Bay, on October 14, 1893. The last enrollment of the *Smith* was issued at Milwaukee on August 31, 1893, and was surrendered at Milwaukee on March 15, 1895; cause of surrender: abandoned.

9. The schooner *Lem Higby*, official no. 14804, was built in 1865 at Sheboygan, Wisconsin, by Amos C. Stokes for Sylvester B. Lyman with two masts at 35.34 tons. She was lengthened during the winter of 1867–68 to 83.3 × 17.0 × 5.3 feet at

52.93 tons by Smith and Hamilton. The last enrollment of the *Higby*, issued at Grand Haven, Michigan, on June 25, 1894, was surrendered at Grand Haven on June 21, 1898; cause of surrender: abandoned.

10. "The *William Aldrich*—She Outlived Her Time," p. 49.

11. The schooner *La Petite*, official no. 15100, was built in 1866 at Huron, Ohio, by F. D. Ketchum with two masts at 122.16 tons. She was enlarged to 172.05 gross tons, 163.45 net tons, with three masts in 1872. On September 7, 1903, she filled with heavy seas and capsized while in tow of the tug *Sydney Smith*; the line was cut, and she drifted ashore about seven miles south of the Sturgeon Bay Ship Canal at Clay Banks. The last enrollment of the *La Petite* was issued at Milwaukee on April 4, 1894, and was surrendered at Milwaukee on September 25, 1903; cause of surrender: vessel lost.

12. Wreck Report, Port of Milwaukee Custom House, November 29, 1911.

13. The steam barge *Helen Taylor*, official no. 96270, was built in 1894 at Grand Haven, Michigan, by Duncan Robertson with measurements of 82.87 gross tons, 55.39 net tons, and 56.4 × 30.2 × 3.8 feet. She foundered at Michigan City, Indiana, on January 1, 1930, with no one on board.

14. The fish tug *Freddie*, official no. 237558, was built in 1901 at Manitowoc, Wisconsin, by Burger with dimensions of 8 gross tons, 6 net tons, and 32.1 × 9.4 × 3.2 feet. The *Freddie* was abandoned in 1945.

NOTES—Chapter Twelve

1. "The *William Aldrich*—She Outlived Her Time," p. 49.

2. "Shipbuilding at Little Sturgeon Bay, 1866 to 1874," p. 22.

3. The schooner *Our Son*, official no. 19437, was built at Black River, Ohio, in 1875. On September 26, 1930, she waterlogged 40 miles west-southwest of Big Point Sable and foundered off Sheboygan in a gale with a load of pulpwood. The crew of seven were saved by the steamer *William Nelson*, Capt. Charles H. Mohr.

4. The schooner *Lucia A. Simpson*, official no. 140097, was built at Manitowoc, Wisconsin, in 1875. She lost her mizzenmast in a sudden squall about 12 miles off Algoma, Wisconsin, in 1929 and was towed to the boneyard in Sturgeon Bay, where she burned in the great fire at the yard of the Sturgeon Bay Shipbuilding and Dry Dock Company on the night of December 3, 1935.

5. The schooner *Mary Ellen Cook*, official no. 90763, was built at Grand Haven, Michigan, in 1875. She was used as a landing dock for yachtsmen in front of the Door County Country Club at Sturgeon Bay and was reported abandoned in 1923.

6. Port of Milwaukee July 19, 1856, enrollment no. 53. National Archives, Industrial and Social Branch, Washington, D.C. 20408.

7. "Marine Casualties 1863 to 1873," Microcopy No. T729; National Archives, Industrial and Social Branch, Washington, D.C. 20408.

8. The side-wheel steamer *Sarah Van Eps*, official no. 22585, was built at Green Bay, Wisconsin, in 1862 and was abandoned in 1878.

9. The schooner *Josephine Lawrence*, official no. 12976, was built at Milwaukee, Wisconsin, in 1854 with measurements of 110²⁶⁄₉₅ tons old measure, length 85 feet, breadth 21⁹⁄₁₂ feet, and depth 7 feet with two masts. The last enrollment of the *Lawrence* was surrendered at Milwaukee on October 16, 1880; cause of surrender: total loss, stranded near Bailey's Harbor, Wisconsin, October 16, 1880.

10. The schooner *L. J. Conway*, official no. 15955, was built at Manitowoc, Wisconsin, in 1873. Her measurements were 90.45 gross tons, 85.93 net tons, and 80.6 × 21.6 × 6.4 feet with two masts. The *Conway* foundered seven miles north of White Lake, Michigan, near Fowler Creek on November 17, 1886, losing the entire crew.

11. The schooner *Lettie May*, official no. 140063, was built at Fort Howard, Wisconsin, in 1874 by Simeon Vaughan of Fort Howard for M. F. Kalmbach of Fort Howard. Her measurements were 47.4 × 14.2 × 7.0 feet at 29.21 total tons with two masts. The last document of the *Lettie May* of St. James, Michigan, was surrendered at Grand Haven on September 25, 1906; cause of surrender: struck a rock off Skilligallee Light, Michigan, October 5, 1905.

12. The schooner *Cascade*, official no. 4573, was built in 1853 at Black River, Ohio, by William Jones for Charles Hickox

of Cleveland, Ohio. Her measurements were 335³⁵/₉₅ tons old measure, length 129²/₁₂ feet, breadth 25²⁵/₁₂ feet, and depth 11¹/₁₂ feet with two masts. The last enrollment was surrendered at Cleveland on August 31, 1899; cause of surrender: vessel sank.

13. The schooner *James Platt*, official no. 13302, was built in 1863 at Oswego, New York, by George Goble for himself and Daniel G. Fort as equal owners. Her measurements were 441⁸⁷/₉₅ tons old measure, length 139 feet, breadth 26 feet, and depth 13¹/₁₂ feet with two masts. The *Platt* went ashore on South Fox Island on November 24, 1881, becoming a total wreck. The captain and woman cook were drowned; the remainder of the crew was rescued by the lightkeeper after being exposed to the elements for 48 hours.

14. The schooner *Peoria*, official no. 19668, was built at Black River, Ohio, in 1854 by A. Gilmore for Charles H. Livingston and E. P. Frink as equal owners, both of Black River. Her measurements were 226⁴/₉₅ tons old measure, length 113⁷/₁₂ feet, breadth 24⁴/₁₂ feet, and depth 8¹¹/₁₂ feet with two masts. The last enrollment of the *Peoria* of Charlevoix was surrendered at Grand Haven, Michigan, on December 20, 1901; cause of surrender: wrecked—total loss.

15. The schooner barge *Brunette*, official no. 2756, was built in 1871 at Gibralter, Michigan, by Linn & Craig with measurements of 738.64 gross tons, 711.21 net tons, and 215.8 × 35.5 × 13.1 feet with three short masts. She was renamed *Buffalo* in 1902 and was sold Canadian in 1913.

16. The steamship *W.L. Wetmore*, official no. 80196, was built in 1871 at Cleveland by Quayle and Martin for George W. Bissell of Detroit with measurements of 850.57 gross tons, 785.00 net tons, and 215.4 × 33.4 × 14.2 feet. The last document of the *Wetmore* was surrendered at Buffalo on January 25, 1902; cause of surrender: vessel lost.

17. The tug *A.W. Lawrence*, official no. 105948, was launched in May 1880 at Sturgeon Bay by John Gregory of Chicago for the Sturgeon Bay Lumber Company. The boiler of the *Lawrence* exploded off Milwaukee on October 30, 1888, and she became a total loss.

18. The tug *Balize*, official no. 2714, was built in 1863 at Cleveland, Ohio, as the *Mary Grandy*. She was bought by the U.S. Navy on August 2, 1864, for $56,100 and was renamed *Bignonia*. After the war, she was sold at auction for $22,500, was redocumented *Balize* on September 19, 1865, and came to Detroit in 1867. In 1903, the *Balize* was sold Canadian, C100306, and was last shown in Canadian Merchant Vessels 1919 as owned by John Charlton, Lynedock, Ontario.

19. The tug *Alfred P. Wright*, official no. 105722, was built in 1877 at Buffalo, New York, with measurements of 56.18 gross tons, 28.09 net tons, and 71.1 × 16.8 × 9.0 feet. She stranded three miles north of Manistee, Michigan, on November 29, 1886, and the last document of the *Wright* was surrendered

at Grand Haven on December 17, 1886; cause of surrender: abandoned.

20. The tug *John Gregory*, official no. 76205, was built in 1878 at Green Bay, Wisconsin, by John Gregory of Chicago with measurements of 75.25 gross tons, 46.34 net tons, and 80.0 × 17.0 × 9.3 feet. On November 13, 1904, the tug capsized at the entrance to Cleveland Harbor during strong winds, drowning her captain and blocking the harbor. The last document of the *Gregory* was surrendered at Cleveland on January 24, 1905; cause of surrender: vessel lost.

21. The tug *John Leathem*, official no. 76064, was built in 1878 at Sturgeon Bay by John Gregory of Chicago for Scofield & Co. of Sturgeon Bay with measurements of 75.25 gross tons, 38.61 net tons, and 80.0 × 17.0 × 8.5 feet. She was renamed *Holliswood* in 1921 and went to the East Coast, where she stranded in New Jersey in 1925.

22. The tug *W.C. Tillson*, official no. 80599, was built at Sheboygan, Wisconsin, in 1876 by Charles Huntley with measurements of 49.44 gross tons, 24.72 net tons, and 53.6 × 15.7 × 7.0 feet. The *Tillson* was destroyed by fire on October 30, 1889, while towing two rafts of logs from Peshtigo, Wisconsin, to Sturgeon Bay, the accident happening only about one mile from the mouth of the bay. The last document of the *Tillson* was surrendered at Milwaukee on November 6, 1889; cause of surrender: total loss.

23. The tug *Leviathan*, official no. 14612, was built in 1857 at Buffalo, New York, by Buel B. Jones. She was a large and powerful wrecker with new measurements of 232.44 gross tons, 129.05 net tons, and 126.0 × 25.8 × 9.0 feet. On November 12, 1891, the *Leviathan* burned at Cheboygan, Michigan, and was a total loss.

24. The tug *Caroline Williams*, official no. 5811, was built in 1868 at Buffalo, New York, by Henry Williams for John Canfield of Manistee, Michigan. She burned on April 22, 1884, about 15 miles southwest of Grand Point Sable while towing the wrecked schooner *Watertown* from Manistee to Chicago.

25. The tug *Satisfaction*, official no. 116628, was built in 1894 at Sheboygan, Wisconsin, with measurements of 47.75 gross tons, 23.88 net tons, and 64.0 × 16.0 × 8.0 feet. In 1946, she was abandoned and dismantled at Green Bay, and her remains were deposited alongside the tug *Bob Teed* in the boneyard on the Fort Howard side.

26. The schooner *Rouse Simmons*, official no. 110024 (to 1884) and 110087 (from 1885), was built in 1868 at Milwaukee, Wisconsin, and foundered off Two Rivers, Wisconsin, with a cargo of Christmas trees on November 23, 1912.

27. From the *Edward E. Skeele* file of the Wisconsin Marine Historical Society Collection, Milwaukee Public Library, Milwaukee, Wisconsin.

28. "Where is the *Two Friends?*—A Story of North Bay," p. 3.

APPENDIXES

APPENDIX A

Data for Vessels
Built or Rebuilt
at Little Sturgeon Bay

NAME	OFFICIAL NO.	BUILT	BY	TONS	LENGTH	BREADTH	DEPTH	RIG
F. B. GARDNER		1855	A. Gilson	$460^{78}/_{95}$	$138^{7}/_{12}$	$31^{6}/_{12}$	$11^{7}/_{12}$	Brig – 2 mast
(Rebuilt)	9198	1866	T. Spear	422.51	172.6	31.3	10.6	Barque – 3 mast
UNION		1862	S. C. Fowles	118	110.0	26.0		Tug
(Rebuilt)	25047	1866		118.95	111.0	16.9	6.0	Steamer
JOHN SPRY	75599	1866	T. Spear	55.46	92.0	15.0	5.0	Steamboat
OZAUKEE		1857		$102^{70}/_{95}$	92.8	17.5	6.5	Tug
(Rebuilt)	19002	1868		66.57	94.0	17.5	6.2	Steamer
PENSAUKEE later *JAMES G. BLAINE*	20195	1867	T. Spear	579.23	177.0	33.7	12.8	Barque – 3 mast later Schooner – 3 mast
LAKE FOREST	15578	1869	T. Spear	332.44	146.7	29.0	11.1	Schooner – 2 mast later 3 mast
NORMAN		1848	Ellenwood	$345^{53}/_{95}$	135.25	26.0	10.5	Barque – 3 mast
(Rebuilt)	18101	1871		251.74	134.35	26.0	9.9	Schooner - 3 mast
HALSTED	95260	1873	T. Spear	496.53	171.1	33.4	12.4	Schooner – 3 mast
ELLEN SPRY	8983	1873	A. M. Spear	545.68	172.75	33.0	13.1	Schooner – 3 mast
J. W. DOANE	75660	1874	A. M. Spear	617.02	183.5	33.3	13.6	Schooner – 3 mast

All of the above vessels were built or rebuilt at Little Sturgeon Bay for F. B. Gardner, with the exception of the *Lake Forest* and the *Halsted*. The *Lake Forest* was built for E. Bailey and T. Vincent. The construction of the *Halsted* was ordered by F. B. Gardner, but because of business reverses was constructed for H. S. Halsted of Chicago.

APPENDIX B

Enrollments and Registers (R)
for Vessels Built or Rebuilt
at Little Sturgeon Bay

PORT	DATE	DOCUMENT NO.	MANAGING OWNER	MASTER	RIG
		F. B. GARDNER, Official No. 9198			
Chicago	October 11, 1855	104	F. B. Gardner	James Flood	Brig
Chicago	July 2, 1857	82	S. Lird	C. Childs	Brig
Chicago	April 10, 1858	8	F. B. Gardner	C. Childs	Brig
Chicago	September 17, 1861	83	Hugh T. Dickey	William Casey	Brig
Chicago	April 25, 1865	265	F. B. Gardner	Nicholas Morgan	Brig
Chicago	July 28, 1866	30	F. B. Gardner	Nicholas Morgan	Barque
Chicago	April 20, 1867	343	J. P. Merrill	George O. Baker	Barque
Chicago	April 18, 1868	296	Henry K. Elkins	George O. Baker	Barque
Cleveland	April 29, 1872	8(R)	Henry K. Elkins	George O. Baker	Barque
Chicago	May 13, 1872	138	Henry K. Elkins	George O. Baker	Schooner
Port Huron	April 24, 1874	4(R)	Henry K. Elkins	J. B. Gibbs	Schooner
Chicago	August 4, 1874	12	Henry K. Elkins	J. B. Gibbs	Schooner
Chicago	April 9, 1877	32	William Weinert	J. B. Gibbs	Schooner
Chicago	August 12, 1879	15	Henry S. Halsted	John Foster	Schooner
Chicago	October 14, 1879	44	Henry S. Halsted	John Foster	Schooner
Buffalo	March 24, 1884	28	John Connelly	William Williams	Schooner
Port Huron	February 16, 1901	25	John C. Pringle	John C. Pringle	Schooner
Port Huron	March 4, 1902	34	John C. Pringle	J. Burk	Schooner

Surrendered at Port Huron September 16, 1904. Vessel burned off Forester, Lake Huron, September 15, 1904.

PORT	DATE	DOCUMENT NO.	MANAGING OWNER	MASTER	RIG
		UNION, Official No. 25047			
Chicago	November 7, 1865	570	F. B. Gardner	John Howlett	Steamer
Milwaukee	June 6, 1866	208	A. C. Brown	Joseph A. Monroe	Steamer
Milwaukee	September 4, 1867	23	William J. Fisk	Martin Goldin	Steamer
Milwaukee	September 25, 1869	32	Lewis J. Day	Thomas Hawley	Steamer
Milwaukee	June 23, 1874	178	Thomas Hawley	Thomas Hawley	Steamer
Milwaukee	May 16, 1876	117	Thomas Hawley	Thomas Hawley	Steamer

Surrendered June 30, 1881, at Milwaukee. Vessel dismantled and abandoned.

PORT	DATE	DOCUMENT NO.	MANAGING OWNER	MASTER	RIG
		JOHN SPRY, Official No. 75599			
Chicago	April 25, 1873	237	F. B. Gardner	F. B. Gardner	Steamboat
Chicago	May 16, 1876	103	F. B. Gardner	F. B. Gardner	Steamboat
Milwaukee	May 3, 1877	81	William H. Baptist	William H. Baptist	Steamer
Milwaukee	June 22, 1878	111	William H. Baptist	William H. Baptist	Steamer
Milwaukee	October 6, 1882	34	F. J. Page	F. J. Page	Steamer
Milwaukee	June 30, 1885	91	A. J. Cointe	A. J. Cointe	Steamer

Surrendered November 23, 1885, at Milwaukee. Vessel burned, total loss.

PORT	DATE	DOCUMENT NO.	MANAGING OWNER	MASTER	RIG
		OZAUKEE, Official No. 19002			
Chicago	July 7, 1857	84	Alva Trowbridge	L. L. Slyfield	Tug
Chicago	July 21, 1860	57	Jakob Beidler	Jakob Beidler	Tug
St. Louis	October 6, 1865	181	Isaac Walton	Isaac Walton	Steamer
Chicago	September 6, 1867	63	F. B. Gardner	F. B. Gardner	Tug Propeller
Chicago	February 6, 1868	179	Erastus Bailey	Erastus Bailey	Tug Propeller

*Names are written here as they appeared in the documents. As a result, spellings vary.

PORT	DATE	DOCUMENT NO.	MANAGING OWNER	MASTER	RIG
Chicago	May 3, 1870	201	F. B. Gardner	William H. Baptist	Tug
Milwaukee	May 7, 1879	103	J. R. Shepard	Charles Call	Tug
Marquette	February 11, 1880	11	H. J. James	H. J. James	Tug
Marquette	March 29, 1883	15	H. J. James	H. J. James	Paddle Steamer

Surrendered June 11, 1884, at Marquette. Loss of Steamer at Bad River, May 27, 1884.

PENSAUKEE, *Official No. 20195*
(later JAMES G. BLAINE)

PORT	DATE	DOCUMENT NO.	MANAGING OWNER	MASTER	RIG
Chicago	July 8, 1867	10	F. B. Gardner	Childs	Barque
Erie	August 2, 1869				
Chicago	August 16, 1869	32	F. B. Gardner	P. Myers	Barque
Chicago	July 22, 1872	15	J. S. Dunham	P. Myers	Barque
Buffalo	July 26, 1873	3(R)	Pat. Myers	Pat. Myers	Barque
Chicago	August 6, 1873	16	J. S. Dunham	P. Myers	Barque
Chicago	October 9, 1874	25	J. S. Dunham	T. Fountain	Schooner
Chicago	May 6, 1878	94	T. Fountain	T. Fountain	Schooner
Chicago	April 25, 1879	32			
Chicago	March 29, 1887	52	J. S. Dunham	William Griffin	Schooner
Chicago	December 11, 1890	41	J. S. Dunham	J. S. Dunham	Schooner
Chicago	April 5, 1900	114	Waide Transpor. Co.	Arnold Green	Barge
Oswego	March 24, 1902	2	Charles H. Ripsom		Barge
Buffalo	April 15, 1904	62	Walter K. Fullum		Barge
Buffalo	May 23, 1907	119	Geo. Hall Coal Co.		Barge
Ogdensburg	May 28, 1907	7	Geo. Hall Coal Co.	Samuel LaFlam	Barge

Surrendered March 31, 1909, at Ogdensburg. Vessel wrecked, total loss.

LAKE FOREST, *Official No. 15578*

PORT	DATE	DOCUMENT NO.	MANAGING OWNER	MASTER	RIG
Chicago	May 19, 1869	281	Erastus Bailey	R. J. Stubbs	Schooner
Chicago	March 19, 1870	134	F. B. Gardner		Schooner
Chicago	March 21, 1870	136	Henry S. Halsted	F. Brown	Schooner
Chicago	January 5, 1876	40	W. Winert	W. Nelson	Schooner
Grand Haven	April 10, 1879	46	J. Guilick	H. H. Kramer	Schooner
Milwaukee	March 27, 1882	102	H. H. Kramer	C. Rayman	Schooner
Chicago	October 29, 1886	21	W. D. Hitchcock	William Mahlman	Schooner
Chicago	July 31, 1891	9	W. D. Hitchcock	G. H. Mahlman	Schooner
Chicago	April 4, 1892	43	W. D. Hitchcock	G. H. Mahlman	Schooner
Chicago	April 15, 1893	74	W. D. Hitchcock	A. Waskow	Schooner
Chicago	March 21, 1896	76	Charles E. Hinds	A. Waskow	Schooner
Chicago	May 23, 1898	61	Charles E. Hinds	A. Waskow	Schooner
Chicago	January 23, 1900	84	James T. Johnson	James T. Johnson	Schooner
Milwaukee	April 1, 1902	87	James E. Erickson	James E. Erickson	Schooner
Milwaukee	April 14, 1908	68	Christ. Nerdrum	Christ. Nerdrum	Schooner

Surrendered March 7, 1910, at Chicago. Dismantled and converted into a barge.

NORMAN, *Official No. 18101*

PORT	DATE	DOCUMENT NO.	MANAGING OWNER	MASTER	RIG
Oswego	October 6, 1848	49	D. C. Littlejohn		Barque
Oswego	April 4, 1853	10	James Peck	J. H. Redfield	Barque
Chicago	April 1, 1854	25	James Peck	Andrew I. Sucas	Barque
Chicago	March 5, 1862	9	Jabiz K. Botsford	Jabiz K. Botsford	Barque
Chicago	March 5, 1862	11	Samuel Howe	Samuel Howe	Barque
Chicago	May 13, 1862	85	Howard C. Gardiner	T. M. Hansen	Barque
Chicago	April 25, 1865	266	F. B. Gardner	Patrick Meyers	Barque
Chicago	April 24, 1867	354	Joseph McGee	P. Myers	Barque
Chicago	April 21, 1870	191	F. B. Gardner	Thomas Myers	Barque
Chicago	April 25, 1873	236	J. S. Dunham	Thomas Meyers	Schooner
Troy	April 29, 1878	42	Alfred Mosher	J. C. Dickson	Schooner

PORT	DATE	DOCUMENT NO.	MANAGING OWNER	MASTER	RIG
Chicago	May 2, 1879	37(R)	J. C. Dickson	J. C. Dickson	Schooner
Chicago	February 25, 1881	62	John Hanson	John Hanson	Schooner
Chicago	March 30, 1883	56	John Hanson	John Hanson	Schooner
Chicago	April 3, 1884	50	John Hanson	John Hanson	Schooner
Chicago	March 25, 1892	38	John Hanson	Christian Larson	Schooner
Chicago	August 14, 1895	23	Henry Hust	Christian Larson	Schooner

Surrendered June 22, 1901, at Chicago. Dismantled and abandoned as unfit for service.

HALSTED, Official No. 95260

PORT	DATE	DOCUMENT NO.	MANAGING OWNER	MASTER	RIG
Chicago	May 23, 1873	254	Henry S. Halsted	John G. Keith	Schooner
Chicago	May 29, 1874	229	Henry S. Halsted	John G. Keith	Schooner
Marquette	June 16, 1877	1(T)*	Henry S. Halsted	John G. Keith	Schooner
Chicago	July 16, 1877	5	Henry S. Halsted	John G. Keith	Schooner
Chicago	August 29, 1888	21	Annie Halsted	George Pollock	Schooner
Chicago	September 6, 1892	16	John Kelley	T. E. Johnson	Schooner
Marquette	September 24, 1892	21	E. A. Shores	T. E. Johnson	Schooner
Chicago	April 19, 1899	67	Soper Lumber Co.	Alex. C. Soper	Schooner
Chicago	March 31, 1900	109	Soper Lumber Co.	John Lundberg	Schooner
Chicago	February 11, 1901	23	Soper Lumber Co.	John Lundberg	Schooner-barge
Chicago	April 30, 1912	80	Soper Lumber Co.	James P. Soper	Schooner-barge
Chicago	August 22, 1912	9	Soper Lumber Co.	Rudolph Peterson	Schooner-barge
Milwaukee	June 29, 1914	364	Greiling Bros. Co.	Herman A. Greiling	Schooner-barge
Marquette	May 10, 1916	14	National Pole Co.	Carl Johnson	Schooner-barge
Chicago	May 4, 1917	49	National Transit Co.	Homer J. Carr	Schooner-barge
Chicago	April 19, 1920	35	National Transit Co.	Floyd A. Deahl	Schooner-barge
Chicago	June 29, 1922	51	National Transit Co.	M. E. Brown	Schooner-barge
Cleveland	June 19, 1923	58	Smeed Box Co.	G. F. Forrest	Schooner-barge

Surrendered at Cleveland December 29, 1930. Abandoned, sold for junk.

ELLEN SPRY, Official No. 8983

PORT	DATE	DOCUMENT NO.	MANAGING OWNER	MASTER	RIG
Chicago	September 24, 1873	63	F. B. Gardner	H. Ruther	Schooner
Chicago	April 27, 1874	209	John Spry	T. Myers	Schooner
Buffalo	May 10, 1876	7(T)	John Spry	T. Myers	Schooner
Chicago	May 29, 1876	107	John Spry	T. Myres	Schooner
Chicago	September 6, 1883	14	H. H. Gardner	A. C. Wilson	Schooner
Chicago	April 26, 1884	90	William G. Keith	A. Eade	Schooner
Chicago	May 7, 1885	63	William G. Keith	Alf. Eado	Schooner
Chicago	April 14, 1886	48	William G. Keith	Fred Ahlstrom	Schooner

Surrendered December 11, 1886, at Chicago. Vessel lost. Foundered in Lake Michigan November 6, 1886.

J. W. DOANE, Official No. 75660

PORT	DATE	DOCUMENT NO.	MANAGING OWNER	MASTER	RIG
Chicago	May 18, 1874	227	F. B. Gardner	P. Myres	Schooner
Chicago	July 15, 1874	4	G. Kent	P. Myers	Schooner
Chicago	February 17, 1880	71	Wiley M. Egan	R. H. Long	Schooner

Surrendered December 6, 1883, at Chicago. Vessel lost near Buffalo, N.Y., in November 1882. Total wreck.

*Temporary enrollment

BIBLIOGRAPHY

U.S. Government Documents,
National Archives, Washington, D.C.

Master Abstracts of Enrollments issued at: Milwaukee, Chicago, Green Bay, Toledo, Detroit, Michilimackinac, Sault Ste. Marie, Buffalo, Cleveland, Sandusky, Port Huron, Grand Haven, Duluth, Marquette, Oswego, Ogdensburg, Erie, Suspension Bridge, Cape Vincent, Dunkirk, French Creek, Rochester, and Sacketts Harbor.

Certificates of Enrollment issued at: Milwaukee, Chicago, Green Bay, Detroit, Michilimackinac, Sault Ste. Marie, Buffalo, and Sandusky.

Registers issued at Great Lakes' ports.

Annual Reports of the U.S. Life-Saving Service, 1876 through 1913.

Collectors of Customs Reports of Casualty from the Custom House Districts (Wreck Reports): Chicago, Detroit, Duluth, Erie, Milwaukee, and Oswegatchie.

Newspapers

Door County Advocate, Sturgeon Bay, Wisconsin, 1862 to present.

Milwaukee Sentinel, 1837 to present.

Milwaukee Sentinel Index, 1837 to 1890, Local History and Marine Room, Milwaukee Public Library.

Chicago Inter-Ocean, 1872 to 1914.

Chicago Tribune, 1860 to present.

Detroit Free Press, 1858 to present.

Insurance Records

1860. Lake Vessel Register, Board of Lake Underwriters. Buffalo, New York.

1866. Lake Vessel Register, Board of Lake Underwriters. Buffalo, N.Y.: Matthews and Warren.

1875. Classification, National Board of Lake Underwriters. Buffalo: Printing House of Matthews & Warren.

1879. Lake Hull Register, Association of Lake Underwriters. Detroit: Free Press Book and Job Printing House.

1882. Vessel Classification of The Inland Lloyds. American Hulls. Buffalo: Printing House of Matthews, Northrup & Co.

1884. Vessel Classification of The Inland Lloyds. American Hulls. Buffalo, New York. Printing House of Matthews, Northrup & Co.

1885. Vessel Classification of The Inland Lloyds. American Hulls. Buffalo, New York. Printing House of James D. Warren.

1887. The Inland Lloyds Vessel Register. Buffalo, N.Y. Printing House of James D. Warren's Sons.

1889. The Inland Lloyds Vessel Register. Buffalo, N.Y. Art-Printing Works of Matthews, Northrup & Co.

1890. The Inland Lloyds Vessel Register. Buffalo and New York. Art-Printing Works of Matthews, Northrup & Co.

1891. The Inland Lloyds Vessel Register. Buffalo and New York. Art-Printing Works of Matthews, Northrup & Co.

1893. The Inland Lloyds Vessel Register. Detroit, Mich.: Wm. Suckert & Sons, Blank Book Manufacturers, Printers &c.

1894. The Inland Lloyds Vessel Register. Cleveland, Ohio, W. R. Smellie, Printer and Blank Book Manufacturer.

1895. The Inland Lloyds Vessel Register. Cleveland, Ohio, W. R. Smellie, Printer and Blank Book Manufacturer.

1897. The Inland Lloyds Vessel Register. Buffalo, N.Y. Printing House of James D. Warren's Sons.

1899. The Inland Lloyds Vessel Register. The Buffalo Commercial Fire-Proof Printing House, James D. Warren's Sons, Proprietors.

1906. The Inland Lloyds Vessel Register. The Buffalo Commercial Fire-Proof Printing House, James D. Warren's Sons, Proprietors.

Others

The Marine Collection of the Wisconsin Marine Historical Society, Local History and Marine Room, Milwaukee Public Library.

Great Lakes Maritime History: Bibliography and Sources of Information by Dr. Charles E. Feltner and Jeri Baron Feltner, First Edition, December 1982, Seajay Publications, P.O. Box 2176, Dearborn, MI 48123.

INDEX OF VESSELS *

A. P. Nichols, 566, barque, schooner 33,*34*, 36, 38, 40, 42

A. W. Lawrence, 105948, tug 18, 82, 107

Active, 105087, schooner 69

Agnes Behrmann, 106189, scow schooner 97

Albert Soper, 105977, steam barge 28

Alfred P. Wright, 105722, tug 107

Alpena, 404, side-wheel steamer 3, *3*, 33

America, 105244 and 105337, schooner 81, *81, 83*

Andrew Johnson, U.S. revenue cutter 91,*92*

Ann Maria, 387, schooner 18

Annie Laura, 105106, steam barge 51

Arctic, 359, schooner 95

Arctic, 106040, tug *92*

Argo, steam sloop 43

Argo, 1427, side-wheel steamer 43

Argosy, 29296, barge 19

Arthur Orr, 107005, steel steamer 58

Balize, 2714, later Canadian 100306, wrecking tug 107

Black Hawk, 2140, schooner *100*

Brunette (later *Buffalo*), 2756, schooner barge 107, *107*

Buena Vista, 2241, schooner *36*

Buffalo (ex-*Brunette*), 2756, schooner barge *107*

Burt Barnes, 3193, later Canadian 150489, schooner 96, *96*

C. Amsden, 5054, schooner *85*

C. Harrison, 4569, schooner 40

C. Williams, also known as *Caroline Williams*, 5811, tug 76, 109

Canada (later *Schilde, Eureka*), Canadian 100392, propeller 53

Carrier, *4334*, barque, schooner 78

Cascade, 4573, schooner 106

Challenge, 4349, schooner 27, *27*, 49, *111*

Champion, 5720, wrecking tug 5, 19

Charles E. Wyman, 126005, later Canadian 134245, schooner 78

Charley J. Smith, 125749, scow schooner *95*

Christina Nilsson, 125293, schooner 92, 93, *93*

City of Madison, 4350, propeller 29

City of Painesville, 5394, barque, schooner 24, *25*

Col. Ellsworth, 4354, barque, schooner 4

Columbia, Canadian propeller 55

Conqueror (ex-*Wm. L. Proctor*), Canadian 138233, tug 19

Corona, 125091, side-wheel steamer 100, *101*

Crusader, 125252, tug 25

D. Leuty, 157065, steam barge 16, *17*

D. A. Wells, 6843, schooner *46*, 47

Delos DeWolf, 6327, schooner 100

Democrat, 6932, schooner 40

Detroit, 6150, ferry boat 44

Dionne (ex- and later *M. A. Gagnon*), U.S. government tug 45

E.C.L., 7294, barque, schooner 7, 9

E. G. Crosby (2nd), 127731, steel steamer *60*

E. P. Royce, 8912, schooner 47, 86

Ebenezer (ex-*Watts Sherman*), 26168, schooner 63, *64*, 66, 78

Ebenezer, 7518, schooner 66, 68

Ebenezer, 136136, scow schooner 68, 69, *70*

Ebenezer, undocumented, schooner 70

Edward E. Gillen (1st) (ex-*J. J. Hagerman*), 75591, tug 78

Edward E. Skeele (ex-*Pauline, John Mee*), 76264, schooner 66, 105, *110, 112, 113, 114, 115*

Elbe, 7519, schooner *36*

Eleanor, 7298, schooner 50

Elizabeth, 135939, scow schooner 89

Ellen Spry, 8983, schooner 28

Ellen Williams, 7308, schooner 31, *31*

Emily and Eliza, 36582, scow schooner 95, *95*

Emma L. Nielsen, 135665, schooner 85, *85, 86, 88, 89*

Eureka (ex-*Schilde, Canada*), 116578, schooner 53

F. & P. M. No. 1 (later *Wisconsin*), 120499, steamer *85*

F. B. Gardner, 9198, brig, barque, schooner 15, 16, *16, 17*

Fanny Gardner, 9199, brig 15

Farrand H. Williams, 120474, scow schooner 169, 91

Favorite (1st), 9201, tug *92*

Fleetwing, 9883, schooner 71

Floretta, 9688, schooner 4, 72

Flying Cloud, 9196, schooner 91

Forest, 9740, scow schooner 33, *34*, 35, 39, 40

Francis Hinton, 120754, steam barge *85*

Frank B. Stevens (ex-*St. Joseph*), Canadian 134517, steam barge 23

Freddie, 237558, fish tug 103

G. Pfister, also known as *Guido Pfister*, 85304, schooner 4, 5

G. D. Norris, 10336, schooner 38

George H. Warmington, 85217, later Canadian 122015, schooner 8, 9

George L. Dunlap, 10347, side-wheel steamer 23

George L. Wren, 10816, schooner 40, *41*

George Murray (later *George*), 85305, schooner 4

George Nelson, 85946, tug 12, 52

George T. Nelles (ex-*Welcome* 1st), 202985, tug 75, 78

Gertrude, 10202, schooner 50

Glen Cuyler, 10338, schooner *94*, 95

Grace Williams, 85882, steam barge 95

Graham Brothers, 85375, schooner 28, *74*

H. M. Scove, 95256, schooner 29

Halsted, 95260, schooner, schooner barge 24, *24*, 26, *26*, 28, 105

Hans Crocker, 11174, barque 30

*The vessel's official number appears immediately after its name. United States official numbers were first assigned in 1867, Canadian numbers in 1855. Vessels lost before these dates had no numbers.

Harvey Bissell, 11281, schooner 72, *73*

Hattie, 11989, schooner 66

Helen Taylor, 96270, steam barge 102, *103*

Henry Marshall (later *Jesse Spaulding, Sioux*), 95759, tug 12

Henry S. Sill, 95382, tug 91, *94*

Holliswood (ex-*John Leathem*), 76064, tug 52, 108

Home, 11210, tug 7

Honest John, 11180, scow schooner 36, *36*

I. N. Foster, 100031, schooner, steam barge 59

Ida, 12140, schooner *85*

Industry, 100023, schooner 95

Ivy M. Leathem (later *Violet H. Raber*), 100509, tug 53, *54*

J. Maria Scott (later *White Star*), 75610, schooner 25

J. B. Kitchen, 75511, later Canadian 116814, schooner 21

J. C. Evans (ex-*James McGordon*), 75867, tug 59

J. E. Gilmore, 13307, schooner 33, *34*, 35, 38, 42

J. H. Outhwaite, 76636, steamer 42

J. H. Stevens, 12787, sloop, schooner 27, *28*

J. I. Case, 75720, later Canadian 141595, schooner 91, *91*

J. J. Hagerman (later *Edward E. Gillen* 1st), 75591, tug 75

J. K. Stack, 75805, schooner 69

J. S. Crouse, 77313, steamer 78

J. U. Porter, 45092, barge, scow schooner 57

J. W. Doane, 75660, schooner 29

James G. Blaine (ex-*Pensaukee*), 20195, schooner, schooner barge 19

James H. Martin, 75114, tug 47

James H. Prentice, 76581, steam barge 26

James McGordon (later *J. C. Evans*), 75867, tug 59

James Navagh, 13304, schooner 71

James Platt, 13302, schooner 106

Jennibel, 12975, schooner 4

Jenny, 76812, scow schooner 69

Jesse Spaulding (ex-*Henry Marshall*, later *Sioux*), 95759, tug 12

Jessie Phillips, 75367, schooner 71

John Gregory, 76025, tug 34, 93, 100, 108

John L. Green, 75777, schooner 72

John Leathem (later *Holliswood*), 76064, tug 52, *52*, 108

John Mee (ex-*Pauline*, later *Edward E. Skeele*), 76264, schooner 105

John Schroeder (later *William A. Hazzard*), 76883, steam barge 56

John Spry, 75599, steamer 17

Josephine Lawrence, 12976, schooner 105, 107

L. J. Conway, 15955, schooner 105

L. L. Barth (ex-*S. S. Wilhelm*), 116266, steam barge 60

L. P. Hill, 141026, fish tug 96

La Petite, 15100, schooner 101, *102*

Lady of the Lake, side-wheel steamer 43

Lake Erie, Canadian, propeller 55, *56*

Lake Forest, 15578, schooner 20, *20*, 21, 22

Laurel, 15409, scow schooner 97, 99

Leathem D. Smith (2nd) (ex-U.S. lightship No. 59), 218159, tug 55

Lem Ellsworth, 140062, schooner 4, *4*

Lem Higby, 14804, schooner 101

Lettie May, 140063, schooner 106, *106*

Leviathan, 14612, wrecking tug 7, 38, 74, 91, 108

Lewis Day, 15410, barque 37, 38

Lewis Ludington, 14804, schooner *36*

Libbie Nau, 14808, schooner *66*

Lily E. (ex-*Louisa McDonald*), 15872, schooner 71, *71, 74, 76, 77, 78, 79*

Linerla, 140732, schooner *100*

Lomie A. Burton, 15958, schooner 65, *66*, 78, 99

Lookout, 14675, schooner 44

Louisa McDonald (later *Lily E.*), 15872, schooner 4, 71

Louisiana, 140882, steamer 26

Lucia A. Simpson, 140097, schooner 60, *60*, 105

Lucy Graham, 15805, schooner 4

Lynx, 202192, scow schooner *74*

M. A. Gagnon (later *U.S. Dionne*), 90728, tug 82

M. C. Hawley (later *City of Green Bay*), 91228, side-wheel steamer 17

Maggie Lutz, 90582, fish tug 96

Major N. H. Ferry, 16631, later Canadian 126130, schooner 78

Mary Booth, 16392, scow schooner 56

Mary Ellen Cook, 90763, schooner 60, *61*, 105

May Richards, 91283, schooner barge *85*

Mediator, 16345, schooner 31

Messenger, 16654, propeller 38

Middlesex (later *Woodlands*), 91307, steamer, tow barge 26

Midnight, 16438, schooner *93*

Minnedosa, Canadian 94884, schooner barge 88

Minnehaha, 90584, schooner 95, *95*

Minnesota, 91272, bulk freighter 9

Monarch, 81218, tug *92*

Montauk, 16403, schooner 4

Nabob (later *Waukesha*), 18175, schooner 79

Naiad, 18100, later Canadian, 116392, barque, schooner 4

Nevada, 130218, steamer *92*

Norman, 18101, barque, schooner 23

Northern Queen (ex-*Robert Holland*), Canadian propeller 53, 55

O. M. Nelson, 155066, schooner 99, *100*

Olive Branch, ferry 43

Orient, 19414, tug 29

Oswego, 19063, tug 5

Ottawa, 19408, schooner *100*

Our Son, 19437, schooner 60, 105

Ozaukee, 19002, tug, steamer 18, 28, 29, 30

Parana, 19765, barque, schooner, tow barge *52, 53, 55, 60*

Parmelia Flood, barque 15

Pauline (later *John Mee, Edward E. Skeele*), 19674, schooner 105

Pensaukee (later *James G. Blaine*), 20195, barque, schooner 18, 19

Pensaukee, 150057, tug 30

Peoria, 19668, schooner *100*, 107, 108

Peter Reiss, 203898, tug *74*

Pewaukee (ex-*Two Friends*), 150233, schooner, propeller, barge 10

Pocahontas, schooner 36

Queen City, 20519, sidewheel steamer 16

Quickstep, 20567, scow schooner 38

Quickstep (ex-*S. Anderson*), 115335, schooner *39, 40*, 68

R. Botsford, 110532, schooner *17*
R. F. Goodman, 110546, tug 29
R. H. Becker, 56207, scow schooner 33, 35, *35*
Robert Holland (later *Northern Queen*), 110043, steam barge,
    propeller 53, *54*, 55, 60
Rockaway, 21475, scow schooner 63
Rosa Bell, 21302, schooner *100*
Rouse Simmons, 110024, schooner 110, *111*
S. Anderson (later *Quickstep*), 115335, schooner 68
S. G. Chase, 22365, tug 29, 30
S. M. Stephenson, 115722, schooner barge, steam barge 53, *53*,
    55
S. S. Wilhelm (later *L. L. Barth*), 116266, steam barge 60
Sarah Clow, 22342, schooner 37
Sarah Van Eps, 22585, side-wheel steamer 105
Satisfaction, 116628, tug *28*, 110
Sea Lark, schooner 36
Sioux (ex-*Jesse Spaulding, Henry Marshall*), 95759, tug 12
St. Joseph (later *Frank B. Stevens*), 23354, propeller 23
St. Maries, 115473, steamer 95
Starke Brothers, 115226, tug 72, 75
Stella, schooner 50
Stuart H. Dunn (ex-*W. R. Taylor*), Canadian 72964, schooner 8
Surprise, 22581, schooner 86
Sweepstakes (later *Sea King*), 22383, tug 19
T. Y. Avery, 24141, schooner 4
Thistle, 145583, steamer *52*
Thomas H. Smith, 145284, steam barge 58
Thomas Spear, 145216, tug 82
Transit, 24231, schooner 95

Trial, 24233, schooner 85
Triumph, schooner 50
Tuscarora, U.S. revenue cutter, later steamer 235600, 102, *102*
Two Fannies, 24144, barque, schooner 16
Two Friends (later *Pewaukee*), Canadian 71279, barque 3
Union, 25047, tug, steamer 16, 23, 30
United, side-wheel steamer, barge 43
Vega (ex-*St. Paul, A. J. Covill*), 22418, schooner *100*
Vermont, 25568, schooner *95*
Violet H. Raber (ex-*Ivy M. Leathem*), 100509, tug *54*
W. C. Tillson, 80599, tug 108
W. L. Wetmore, 80196, steamer 107, *108*
W. R. Taylor (later *Stuart H. Dunn*), Canadian 72964, schooner
    8
Walhalla, 26365, schooner 40
Walter A. Sherman, 62858, barge, schooner barge 19
Watts Sherman (later *Ebenezer*), 26168, schooner 63, *64*, 66, 78
Waukesha (ex-*Nabob*), 18175, schooner 7, 9, *11*
Welcome 1st (later *George T. Nelles*), 80582, tug 75, 78
Willard A. Smith, 80587, schooner 101
William Aldrich, 26362, schooner 49, *49, 50*, 101, 105
William O. Brown, 26915, schooner 36
William R. Crowell, 80531, tug 74
Windsor, 26366 and 62523, side-wheel ferry, barge, schooner
    barge 43
Winslow, 26243, later Canadian 96855, tug *6*, 9, 84
Wm. L. Proctor (later *Conqueror*), 81002, tug 19
Wm. Rudolph, 80762, steam barge 86
Woodlands (ex-*Middlesex*), C138504, schooner barge 26
Wyandotte, 205458, steel steamer *87*, 88

INDEX OF PROPER NAMES*

A. S. Piper & Co. 30, 31
Ahlstrom, Fred 29
Ahnapee (Algoma) 45, 82
Aldrich, James F. 49
Aldrich, William 49
Aldrich, Smith & Co. 49
Algoma (Ahnapee) 81
Allan, McClelland & Co. 51
Alpena, Michigan 21, 88
Alpena Gale 3, 33, 39, 45, 68, 72, 75, 105, 113
American Shipbuilding Co. 79
Amundson, Henry 69
Anderson, Caroline 99
Anderson, Erik 52, 57
Anderson, Frederick 19
Anderson, John 35, 105
Anderson, Julia 97
Anderson, S. 66
Anderson's Pier 69
Anger, William 30
Angwall, Orin W. 112, *115*
Association of Lake Underwriters 3
Austin, Edward 67
Bad River 18
Baetz, Conrad 51
Bailey, A. 36
Bailey, D. E. 36
Bailey, Erastus 20, 22
Baileys (Bailey's) Harbor 9, 12, 45, 53, 63, 65, 68, 85, 92, 96, 99, 105, 107
Baileys Harbor Station (USLSS) 12, 65, 102, 109
Baker, Christ 52
Baltimore Clipper 49
Baptist, William H. 17, 23
Barber, George 105
Barner, Brian *83*
Barnes, C. C. 95
Barr, William 78
Barrie Island, Lake Huron 112, 115
Barton 51
Bates, William W. 49
Bay City, Michigan 18
Bay View 78, 103
Beaver Island, Lake Michigan 59, 91
Beckwith, Edward 36
Behrmann, Henry 97
Beidler, William 59
Bellrichard, Kent 81
Benjamin, Henry M. 107

Bennett, George 107
Bennett, Joseph J. 63
Benton Harbor, Michigan 64
Berntsen, Thorvald "Tom" 109, *110, 113*
Bethel Society 99
Big Bay de Noc, Green Bay 35
Big Summer Island, Lake Michigan 8
Bigelow, Anson A. 55, 57
Bigelow, C. H. 12
Bigelow Lumber Co. 55
Blend, John H. 8
Bolster, Anthony 64, 78, 99
Bonner, Mannus J. 109
Boston, Massachusetts 81
Boutin, Telesfore F. 45
Bowman, E. B. 59
Boyd, James A. 105
Boyne City, Michigan 66, *66*
Bradley, Lyman 31
Brann's Pier 65
Brook, Charles A. 72, 76
Brooks, Nathaniel 36
Brotz, James 81, *83*
Brown, Augustus C. 17
Brown, Jesse T. 45
Brussels 22
Buck, Lawrence A. 110
Buckley, J. A. 68
Buffalo, New York 18, 20, 21, 24, 29, 37, 63, 74, 91, *101*, 106
Buffalo Station (USLSS) 29
Bundy, Herman 99
Burns, Thomas 50
Burtis, John 43
Burton, Allen 99
Butler, James 36
Butteroni, Henry 53
Butters, Daniel 53
Cana Island, Lake Michigan 7, 43, 45, 52, 57, 86
Canadian Point au Sable, Lake Huron 47
Canadian Soo 115
Carlton 81
Case, Jerome I. 91
Cedar River, Michigan 37
Cedar River Reef 38
Celia Shoal, Straits of Mackinac 25
Chamberlin, Aldin 63
Chambers Island, Green Bay 36
Chapin, William W. 105, 109
Charlevoix, Michigan 59, 63, 66, *100*
Charlevoix Station (USLSS) 78
Charlotte, New York 19

*All places for which states are not given are in Wisconsin

Cheboygan, Michigan 8, 18, 25, 38, 84, 91
Chesbrough, A. M. 110
Chicago, Illinois 9, 10, 12, 18, 20, 22, 23, 25, 29, 31, 35, 38, 42, 44, 53, 58, 59, 63, 68, 71, 78, 82, 85, 91, 95, 99, 105, 112
Chicago & Northwestern Rail Road 23, 29
Chicago Company 38
Chicago Fire, 67
Chicago Inter-Ocean 9
Chicago River *40*, 59
Chicago Seamans Bethel 57
Chicago Station (USLSS) 38
Chicago Transportation Company 78, 109
Chicago World's Fair 58
Chipman, Daniel W. 58, 67, 99
Chipman & Raesser's Pier 93
Christensen, Anna 99
Christensen, Anton 99
Claflin, Increase 15
Clauson, Gustav Theodore 65
Clay Banks 67
Cleveland, Ohio 10, 21, 28, 35, 47, 55, 63
Clifton, Raymond D. 79
Clow, Byron 36
Clow, David 36, 37, 38, 41
Clow, David, Jr. 36, 38, 40
Clow, Oscar 36
Clow, Sarah 37
Cobb, Ansel R. 63
Cointe, A. J. 17
Collingwood, Ontario 18, 53
Colwell, John 58
Coplin, Larry 89
Cota, George W. 59
Cousins, Robert 73
Craignair 6
Crandall, David S. 31
Crosby & Dimick's Agency 74
Cross Village, Michigan 101
Crowley, Peter J. 8, 9
Crystal Lake, Illinois 36, 38
Customs Regulations 89
Davenport, Michigan 60
David Vance & Co. 58
Davidson, Thomas 10
Davis, A. B. 91
D. H. Day Dock, Sleeping Bear Bay, Michigan 125
Day, Lewis J. 17, 37
Dean, James 44
Death's Door (Porte des Morts Passage) 4, 11, 18, 26, 33, 38, 42, 91, 96, 102, 105
Detroit, Michigan 37, 43, 44, 84, 93, 107
Detroit & Milwaukee Railway Co. 43
Detroit Harbor 26, 38, 96
Detroit Island, Lake Michigan 11, 33
Detroit River 43
Diederich, H. 80
Dow & Jones 43

Drake, William 85
Duluth, Minnesota 26
Dunham, James S. 18, 23, 59
Dunham Line 59
Dunn, John 57
Eagle Bay 69
Eagle Cliff 95
Eagle Harbor 69, 95, 96
Eagle (Horseshoe) Island 96
Easton, D. J. 72
East Jordan, Michigan 108
East Tawas, Michigan 21
Eaton, Mr. & Mrs. Charles 115
Eberts, Robert M. 49
Edwards, Joseph 72
Egan, Wiley M. 29
Egg Harbor 18, 51, 85, 110
Elk Rapids, Michigan 38
Ellenberger, Wm. J. 28
Ellingsen, Jens 52
Elliott, Samuel 47
Ellison Bay 34, 110
Emmons, N. J. 43
Engelmann, Michael 72, 74
Ephraim 37, 68, *70*, 95, 97
Epoufette, Michigan 60
Erickson, H. 86
Erickson, James E. 21
Erie, Pennsylvania 29, 36
Erskine, Linc (Lincoln) 107
Escanaba, Michigan 8, 10, 17, 21, 24, 26, 30, 36, 42, 47, 75, 82, 92, 110, 115
Escanaba Towing & Wrecking Co. 42
Etna Insurance Company 92
Evanston, Illinois 92
Evanston Station (USLSS) 25
Evenson, John E. 73
Evergreen Beach Hotel 69
F. B. Gardner & Co. 17, 18, 23, 29
Fairchild, Albert 96
Fairgrieve, Hugh 53
Fairgrieve, John Balmer 53
Fairport 113
Farrell, Thomas 7
Fayette, Michigan 21, 47
Fellows, George Decatur 34
Fellows, Harrison 33
Ferris, David 88
Ferry Village, Maine 32
Fidelity & Deposit Co. 112
Fink, Henry 67
Fish Creek 5, 18, 23, 96
Fisk, William J. 17
Fitzgerald, John 55, 109
Fitzgerald, Robert P. 55
Fitzgerald, William 58
Fitzhugh, Henry 23
Fond du Lac 17

Ford River, Michigan 21, 69
Forester, Michigan 16
Fort Howard (Green Bay) 15, 17, 66
Fowles, S. C. 16
Fox River 17
Franke, Gus 73
Frankfort, Michigan 23, 55, 59
Frankfort Station (USLSS) 21, 23, 59
Fullum, Walter K. 19
Gallagher, David 53
Gandlesen, Edwin 75
Garden Bay, Big Bay de Noc 11, 35
Garden Peninsula, Michigan 11, 21, 47
Gardiner, Howard C. 23
Gardner, D. M. 44
Gardner, Freeland B. 15, 17, 32
Gardner, H. H. 29
Gary, Indiana 28
Geiken, Carry 66
George Hall Coal Co. 19
Georgian Bay 60
Gerlach, John 35
Gifford, W. 36
Gillard, John 99
Gillen, Edward E. 78
Gillen's Point 80
Gills Rock 97
Gilmore, James E. 35
Gilson, Alfred 15
Gladstone, Michigan 113
Glencoe, Illinois 25
Glockner, Wilhelm 101
Goodrich Dock 112
Goodrich Transportation Co. 3, *3*, 23, *101*
Gordon Lodge 5
Gore Bay, North Channel, Lake Huron 115
Goss, Robert A. 67
Grand Haven, Michigan 64
Gray, Harry 91
Gray, John O. 107
Great Northern Transit Co. 53
Great Western Railway 43
Green Bay 15, 17, 22, 30, 32, 36, 69, 105, 113
Green Bay & Menominee Navigation Co. 17
Green Island, Green Bay 15
Greene, George G. 58
Gregory, John 17
Greilick, John 77
Greiling Bros. Co. 28
Greisen, C. 60
Griffin, John M. 71
Gruda, Joab 63
Grummond, Stephen B. 82
Gunderson, Fred 77, 82
Gunderson, Gundervald 66
Gunderson, Gustav 77
Gunderson, James 77
Gunderson, Louis 77

Gunderson, Martha Maria 77
Gunderson, Martin 77
Gunderson, Nels 77
Gunderson, Theodore 77
H. H. Smith & Co. 49
H. M. Benjamin & Co. 86, *86*, 91
Hafer, Henry 67
Hagan, P. 107
Hagen, Julius 10
Hall, Alanson 51
Halsted, Annie 26
Halsted, Henry S. 20, 24
Hamilton, Henry C. 51
Hamilton, Ontario 53
Hamilton, Walter D. 60
Hammer, N. A. 92
Hansen, Chris. 75
Hansen, Hans 39
Hanson, Anton 95
Hanson, James 95
Hanson, Jasper 71
Hanson, Matilda 95
Hanson, Peder ("Big Peder") 97, 99
Hanson, Soren 95
Hanson & Scove 72, 85
Harbridge, James 49
Harder, Charles C. 67
Harris, Joseph 15
Hawley, Thomas 17, 23
Hazen, Eli T. 47
Head, F. H. 11
Hedgehog Harbor 59
Heederik, Andrew M. 80
Henderson's Pier 8
Henry C. Hamilton & Co. 51
Hermann, L. 44
Hessel, Michigan 102
Hill, Homer 66
Hill, John J. 53
Hilty, Michael 11, 64
Hines Lumber Co. 60
Hog Island Reef, Lake Michigan 91
Hogback Reef, Sturgeon Bay 91
Hogenson, Fordel 68, *68*
Holland, Michigan 63
Holland, Robert 53
Holland Station (USLSS) 63
Honey, William 50
Hood, Thomas 81
Horn, William H. 66
Horn's Pier 67
Hornspier Road 67
Horseshoe Bay, Green Bay 97
Horseshoe (Eagle) Island 96
Hourigan, Matt 19
Howard, T. 53
Howland, Thomas H. 72
Hudson, Tim S. 17

Huebel Cedar Co. 60
Hughes, James 71
Hust, Henry 23
Hyde, Jake 101
Inland Lloyds 19, 37, 77
Inland Lloyds Vessel Register 10, 29, 63, 67
Institute *50*, 56
Iversen, Rev. A. M. 37
J. Babcock & Co. 76
J. A. Bryden & Co. 76
J. E. Hathaway & Company 78
Jackson Street Bridge, Chicago, Illinois 59
Jacksonport 45, 86, 96
Jacobson, Anton 99
Jacobson, Caroline 99
Jenkins, J. S. 43
Jennison, Charles 50
Jerome, George 43
Jetzer, James J. 81, *83*
Johnson, A. G. 35
Johnson, Andrew 99
Johnson, Dorothea M. 68
Johnson, Haagen 68
Johnson, Hans 33
Johnson, Harry 57, 58
Johnson, James T. 21
Johnson, Leverisa 75
Johnson, Sam 102
Johnson, William 63, 105
Jones, Alonzo D. 72
Jones, Frederick N. 63
Jones, R. W. 50
Jones Island 73, 79, 103
Jones Mill 71
Jorgenson, Claus S. 77
Jorgenson, Jorgen 64, 66
Jorgenson, Ole 66
Jorgenson, Samuel 77
Julia Bay, North Channel, Lake Huron 112, 114
Kalmbach, Albert 106
Kappelman, Bill *83*
Keith, John G. 24, 29
Keith, William G. 29
Kelderhouse, John 107
Kempton, Samuel 99
Kennedy, W. L. 110
Kenosha 5, 30, 59
Kent, G. 29
Kewaunee 4, 77, 81, *81*, 96, 99
Kingholtz, Richard 50
Kinnickinnic River 7, 73
Kirtland, Charles E. 7, 8
Kirtland, Wolf & Davidson Wrecking Co. 7, 10, 74
Kjeldass, Theodore J. 22
Klingholz, Hugo J. 85
Knapp, F. M. 91
Knickerbocker Co. 31
Knudsen, Arthur 33

Knudsen, Evelyn 33
Knudsen, Martin Nicolai 33, 39, 42
Knudson, Peter E. 69
Kordt, Elizabeth 101
Kramer, H. H. 21
Krause, M. C. 58
Kremer, Charles E. 57, 58
Krones, Frank 59, 101
Krones, Herman 59, 100
Krones, Mary 100
Krones, Minnie 101
Lake Michigan Transit Co. 43
Lane, Theodore 33
Laning, Francis 36
Larsen, James 4, *5*, 113, *115*
Larsen, James Louis 110
Larson, Carl 102
Larson, Louis 105
Larson, Ralph 97
Lawe, John 49
Lawrence, Philip 105
Lawson, O. E. 18
Leathem, John 12, 57, 108
Leathem & Smith Towing & Wrecking Co. 12, 27, 57, 58, 78
LeFlam, Samuel 19
Lester, David 33
Lincoln Park Yacht Club 78
Little Bay, Lake Michigan 7
Little Cedar River 38
Little Harbor, Lake Michigan 47, 86
Little Point Sable, Lake Michigan 113
Little Sister Bay 23
Little Sturgeon Bay 15
Little Suamico 17
Little Summer Island, Lake Michigan 8
Littlejohn, D. C. 23
Lloyds of New York 84
Lockland, John 113
Lockport, New York 31, 51
Long, R. H. 29
Lorain, Ohio 26
Lovell, W. W. 99
Ludington, Michigan 18, 85
M. Engelmann & Co. 72, 74
Macguire, W. 44
Machia, Henry 58
Madden, Edward 63
Madison Dock, Ohio 36
Manistee, Michigan 59, 64, 68, 72, 75, *103*, 105, 107
Manistee Station (USLSS) 76
Manistique, Michigan 21, 23, 55, 110
Manitowoc 12, 19, 34, 44, 49, 58, 66, 67, 71, 72, *74*, 84, 85, *85*, *86*, 87, 91, *92*, 93, 96
Mann, Herman 51
Mann, James R. 30
Mann, Joseph 51
Mann Bros. 51
Marine City, Michigan 53, 88

Marinette 5, 15, 23, 26, 58, *112*, 113
Markham, Geo. C. 58
Marshall, William 5, 6
Marshall's Point 3
Marshall's Reef 5
Masonville, Michigan 40
Masse, John, Jr. 59
Matteson, Charles 73
Matthews, J. S. 21
McDermond, Lemuel 3
McDonald, A. 19
McDonald, Fred 26
McGee, Joseph 23
McKinstry, D. C. 43
McLachlan, Colen 82
McLachlan, L. R. 100
McLean, Angus 29
McLean, Donald 29
McNulty, Martin 47, 86
Medberry, John W. 49
Medberry, Martin B. 49
Menominee, Michigan 12, 15, 16, 23, *49*, 58, 59, 96, 110, 113
Merchant's Dock 58
Mercurt, John 75
Merrill, John B. 8
Metcalf, William 51
Metropolitan Railroad Bridge, Chicago, Illinois 59
Meyer, George 86
Meyers, Patrick 23
Meyers, Thomas S. 23
Meyers, Mr. and Mrs. W. 19
Michael Hilty Lumber Co. 78
Michelson, Halvor 63, *65*
Michigan City, Indiana 82
Michigan Transportation Co. 53
Middle Island Station (USLSS), Lake Huron 88
Miles, Margaret 71
Miller, John 44, 73
Miller Brother's Shipyard 63
Milner, David, Jr. 37
Milwaukee 21, 24, 26, 31, *36*, 38, 51, *52*, 56, 57, 58, 59, 64, 67,
    72, *76*, 77, *77*, 80, 91, 96, 100, *102*, 105, 108, 112
Milwaukee River 7, *86, 114*
Milwaukee Shipyard Co. 108, 115
Milwaukee Station (USLSS) 73, 77
Milwaukee Tug Boat Co. 75
Milwaukee Yacht Club 79
Mission Point, Straits of Mackinac 38
Mississippi River 18
Montague, Charles Z. 58
Montreal, Quebec 53
Moravian Church 69
Morcomb, J. 73
Mott, Thomas S. 35
Mud (Moonlight) Bay, Lake Michigan 7, 68, 85
Mueller Fuel & Coal Co. 100
Muir, Archibald 81
Muir, David 81

Muller, Eli 113
Muskegon, Michigan 11, 63, 85
Muskegon Station (USLSS) 85
Nahma, Michigan 52
National Board of Lake Underwriters 3
National Pole Co. 28
National Transit Co. 28
Neilson, Sam 69
Nelson, Andrew 75
Nelson, C. L. 32
Nelson, John 11, 102
Nerdrum, Christ. 22
Neshoto River 49
New England Manufacturing Co. 50
New England Transportation Co. (N.E.T. Line) 53, *56*
New Franken 22
Newport 33
Newport, Michigan 33
Nichel, John 75
Nichols, John 73
Nielsen, Paul 85, 87
North Bay, Lake Michigan 3, 45, 72, 113
North Channel 115
North Manitou Island Station (USLSS), Lake Michigan 101
North Unity, Michigan 66
Northport, Michigan 8
O. Torrison Co. 96
Oak Creek 36
Oconto 18, 23, 51
Oellerich, Claude H. 8
Ogdensburg, New York 19
Old Chicago Station (USLSS) 21
Oleson, Thomas O. 58
Olson, Andre 105
Olson, Ingar 109
Olson, Louis 109
Olson, Nels 109
Olson, Ole M. 52, 56, 69
Olson, Peter B. 21
Oswego, New York 19, 71
Oswego Station (USLSS) 19
Otto, Charles 68
Palmer, John 63
Pankratz Dock 60
Pankratz Mill, 60
Parker, John 57
Pastors, Peter 51
Pauly, John H. 57
Paust, Mathias 52
Peak, Charlie 74
Peavey Slip 26
Peck, James 23
Pedersen, Andrew B. 52
Pedersen, C. O. 96
Pedersen, Hans 110
Pensaukee 15, 16, 17, 23, 24, 29, 32
Peshtigo 16, 22
Peshtigo Company 16

Peshtigo Fire 22, *22*, 67
Petersen, Christian 59
Petersen, George 35
Peterson, Alfred 101
Petoskey, Michigan 12
Pilot Island, Lake Michigan 33, *33, 34*, 99
Pine Lake, Michigan 66
Plathner, Theodore 86
Plum Island, Lake Michigan 18, 37, 40, 42
Plum Island Station (USLSS) 11, 26, 59, 99
Point au Pelee, Lake Erie 37
Point aux Barques, Lake Huron 88
Point Belle, Lake Erie 37
Point Betsey, Lake Michigan 64
Point Betsey Station (USLSS) 64
Point Epoufette, Lake Michigan 60
Pollock, George 25
Poppe, Albert C. *50*, 51, 56, 57
Port Burwell, Ontario 3
Port Huron, Michigan 55, 81, 89, 107
Port Sanilac, Michigan 16
Port Washington 18, 68, 97, 105
Portage, Michigan 18
Portland, Maine 32
Pottgether, Henry 35
Poverty Island, Lake Michigan 8, 55
Powers, John 63
Prescott, Ontario 19
Prindiville, John 82, *84*
Pripps, Harold W. 112
Quayle & Martin 55
Quinn, James 72
Racine 5, 33, 58, 77, 91, *91, 94*, 99, 113
Racine North Point 58
Raesser, Christopher S. 67, 99
Rand, Greenleaf S. 50
Rand & Burger Shipyard 19, *53*, 58
Rasmussen, Ole M. 4
Ray, Augustine J. 99
Recor, Harry 88
Recor, L. 88
Red River 16, 108
Reinartsen, Lene Gersine 68
Reynolds, Charles 87
Richard Irvin and Co. 6
Riordan, James 75
Ripsom, Charles H. 19
Robertson, A. M. 53
Robeson, David 82
Rock Island, Lake Michigan 8, 44, 99
Roeser's Pier 95
Rounds, W. H. 92
Royce, Eli P. 47
Ruddock, T. S. 44
Russell, George B. 43
S. H. Seaman & Co. 51
Sac Bay, Michigan 47

Sacketts Harbor, New York 23
St. Catharines, Ontario 9
St. Clair, Michigan 88
St. Louis, Missouri 16
St. Martin's Island, Lake Michigan 8
St. Paul Fire & Marine Insurance Company 11, 84
Salvison, Alfred 85
Sanborn, W. E. 36
Sandwich, Ontario 44
Saugatuck, Michigan 47
Sault Ste. Marie *54*, 95, 112
Saveland, John 67
Saveland, Tonnes 105
Saveland, Zacharias 105
Scofield & Co. 108
Seaman, S. H. 51
Sheboygan 15, 20, *28, 35*, 66, *74*, 77, 109, *111.*
Sherman Bay 70
Sister Bay 4, 8, 9, 68, 86, 95
Sister Island, Green Bay 95
Slauson, James R. 36
Smeed Box Co. 28
Smith, D. B. 38
Smith, Hesikiah H. (Deacon) 49
Smith, Thomas H. 12, 57
Snow Island 45
Soper Lumber Co. 26, 27
Sorenson, E. 66
South Bay, Washington Island, Lake Michigan 29
South Chicago, Illinois 106
South Haven, Michigan *41*, 64
South Manitou Island, Lake Michigan 56, 77, 102
South Manitou Island Station (USLSS) 77, 102
South Shore Yacht Club *71*, 78, *78*, 79, 80
South Shore Yacht Club Auxiliary 79
Spanish Mills, Ontario 26
Spaulding, Jesse 17
Spear, Albert Marshall 16, 18, 28, 30, 31
Spear, Amanda Preble 16, 32
Spear, George O. 16, 30, 32, 82
Spear, Thomas 15, 17, 18, 20, 24, 28, 30
Spear Mill 31, 52
Spencer, W. T. 9
Spencer Line 29
Spry, John 28
Starkey, Daniel B. 78
Steele, John R. 81
Steele, George 105
Stephenson, Isaac "Ike" 17, 23
Stephenson, Orville "Dewey" 113
Stephenson, Samuel M. 17
Stetson's Slip, Chicago River 59
Stevenson, Claud 59
Stevenson, Henry 59
Straits of Mackinac 3, 24, 38, 102
Strobel, Peter S. J. 100
Stubbs, John 106

Stubbs, R. J. 20
Sturgeon Bay 11, 12, 15, 18, 22, 28, 31, 33, 45, 52, *52*, 57, 58, 59, 60, *60, 61*, 78, 86, 91, 96, 99, 105, 108, 110
Sturgeon Bay Lumber Co. 7
Sturgeon Bay Ship Canal 18, 29, 31, 45, 53, 72, 87, 92, 96, 100, 101, 105
Suffel, George 3
Swanson, Oliver 31
Swinton, E. 68
Thames & Mersey Co. 19, 74
Thomey, Thomas 82
Thompson, Anne Gurine 77
Thompson, George A. 6
Thompson, John 109
Thompson, Martin 101
Thompson, Michigan 28, 110
Three Mile Bay, New York 35
Thunder Bay, Lake Huron 88
Thunder Bay Island Reef 20
Thunder Bay Island Station (USLSS) 21
Toft Estate 68
Tonneson, Conrad L. 69
Tonneson, Tonnette Amalie 68
Tornado Memorial Park 22
Toronto Marine Historical Society 32
Torrison, Osul 95
Town of Lake 67
Traverse City, Michigan 77, 110
Treiber, John 56
Trotter, Dave 89
Trowbridge, Alva 18
Trowbridge, C. C. 43
Tuttle, John V. 7, 8, 11
Twin River 49
Two Rivers 49, 71, 81
Two Rivers Point 71, 82
Union Dry-Dock Yards 25
Union Towing & Wrecking Co. 26
Upton, J. A. 10
Van Buren Street Bridge, Chicago, Illinois 59
Van Cleve, F. H. 42
Van Dyke & Van Dyke 57

Vermillion, Ohio 63
Vieau, Andrew J. 49
Vincent, Tristam 20, 22
Waide Transportation Co. 19
Wakefield, Al F. 109
Wall, Tom 102
Wanvig, Alida Regine 99
Wanvig, John Daniel 99
Washburn, Arthur 59
Washington Harbor, Washington Island 26, *26*, 99
Washington Island, Lake Michigan 26, 29, 96, 99, 105
Waukegan, Illinois 38, 113
Waukesha 10
Wauwatosa 112
Wegner, Arni *50*, 56
West Shore Line of Green Bay 17
West Twin River 50
Western Seamans Friend Society 57
Whitefish Bay, Door County, Lake Michigan 85
Whitehall, Michigan 20
Whites Town, New York 63
Wilcox, Asa 35
Williams, David 45
Williams, Farrand H. 91
Williams, Francis Porter 91, 93
Williams, Grace 95
Williams, James R. 78
Williamsonville 22
Wiltse's Pier 95
Windsor, Ontario 43
Wing, E. J. 68
Wisconsin Chair Company 97
Wolf, William H. 7, 10, 56
Wolf & Davidson 7, 8, 9, 75, 79
Women's National Relief Association 109
Wood, John 24
Worfel, Harry 47, 86
Wrightstown 17
Wyandotte, Michigan 88
Young, A. J. 88
Young, William 88
Zaleski, Rich 81